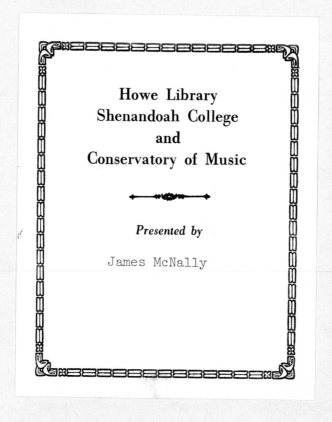

# CONRAD

*Almayer's Folly*
to *Under Western Eyes*

*by* DANIEL R. SCHWARZ

*Cornell University Press*

ITHACA, NEW YORK

First published 1980 by Cornell University Press.

**Library of Congress Cataloging in Publication Data**

Schwarz, Daniel R.
    Conrad, "Almayer's folly" to "Under Western eyes".

    Bibliography:  p.
    1. Conrad, Joseph, 1857–1924—Criticism and interpretation.  I. Title.
PR6005.04Z7927   1980      823'.912      79–48012
ISBN 0–8014–1311–7

Printed in Great Britain

For my mother and father

# Contents

# Acknowledgements

I am indebted to my colleagues at Cornell University for their erudition, judgment, and generosity. In particular, I appreciate the friendship of the late Paul Gottschalk. I am obligated to my Cornell students for their insight and their demands for clarity and precision. I am grateful to my wife, Marcia Schwarz, for advice, encouragement, and understanding, and to my two sons, David and Jeffrey, for the pleasure they bring Marcia and me.

I appreciate grants from the Cornell Humanities Research fund and the Cornell English Department grant-in-aid fund. I am grateful to a number of editors for allowing me to use material that I have published elsewhere. A version of chapter 1 appeared in *Ariel* (Oct. 1977); a version of chapter 3 was published in *Modern British Literature* (Spring 1978); a version of chapter 5 appeared in *Studies in the Novel* (Fall 1972); a version of chapter 7 was published in the *University of Toronto Quarterly* (Fall 1977); and a version of chapter 10 appeared in *The Journal of Narrative Technique* (Spring 1976). *Conradiana* (1975) published a version of the section of chapter 6 that pertains to 'The End of the Tether'; a few paragraphs of chapter 2 discuss material that I published in an article on 'The Idiots' in *Conradiana* (Summer 1969). The discussions of 'An Anarchist' and 'Il Conde' in Chapter 6 contain some material that appeared in *Studies in Short Fiction* (Winter 1969 and Spring 1971). An earlier version of chapter 8 appeared in *Twentieth Century Poetry, Fiction, and Theory*, ed. Harry Garvin (Lewisburg, PA: Bucknell University Press, 1977). With the permission of the University of Tennessee Press, Knoxville, Tennessee, I have used material from an article that I published in Vol. XVI (1971) of *Tennessee Studies in Literature*, pp. 103 – 110, edited by Richard Beale Davis and Kenneth L. Knickerbocker.

*Cornell University*                                       DANIEL R. SCHWARZ
*Ithaca, New York*
*August 1979*

# Abbreviations and a Note on the Text

Occasionally Conrad did not publish his works in the order he wrote them. Within the text, dates in parentheses refer to the year the work was published. The appendix provides the date that each work of fiction was completed.

I have used the following abbreviations for editions of the letters:

*Cunninghame Graham*—C. T. Watts, *Joseph Conrad's Letters to R. B. Cunninghame Graham* (Cambridge: Cambridge University Press, 1969).

*Garnett*—Edward Garnett, *Letters from Joseph Conrad 1895–1924* (Indianapolis: Bobbs-Merrill Company, 1928).

*LL,* i or ii—Georges Jean-Aubry, *Joseph Conrad: Life and Letters,* 2 vols. (Garden City, New York: Doubleday, Page and Company, 1927).

For the novel *An Outcast of the Islands* I have used the abbreviation *OI* and, for Conrad's non-fiction prose, I have used the following abbreviations:

*MS* – *The Mirror of the Sea*
*NLL* – *Notes on Life and Letters*
*PR* – *A Personal Record*

I have used the Kent edition (Garden City: Doubleday, 1926). For the shorter fiction, page numbers in parentheses refer to the collected edition in which the tale appears:

*Tales of Unrest*: 'The Idiots', 'An Outpost of Progress', 'The Lagoon', 'Karain', 'The Return'.

*Youth*: 'Youth', 'Heart of Darkness', 'The End of the Tether'.

*Typhoon*: 'Typhoon', 'Falk', 'Amy Foster', 'Tomorrow'.

*A Set of Six*: 'Gaspar Ruiz', 'The Brute', 'An Anarchist', 'The Informer', 'Il Conde', 'The Duel'.

*'Twixt Land and Sea*: 'The Secret Sharer', 'A Smile of Fortune', 'Freya of the Seven Isles'.

*Within the Tides*: 'The Partner', 'The Inn of the Two Witches', 'The
Planter of Malata', 'Because of the Dollars'.
*Tales of Hearsay*: 'The Black Mate', 'Prince Roman', 'The Warrior's
Soul', 'The Tale'.

# Introduction

Conrad is not only one of the greatest novelists who wrote in English, but he is particularly important for understanding twentieth-century British culture. Although English was his third language, Conrad combined his unique personal background as a Polish emigré and as a seaman with the traditions of his adopted country to change permanently the English novel. He brought a new psychological and moral intensity to the English novel and its traditions of manners and morals. He recognised the role in human conduct of repressed desires, unconscious motives, and unacknowledged impulses. Because he wanted to dramatise how a writer comes to terms with words and meaning, he focused on the teller as much as the tale. Focusing on the problems of how we understand, communicate, and signify experience, he anticipated essential themes in the philosophy, linguistics, criticism, and literature of our era. He understood the potential of the novel for political and historical insights and thus enlarged the subject matter of the English novel. When he dramatised the dilemma of seeking meaning in a universe that is amoral, he addressed the central epistemological problem of the twentieth century. To achieve a more intense presentation of theme and a more thorough analysis of characters' moral behaviour, he adopted innovative techniques, including the meditative self-dramatising narrator and non-linear chronology.

Throughout his career, Conrad stressed that a novel was inseparable from its author. From the first, his aesthetic ideas derived in part from his needs to express his emotional life. In an early letter he wrote, 'You must squeeze out of yourself every sensation, every thought, every image,—mercilessly, without reserve and without remorse: you must search the darkest corners of your heart, the most remote recesses of your brain,—you must search them for the image, for the glamour, for the right expression' (28 Oct. 1895; *LL*, vol. 1, 183). Conrad's presence is embodied in his novels, and the reader experiences that presence on every page. While this is true of every writer, Conrad's presence is more elusive because he never achieved the kind of consistent social and moral character which he could dramatise within his novel as, say, Fielding, Thackeray, and Dickens could. The narrative voice within his novels is often searching for values and self-definition. This search reflects Conrad's sense of himself as a perpetual outsider; his ambivalence both about leaving Poland and abandoning his maritime career; and, above all, his continuing struggle with self-doubt and anxiety.

Conrad knew that his books were the history of his psyche: 'Every novel contains an element of autobiography—and this can hardly be denied, since the creator can only express himself in his creation' (*PR*, pp. xvii–xviii). His fascination with extreme psychological states derives from his having lived through many such states. His novels are intimately related to his life and often reflect his psychic turmoil. Conrad not only transferred his emotional life to his fiction, but he sought to bring coherence to his life by exploring aspects of himself in his works.

Writing enabled Conrad to define his values and his character. He uses his narrators and dramatic personae to objectify his feelings and values. Marlow is a surrogate through whom Conrad works out his own epistemological problems. Marlow's search for values echoes Conrad's. The meaning of several novels, most notably *The Nigger of the 'Narcissus'* and *The Rescue*, depends on understanding the way that Conrad's emotional life becomes embodied in the text. In *Nostromo* the suicidal despair of Decoud reflects a mood that Conrad had known many times in his novel writing years. Even such an objective work as 'The Secret Sharer' becomes more meaningful once we recognise that it has an autobiographical element. At the outset of his voyage, the Captain not only relives emotions Conrad once felt during his first command but reflects the uncertainty and anxiety that Conrad experienced in the period when he wrote it.

Lacking a father, a bachelor until he was thirty-eight, an exile from his native land who felt guilty for deserting not only his homeland but his father's political heritage, Conrad is particularly concerned with loneliness and isolation. Perhaps the Novalis passage that serves as the epigraph to *Lord Jim*, and is repeated in *A Personal Record*, should serve as the epigraph to Conrad's whole career: 'It is certain my conviction gains infinitely the moment another soul will believe in it.' The desperate reaching out to an alter ego who might sympathetically respond to his frustrations—the pattern of his letters to Edward Garnett, and R. B. Cunningham Grahame—defines a central structural and thematic component of his work: A lonely soul—be it

Marlow, Jim, the Captain in 'The Secret Sharer', Razumov, Heyst, or Captain Anthony—reaches out for an other who he hopes will recognise, understand, and authenticate him.

The pervasive gloom that haunts Conrad's novels reflects his personal travail. He was beset by self-doubt, physical illness, and debt. Despair, anguish, and a sense of failure were his constant companions during his writing career. Yet, while inability to write is a constant theme of his letters, he was in fact a prolific novelist, especially for a man who did not devote his full energies to writing until he was thirty-six. Few major writers have been more productive than Conrad was between 1894 and 1900, when, in addition to *Almayer's Folly* and *An Outcast of the Islands* and several important short stories, including 'The Lagoon', 'Karain', and 'An Outpost of Progress', Conrad completed *The Nigger of the 'Narcissus'* and the three major Marlow tales—'Youth', 'Heart of Darkness', and *Lord Jim*. Yet because in those years he was unable to complete *The Rescue* (originally titled *The Rescuer*) and abandoned in its early stages another novel, *The Sisters*, Conrad convinced himself that he was making poor progress on his work.

The act of writing placed the most excruciating pressure on Conrad's psyche. Speaking of the composition of *Nostromo*, he wrote:

> I had, like the prophet of old, 'wrestled with the Lord' for
> my creation. . . . These are, perhaps, strong words, but it is
> difficult to characterise otherwise the intimacy and the strain of
> a creative effort in which mind and will and conscience are
> engaged to the full, hour after hour, day after day, away from
> the world, and to the exclusion of all that makes life really
> lovable and gentle . . . . (*PR*, pp. 98–9)

When dissatisfied about the progress of his work, Conrad quite frequently felt as if he were suffering from a physical illness that must be endured until the work's completion (its birth) allowed him to recover from his agony.

For Conrad, writing became at times more real than the life he was leading with Jessie and his sons. In a revealing passage, he noted: 'The writer's substance is his writing; the rest of him is but a vain shadow, cherished or hated on uncritical grounds' (*PR*, p. 107). To preserve in his own mind the continuity between writing and his career at sea,

Conrad used the term 'literary action' to describe his writing. He claimed that he carried over into his writing 'that full possession of myself which is the first condition of good service' (*PR*, p. xix). For Conrad, writing was life. He conceived writing not only in terms of a voyage to be completed, but in terms of an irrational need to produce as if that alone would keep him alive: 'I dare say I am compelled, unconsciously compelled, now to write volume after volume, as in past years I was compelled to go to sea, voyage after voyage. Leaves must follow upon each other as leagues used to follow in the days gone by . . .' (*PR*, p. 18). How revealing that the creative act is described in terms which suggest both Marlow's own debilitating journey in 'Heart of Darkness' (modelled on Conrad's own experience) and Marlow's quest for the appropriate language and epistemology to narrate that experience: 'Least of all can you condemn an artist pursuing, however humbly and imperfectly, a creative aim. In that interior world where his thought and emotions go seeking for the experience of imagined adventures, there are no policemen, no law, no pressure of circumstance or dread of opinion to keep him within bounds' (*PR*, p. xx).

Conrad's pessimism and nihilism have been over-emphasised, while his humanism has been neglected. Like Hardy, Conrad posits an amoral cosmos that is indifferent to man's aspirations, but unlike Hardy he does not posit a malevolent universe. He perceived the universe in terms of an indifferent mechanism that man cannot control:

There is a—let us say—a machine. It evolved itself (I am severely scientific) out of a chaos of scraps of iron and behold!—it knits. I am horrified at the horrible work and stand appalled. I feel it ought to embroider,—but it goes on knitting. You come and say: 'This is all right: it's only a question of the right kind of oil. Let us use this,—for instance—celestial oil and the machine will embroider a most beautiful design in purple and gold.' Will it? Alas no! You cannot by any special lubrication make embroidery with a knitting machine. And the most withering thought is that the infamous thing has made itself; made itself without thought, without conscience, without foresight, without eyes, without heart. It is a tragic accident,— and it has happened. You can't interfere with it. The last drop of bitterness is in the suspicion that you can't even smash it. In virtue of that truth one and immortal which lurks in the force

that made it spring into existence it is what it is—and it is
indestructible! (20 Dec. 1897; *LL*, vol. i, p. 216)

Yet within Conrad's morally neutral universe, man can for a time
create his own islands of satisfaction and meaning. Conrad's values
have often been explained in terms of his sea ethos, to the exclusion of
his other concerns. To be sure, fidelity, courage, responsibility to
one's fellows, and dedication to the task for its own sake are crucial
values. But he also dramatises how creative action, family relationships, and passionate love enable people to escape the psychological imprisonment of fears, doubts, obsessions, compulsions,
and fixations. Perhaps because he was an orphan and an emigré, the
importance of restoring personal and family ties is a major theme
throughout his career, a central value of the political novels, and the
cornerstone of his humanism. As he came to respect the English
tradition of manners, particularly in his later work, he emphasised
such private virutes as consideration to others, tact, sensitivity,
flexibility, and tenderness. Conrad's belief in the efficacy of fiction
underlines his humanism. The 1897 Preface to *The Nigger of
'Narcissus'* stresses the ability of fiction to make man see with more
clarity, insight, and understanding. A decade later in *A Personal
Record*, he contended: 'And what is a novel if not a conviction of our
fellow-men's existence strong enough to take upon itself a form of
imagined life clearer than reality and whose accumulated verisimili-
tude of selected episodes puts to shame the pride of documentary
history?' (*PR*, p. 15).

In a sense, the subtitle of this study could have been *Conrad's
Humanism*. As readers, we feel Conrad's living presence within his
fiction. Frequently, he is expressing his deep sympathy for suffering
humanity. At other times, he is struggling to discover the appropriate
form with which to render his concern and values. Surely his
dramatisation of diverse perspectives derives from his profound need
to understand humanity. For all his personal agony, Conrad
recognised both the grandeur and pathos of human life. From his
Polish heritage he claimed:

An impartial view of humanity in all its degrees of splendour
and misery together with a special regard for the rights of the
unprivileged of this earth, not on any mystic ground but on
the ground of simple fellowship and honourable reciprocity of
services . . . . (*PR*, p. ix)

He conceived of his art as homage to mankind: 'An imaginative and exact rendering of authentic memories may serve worthily that spirit of piety towards all things human which sanctions the conceptions of a writer of tales, and the emotions of the man reviewing his own experience' (PR, p. 25). Yet, throughout his career, Conrad's humanism conflicted with his scepticism. In his works he showed how the urge to self-fulfilment often interfered with a person's moral responsibilities to his fellows. As Aileen Kelly wrote of Tolstoy, 'Those of his characters who devote themselves to deliberate and reasoned altruism, whether in their personal relations or in social action, are shown as both impotent in their efforts to divide the ocean of good and evil and sterile in their inner lives.'[1] Gould, Jim, Peter Ivanovitch are in this category. But a more reflective and modest group, including Marlow, Monygham, and the language teacher in *Under Western Eyes*, redeem themselves by an instinctive commitment to ideals, values, and other persons.

This book is not only for students and teachers, but for all those who read Joseph Conrad. Unlike most recent critics whose books focus on one or another theme or group of Conrad's works, I consider the entire canon of Conrad's fiction from *Almayer's Folly* to *Under Western Eyes*, except for his collaborations with Ford and the fragment entitled *The Sisters*. In a subsequent volume entitled *Conrad: The Later Fiction*, I shall discuss the remainder of Conrad's work. Explicitly and implicitly, I also address central issues of Anglo-American fiction criticism and make suggestions about how to read novels. The book gradually presents a strikingly different Conrad from the one we have known. Yet it can be usefully consulted by teachers and students for discussions of individual works. I have intentionally avoided imposing an arbitrary pattern or thesis on Conrad's work. Rather, I have first considered each work as a unique imagined world with its own aesthetic and moral geography and only then asked how that work contributed to our understanding of Conrad. I think Conrad would have approved of this method, for in 'Books' (1905) Conrad wrote:

> After all, the creation of a world is not a small undertaking except perhaps to the divinely gifted. In truth every novelist must begin by creating for himself a world, great or little, in which he can honestly believe. This world cannot be made otherwise than in his own image: it is fated to remain

individual and a little mysterious, and yet it must resemble something already familiar to the experience, the thoughts and the sensations of his readers. (*NLL*, p. 6)

NOTE

1. Aileen Kelly, 'Tolstoy in Doubt', *The New York Review of Books*, vol. xxv (29 June 1978), p. 23.

# Part One
# Quest for Identity

# 1 Acts of initiation: *Almayer's Folly* and *An Outcast of the Islands*

I

Conrad's first two novels, *Almayer's Folly* (1895) and *An Outcast of the Islands* (1896), reflect his state of mind and reveal his values.[1] In these early novels Conrad tests and refines themes and techniques that he will use in his subsequent fiction. In what will become a characteristic of Conrad's early works, he uses fictional material from his own adventures as his source material. He not only draws upon his experience when he sailed as mate with the *Vidar* (1887–88), but bases the title character of his first novel on a man he actually knew. While these two novels seem to be about remote events, they actually dramatise his central concerns. While not ignoring the substance of *Almayer's Folly* and *An Outcast of the Islands*, this chapter will define issues and concerns which led to the development of Conrad's major work.

Sambir, the setting for *Almayer's Folly* and *An Outcast of the Islands*, is the first of Conrad's distorted and intensified settings. Like the Congo in 'Heart of Darkness' and Patusan in *Lord Jim*, Sambir becomes a metaphor for actions that occur there. It is also a projection of Conrad's state of mind as it appears in his 1894–6 letters: exhaustion and ennui alternate with spasmodic energy.[2] Conrad's narrator is in the process of creating a myth out of Sambir, but the process is never quite completed. Like Hardy's Egdon Heath, Sambir is an inchoate form that can be controlled neither by man's endeavours nor by his imagination. The demonic energy that seethes within the forests is a catalyst for the perverse sexuality of the white people and their subsequent moral deterioration. With its 'mud soft and black, hiding fever, rottenness, and evil under its level and glazed surface', Sambir refutes the Romantic myth that beyond civilisation

3

lie idyllic cultures in a state of innocence (pp. 325–61). Sambir's river, the Pantai, is a prototype for the Congo; the atavistic influence it casts upon white men, drawing out long repressed and atrophied libidinous energies, anticipates the Congo's effect on Kurtz. Sambir's primordial jungle comments on the illusion shared by Dain and Nina, as well as by Willems and Aissa, that passionate love can transform the world. Sambir's tropical setting seems to be dominated by the processes of death and destruction, and the jungle's uncontrollable fecundity expresses itself in devolution rather than evolution. The dominance of the Pantai and the forest implies that Conrad's cosmos is as indifferent to man's aspirations as the cosmos of his contemporary Hardy whose *Jude the Obscure* was published in 1895.

Had Conrad not gone on to write 'Heart of Darkness', we might be more attentive to the extent to which Sambir embodied Conrad's nightmare of various kinds of moral degeneracy and how it is for him a grim Dantesque vision of damnation. In Sambir, the (relatively) strong prey on the weak, the young upon the old, and the rich upon the poor. Illness, ageing, and death dominate life in Sambir. In *Outcast*, a tired worn-out generation gives way to another; Lakamba displaces Patalolo because the latter is ageing, Abdulla replaces Lingard; Mahmat Banjer displaces the 'very aged and feeble' Hinopari, and the old woman servant who remains with Willems and Aissa has been all but discarded to die (*OI*, p. 309). In *Almayer's Folly* Babalatchi is very conscious that he and Lakamba lack the energy they once had. Lakamba, Abdulla, and Almayer are older and moving toward their own inevitable death. The span of twenty years, a generation, has brought no discernible progress to Sambir. As Chapter 11 of *Almayer's Folly* opens and Dain awaits Nina with whom he will elope, Dain is depicted as a diminutive and anonymous figure who is dwarfed by the size and energy of the forest. While Dain and Nina rendezvous, 'the intense work of tropical nature went on: plants shooting upward, entwined, interlaced in inextricable confusion, climbing madly and brutally over each other in the terrible silence of a desperate struggle towards the life-giving sunshine above—as if struck with sudden horror at the seething mass of corruption below, at the death and decay from which they sprang' (*AF*, p. 71).

Upon the anarchical and primordial Sambir, man seeks to impose his order. Lacking wife and parents, and bereft in England of any family ties, Conrad proposes family and personal relationships as an alternative to the greed and hypocrisy that dominate Sambir life. Throughout Conrad's early work, the search for someone to legitimise one's activities by an empathetic response to one's motives and feelings is dramatised. We see this in Jim's need to be understood by Marlow and Marlow's to be understood by his audiences, as well as Conrad's desperate early letters to Garnett. As his letters indicate, Conrad's personal quest for identity involves rendering an account to such putative fathers as Garnett and Cunninghame Graham, who both took the place of Thaddeus Bobrowski after his uncle's death in 1894. It is as if within the artistic and intellectual realm Conrad felt himself an adolescent in relation to peers and contemporaries whom he *required* as approving authority figures. The tone of Bobrowski's letters implies that even in his mid-thirties Conrad accepted the role of an adolescent in that relationship. The 1895 letters to Garnett are as self-revealing as they are painful to read. Typically, he writes: 'I suffer now from an acute attack of faithlessness in the sense that I do not seem to believe in anything, but I trust that by the time we meet I shall be more like a human being and consequently ready to believe any absurdity . . .' (July 1895; *Garnett*, p. 39). The protagonists of his first novels—ineffectual, self-deluding indolent men who are the victims of their own imagination—objectify the self-consciousness about his ability and worth that he projects in his early letters. Since the orphaned Conrad regarded his uncle as a father figure, Conrad would have taken very seriously his uncle's rebuke that he lacked 'endurance and steadfastness of decision' and the implication that he had inherited from his father's side a tendency to '[plunge] in[to] plans of various kinds, the most diverse, mostly of a fantastic nature'.[3] In the Sambir novels each person seems to require someone else to share his confidence. This takes the form of a search for the missing family. As an orphan, who felt guilty for betraying his personal and national paternal heritage by living in England, Conrad was concerned from the outset with the relationship between parent and child. Almayer and Willems lack a father and seek to compensate for the absence of someone in whom to confide. The Malays' search for the restored family parallels that of the white protagonists: Omar is a father figure to Babalatchi, and the latter plays that role for Lakamba.

Conrad ironically uses the biblical concept of symbolic paternity in which God the father or a patriarch confers his blessing almost as if by magic. Both Almayer and Willems, for whom blessing is equated with wealth, depend on Lingard for such a symbolic paternity. Almayer and Willems define even the most fundamental human relationships in economic terms. Almayer calls Lingard 'father' because he wants to establish a filial relationship with the man who offers the promise of wealth in exchange for marrying his adopted daughter. Willems has married Hudig's illegitimate half-caste daughter in exchange for economic amenities. Lingard does not deny Willems's accusation that he has sold his soul: 'Well, whatever I have sold, and for whatever price, I never meant you—you of all people—to spoil my bargain' (*OI*, p. 91). Pathetically, Willems and Almayer believe in Lingard's omnipotence, for Lingard is the man both men would like to be. At one point, the disreputable Willems parodies Lingard's colonial impulse, an impulse that Conrad understood as perverse paternalism: 'In exchange for [fulfilling their economic needs], he had their silent fear, their loquacious love, their noisy veneration. . . . His munificence had demoralized them' (*OI*, pp. 4–5). Even more than the natives who confer on Lingard the name, 'King of the Sea', Almayer believes in him. Willems acknowledged Lingard's role as a father figure: 'In the whole world there was only one man that had ever cared for me. Only one white man. You!' (*OI*, p. 274). Lingard himself has a need for the surrogate children. He adopts Willems and Mrs Almayer, requests that Almayer call him father, and dotes on Nina. Ironically, he mistakenly believes that Willems is his surrogate son because he has qualities that resemble his own ('How he had liked the man: his assurance, his push, his desire to get on, his conceited good humour, and his selfish eloquence' (*OI*, p. 223)). Furthermore, because he thinks of Willems as a man whom he has 'brought up', Lingard feels Willems's conduct as a personal shame (*OI*, pp. 262, 277).

In *An Outcast* the narrator tentatively proposes and discards Lingard not only as a hero but as the centre of the novel's attention. Lingard's courage, straightforwardness, and willingness to accept the consequences of his behaviour provide standards by which we measure Almayer and Willems. At first, Lingard is a sympathetic figure, because he seems to represent a separate and distinct alternative to Willems. Lingard egotistically speaks of 'that river of mine' and thinks that his 'word is law' (*OI*, p. 43), but he really has little control over Sambir events. Having discovered the river 'for his own benefit only', he begins to equate Sambir's destiny with his own: 'He dreamed of Arcadian happiness for that little corner of the world which he loved to think all his own. His deep-seated and immovable conviction that only he—he, Lingard—knew what was good for them was characteristic of him, and after all, not so very far wrong. He would make them happy whether or no, he said, and he meant it' (*OI*, p. 200). Gradually and almost reluctantly Conrad acknowledges that Lingard's egomania is a serious flaw. The first of the apparent *übermenschen* that fascinated Conrad, Lingard equates himself with Law and Justice. The ageing Lingard represents a kind of independent, self-sufficient man who benefits from the East's geographical and moral spaces. He is the embodiment of the childhood fantasy that desires may determine one's morality, a fantasy which takes more pernicious forms in Kurtz and Jim. Lingard does have the sense of self, confidence, authority, and ability to act unselfconsciously that his creator lacked in his new writing career. Lingard may respond amorally and egocentrically, but he knows who he is and has the kind of stature that enables him to transform a situation by his very presence. What sustains Lingard is his self-confidence and the intensity of his imagination. At times he behaves as if his very words were capable of transforming his wish into reality. In a sense he is both the artist Conrad wishes to be and the idealised man of action who regretfully must be left behind.

Lingard anticipates Kurtz in the Congo, Jim on Patusan, and Gould in Costaguana as men who are finally unable to conquer themselves by means of conquering their environment. As Kurtz will in the Congo and Jim on Patusan, Lingard plays God in Sambir; indeed, the natives believe that he had magic powers 'to be in two places at once' or to 'make himself invisible' (*OI*, p. 317). Lingard regards Sambir as a kind of Utopia because of his delusion that his will is dominant and his word law; however, Sambir is less a primitive Xanadu than a mare's nest of petty intrigue. After he loses his boat and control over the river, he subsequently disappears. His identity as the 'King of the Sea' is demythologised; Lingard proves no more able than another man to transform his fictions into action. The ineffectuality and disappearence of the potential hero indicate Conrad's reluctance to depend on this vestige of his previous life as an ordering principle within his fiction.[4] Yet the temptation to allow Lingard's autonomy to become the ultimate moral value, as it almost does in the final confrontation with Willems, must have been great.

Unmarried until his late thirties, Conrad idealised heterosexual love; he wistfully and poignantly remarked: 'There is love. . . . Still one must have some object to hang his affections upon—and I haven't' (7 June 1895, *LL*, vol. i, p. 175). From the outset of his career, the early Conrad explores heterosexual love as a possible alternative to isolation and self-doubt. Yet Conrad's idealisation of heterosexual love is undermined by his obsessive treatment of Victorian sexual taboos: miscegenation, incest, and adultery. That sexuality so frequently focuses on these taboos reflects his unconscious discomfort with the subject of sex. Sambir becomes Almayer's and Willems's personal nemesis once they violate sexual taboos. Aissa is equated with Sambir because her sexuality is frightening not only to Willems, but to the propriety and decorum of Conrad's standards. Conrad is both titillated and shocked by interracial heterosexuality, a response that plays an important part in 'Heart of Darkness' and *Lord Jim*. Conrad depicts Willems's love for Aissa as a turning towards decay and moral darkness. Significantly, Willems perceives her as 'the very spirit of that land of mysterious forests' (*OI*, p. 70). Once Willems has sexual intercourse with Aissa, he has 'a depraved sense of pleasure at the after-taste of slime in the water' (*OI*, p. 73). Like Sambir her facade is appealing, while containing the threat of the forbidden and destructive: 'He had been baffled, repelled, almost frightened by the intensity of that tropical life which wants the sunshine but works in gloom; which seems to be all grace of colour and form, all brilliance, all smiles, but is only the blossoming of the dead; whose mystery holds the promise of joy and beauty, yet contains nothing but poison and decay' (*OI*, p. 70). The catalytic effect of his passion for Aissa upon his repressed libidinous needs leads to Willems's atavistic behaviour. Describing how passionate, forbidden sexual love causes Willems to put behind him his last vestige of the civilised man he believed he was, Conrad struggles to control his ironic distance and his language. He punishes his character Willems by having him imagine his own nullification. Willems saw himself 'going away from him and diminishing in a long perspective of fantastic trees. . . . He felt a desire to see him vanish' (*OI*, p. 175).

These first novels introduce the essential Conrad theme, that man necessarily lives in a world of his own illusions. Each of the major characters creates narratives of the future in which he or she believes. The novels trace Almayer's and Willems's response to the destruction of the putative future that each man imagines to keep himself going. In making an imagined world the basis of their existence while they are oblivious to empirical reality, Almayer and Willems anticipate Jim and Kurtz. The opening of each novel stresses the fictions in which both men live: Almayer's 'dream of splendid future' and Willems's illusions that his step off the 'straight and narrow path' will be a 'short episode' (*AF*, p. 3; *OI*, p. 3). The language focuses on self-delusion. Almayer is 'absorbed' in his dream; Willems 'imagined' and 'fancied' that his life will continue as it has (*AF*, p. 3; *OI*, p. 3). Almayer fantasises a future which will compensate for his present degradation; prior to his dismissal, Willems complacently assumes the invulnerability of the position on which he predicates his present self-

satisfaction. The flashback technique—temporarily moving to the
past but always returning to the present—is an appropriate formal
metaphor for Almayer whose alternating fantasies and reminiscences
cannot permanently exclude the present any more than the narrative
can. Once he is disgraced, Willems responds to his repressed
libidinous needs by creating a fantasy in which sexual love becomes
synonymous with life. Ignoring evidence of her real attitude to him,
her mother's growing influence, and her psychosexual needs,
Almayer creates a fiction of Nina that is not congruent with the facts.
Just as Lingard unsuccessfully tries to play Pygmalion with Mrs
Almayer, so does Almayer with his daughter. Living in a fictive
world purged of moral sanctions not only makes Almayer ineffective
in dealing with present exigencies, but it permits him to form
subconsciously a forbidden relationship with his daughter:

> Almayer was absorbed in the preparations, walking amongst
> his workmen and slaves in a kind of waking trance, where
> practical details as to the fitting out of the boats were mixed up
> with vivid dreams of untold wealth, where the present misery
> of burning sun, of the muddy and malodorous river bank dis-
> appeared in a gorgeous vision of a splendid future existence for
> himself and Nina. (*AF*, p. 62)

As will occur later in *Lord Jim*, *An Outcast of the Islands* begins with a
prologue (in this case, the first three chapters) in which the central
character's moral identity is defined. The rest of the novel is a
working out of the consequences of what happens to a man once he
has given in to his inherent weaknesses; Willems unwillingly
surrenders to savagery and moral darkness after he is revealed as an
embezzler. His 'indiscretion' is deliberately described in terms which
blur the distinction between civilisation and savagery: the 'track' of
his 'peculiar honesty' was so 'faint and ill-defined . . . that it took him
some time to find out how far he had strayed amongst the brambles of
the dangerous wilderness he had been skirting for so many years' (*OI*,
p. 21). Even before Willems departs for the wilderness of Sambir, he
is morally correlated with that grotesque place. Like the original 'path
from which he had strayed', the path to Aissa is almost allegorical:
'at the end of the first turning', Willems had 'a vision of blackness
darker than the deepest shade of the forest' (*OI*, p. 68). The man who
had equated *the* world with *his* world, soon discovers as Jim and
Razumov will, 'that the world was bigger, the night more vast and
more black' (*OI*, p. 30). Yet he is transformed in his own eyes into

another man. As Willems understands after his disgrace, he has become 'Another man—and another life with the faith in himself gone' (*OI*, p. 23). Like a snake (an image which the narrator associates several times with Willems [*OI*, pp. 328, 358]) shedding its cover, Willems casts off the remnants of his superego. The change in circumstances obliterates his façade of self-respect and makes him prey to libidinous impulses which he had barely sublimated in his compulsively aggressive pursuit of money. Willems is afraid of his transformation. With Victorian fastidiousness, he insists on affirming his marriage tie to a woman he despises and whom he regards as a 'limp weight' and an 'encumbrance'. As the ironic narrator makes clear, Willems is the man who has no principles and who takes economic success as a synecdoche for moral and emotional well-being. Like Jim, he takes solace in being white. As Part One ends, Willems despises his reversion to savagery; but he cannot help himself. Later, he irrationally and paranoically attributes demonic powers to Aissa. 'I did not belong to myself. She did. I did not know there was something in me she could get hold of. . . . She found out something in me. She found it out, and I was lost. I knew it. She tormented me.' (*OI*, p. 269)

Omar's murder attempt on Willems may be externalisation of Conrad's own subconscious self-condemnation for permitting his character to have a sexual affair with a Malay woman. The man who violates sacrosanct moral laws brings upon himself his own nemesis. Perhaps that is the real clue to why Omar's murderous passion finally casts Willems completely adrift from his psychic moorings; Willems had an 'unreasoning fear of this glimpse into the unknown things, into those motives, impulses, desires he had ignored, but that had lived in the breasts of despised men. . . . It was not death that frightened him: it was the horror of bewildered life where he could understand nothing and nobody round him; where he could guide, control, comprehend nothing and no one—not even himself' (*OI*, p. 149). Willems becomes a totem to warn man and to remind man of what happens when he gives into his repressed impulses. Covered with blood from Lingard's attack, Willems 'seemed as though he had been set up there for a warning, an incomprehensible figure marked all over with some awful and symbolic signs of deadly import' (*OI*, pp. 263–4).

Violating the incest taboo evokes a similar nemesis. It is not impossible that Conrad's heterosexual interest in Mme Poradowska, a distant relative by marriage, accounts for the narrator's relatively compassionate view of Almayer's love for his daughter. When Almayer's marriage proves disastrous, he unconsciously begins to transform his daughter into a wife. He rationalises that his quest for gold is entirely a quest to transform his daughter's status. His obsessions with gold and racial status are in part sublimations by which he circumvents the incest taboo. Ironically, Almayer, who has sold himself to Lingard as a husband for his adopted daughter in exchange for the promise of gold, wants to use the gold to purchase back his status and that of his daughter, and thus reverse the descent in status that interracial sexuality implies to him. Gold becomes the means by which he can pay homage to his daughter in a socially acceptable way. His passion for Nina evolved from his apotheosising her when she was a young child; Almayer 'appeared strangely impressive and ecstatic; like a devout and mystic worshipper, adoring, transported and mute; burning incense before a shrine, a diaphanous shrine of a child-idol with closed eyes; before a pure and vaporous shrine of a small god—fragile, powerless, unconscious and sleeping' (*OI*, p. 320). Almayer's ecstatic child-worship, recalling the idolatry of primitive cultures, underlines the equation of sexuality and atavism. This equation is at odds with Conrad's efforts to establish heterosexual love as a paradigm and with his contention that there is no substantial distinction between primitive and civilised man.

In two of the more significant readings of *Almayer's Folly* written in the last decade or so, John H. Hicks and Royal Roussel have stressed the affirmative nature of the heterosexual relationship between Nina and Dain.[5] Hicks argues that what begins as a 'spontaneous and irrational passion' evolves into a mature relationship; while Dain reconciles his desire for Nina with his 'responsibilities as seaman, prince, and future ruler', Nina combines her own individuality with a socially valid identity.[6] Roussel speaks even more enthusiastically of how through 'mutual surrender two people can achieve such a miraculous continuity and enter an existence in which any distinction between self and other disappears'.[7] Yet the narrative structure indicates that Nina is as much a dreamer as Almayer. Nina's wish to escape with a passionate lover to a land unpolluted by white men and sordid searches for wealth is an ironic inversion of her father's. While Almayer dreams of wealth and triumph in the white world with himself as her companion, she dreams of leaving him behind. The fulfilment of her dream is inevitably the destruction of his. How often in Conrad does one person seem to thrive at the expense of others, as if by a weird principle of human energy one person's happiness necessarily implies another's destruction. But both dreams are the function of a psychic need to escape a claustrophobic existence. Psychologically, Nina is prepared for virtually any alternative to her intolerable existence of the past three years. Disillusioned by the civilised world at Singapore, she responds to her mother's fictions rather than her father's and believes she has found the ideal Malay chief of her mother's tradition. Well aware that her response to Dain is a function of disappointment, sexual frustration, and ennui, the narrator renders her awakening with gentle irony and intentionally melodramatic language: 'She understood now the reason and the aim of life; and in the triumphant unveiling of that mystery she threw away disdainfully her past with its sad thoughts, its bitter feelings and its faint affections, now withered and dead in contact with her fierce passion' (*AF*, p. 152). Dain's impulsiveness, immoderation, his enthusiasm, and his recklessness appeal to her because these qualities contrast to her father and the hypocrisy of the white world in Singapore where she had been slighted for her colour. That the characters arrive for Dain's and Nina's elopement in reverse order of their original presentation— Dain first, then Nina, finally, in pursuit, Almayer—shows how Dain has rendered Almayer obsolete and cast him out of the primary position he once occupied not only in Nina's consciousness but in the novel's form.

In an early version of *The Secret Sharer* motif, Dain and Nina mythicise one another. Even before he knows her, he is not only captivated by her looks, but certain that they are of a common mind. No sooner does Nina behold Dain than she feels 'born only then to a knowledge of a new existence' (*AF*, p. 64). Yet when they meet to elope, 'She was thinking already of moulding a god from the clay at her feet. A god for others to worship' (*AF*, p. 172). She is unintentionally miming her father's attitude towards her. She has a touch of her father's egoism and more than a touch of his hyperbolic imagination; she tells her father: 'I shall make him great. His name shall be remembered long after both our bodies are laid in the dust' (*AF*, p. 180). The reader understands that she may repeat Almayer's effort to shape another human being according to one's own whims, an effort which, perhaps more than anything, is 'Almayer's folly'.

But do Dain's and Nina's mutual fictions imply that they will really live a transformed life? Isn't Dain's love for her an expression of his immoderate and spontaneous nature rather than a guarantee of future bliss? Like Almayer and Willems, Dain barters for his wife. He is, like them, choosing a wife who is culturally incompatible. For psychological reasons, Nina chooses a racial antitype as a means of passage away from a world she finds stifling and disgusting. Where is there an indication of a mature love? After all, Mrs Almayer suggests that, despite Dain's present enthusiasm, 'there will be other women' (*AF*, p. 153); she implies that Nina should merely accept this, unless he is in love with one specific woman in which case she recommends that Nina murder her rival. True, Nina will be the wife of a mighty prince, but isn't Mrs Almayer's recollection of 'the usual life of a Malay girl—the usual succession of heavy work and fierce love, of intrigues, gold ornaments, of domestic drudgery, and of that great but occult influence which is one of the few rights of half-savage womankind'—proleptic of Nina's life? (*AF*, p. 22). In any case she will be part of a world in which war, intrigue, and violence are perpetual. Lakamba and Babalatchi have few scruples about murdering both Almayer and Dain. Mrs Almayer's vision of Malay life is a violent one; in her Polonius role before the elopement, she encourages her daughter to insist that 'men should fight before they rest' (*AF*, p. 152), and she imagines that he will be perpetually fighting white men. Her view of Malay heterosexual love is one in which the woman serves her man by day and dominates him sexually at night. Clearly, the reader is shown aspects of Nina's future life that do not conform to her fictions.

Nina's own fastidiousness and timidity about leaving her father show that she does not share her mother's temperamental enthusiasm for this world. Ironically, her acculturation makes her unfit for the Malay world as well as the white world. While she romanticises the future into a paradise, the narrative implies that Dain's life may be hardly more than a series of military adventures. Indeed, Conrad would have us understand that her speech to her father about the impossibility of two people understanding one another is appropriate to *any* human relationship: 'No two human beings understand each other. They can understand but their own voices. You wanted me to dream your dreams, to see your own visions. . . . But while you spoke I listened to the voice of my own self' (*AF*, p. 179). Like Almayer and Willems, Nina inhabits a world of her own sensory perceptions from which she desperately tries to escape by seeking a sympathetic other. Nina's speech undermines the very belief in mutual love to which she commits herself by implying that each person narcissistically responds to his or her own voice. When Dain is baffled by her tears, the narrator stresses the necessary disparity between Dain and Nina, and by implication, any two people: 'He was uneasily conscious of something in her he could not understand. . . . No desire, no longing, no effort of will or length of life could destroy this vague feeling of their difference' (*AF*, p. 187). Clearly, Nina has not found the sympathetic other that she seeks.

Conrad understood that man can only pursue, and never capture, one's dream. Temporarily, Nina and Dain may '[enter] a land where no one can follow us' but the exigencies of survival, the passage of time, and the ephemeral nature of sexual love are continual threats to their present bliss (*AF*, p. 179). Love, then, is as temporary an illusion for Nina as it is for Aissa, Willems and Dain, all of whom face an extremely problematic future. The emphasis upon man's diminutive stature in relation to nature, the stress on man's temporality, the indifference of nature to man's aspirations, and perhaps even the meanness of the human spirit as illustrated by white men and natives show the impossibility of love's creating a new existence.

## II

Before he created Marlow, Conrad had difficulty controlling the personal turmoil that we see in his letters of the 1894–96 period; he feels isolated in a meaningless universe; he is cynical about man's motives and purposes on this earth; he senses that he is an artistic failure; he doubts his ability to communicate, even while expressing his desperate need to be understood. If it does not always seem that the commentary is appropriate to the dramatic action which evokes it, it is because Conrad is using his speaker to explore his own bafflement in a universe he regards as amoral, indifferent, and at times hostile. In the first two novels, when Conrad's surrogate, his narrator, places an episode in an intellectual and moral context, he is often testing and probing to discover what an episode means. Conrad subsequently learns to capitalise on his reluctance to be dogmatic; he dramatises Marlow's process of moral discovery, and shows how Marlow continually formulates, discards and redefines his beliefs through experience. But because in 1894–5 Conrad had difficulty in embracing a consistent set of values, his narrators' commentary does not always move towards a consistent philosophic position, but rather may posit contradictory perspectives. Quite frequently, the omniscient voice of the first two novels, *Almayer's Folly* and *An*

*Outcast of the Islands*, explores characters and action from the perspective of a man committed to family ties, the work ethic, sexual constraint, individual responsibility, and racial understanding. Yet these basic humanistic values are often at odds with the artistic tentativeness and moral confusion that derive from Conrad's uncertainty and anxiety. The unresolved tension between, on the one hand, Conrad's own personal concerns and, on the other, his attempt to objectify moral issues is revealed in conflicts between the values expressed by the narrator and the implications of his plot and setting. At times, one of the narrator's comments may very well be in some conflict with another. Or one of his comments may be more an outburst of intellectual energy than a reasoned through discussion of the novel's action. For example, the narrator uses the occasion of verbal fencing between Babalatchi and Willems to make the following meditative comment that barely pertains to the action, but reflects Conrad's own ennui and pessimism.

> Babalatchi's fatalism gave him only an insignificant relief in his suspense because no fatalism can kill the thought of the future, the desire of success, the pain of waiting for the disclosure of the immutable decrees of Heaven. Fatalism is born of the fear of failure, for we all believe that we carry success in our own hands, and we suspect that our hands are weak. (*OI*, p. 126)

When Aissa feels her isolation, Conrad characteristically defines it in terms of *his own* loneliness which he generalizes into mankind's common plight:

> Her hands slipped off Lingard's shoulders and her arms fell by her side, listless, discouraged, as if to her—to her, the savage, violent, and ignorant creature—had been revealed clearly in that moment the tremendous fact of *our* isolation, of that loneliness impenetrable and transparent, elusive and everlasting; of the indestructible loneliness that surrounds, envelops, clothes *every human soul* from the cradle to the grave, and, perhaps, beyond. (*OI*, p. 250; emphases mine)

When he launched his writing career, Conrad was not only a complex personality almost paralysed by self-doubt, but an expatriate with an ambiguous attitude toward the English intellectual and moral milieu of the 1890s. In his early novels, the conservative standards of the British merchant marine are qualified by the values and attitudes of bourgeois culture as well as the ennui and cynicism of the *fin de siècle*. The tradition of English manners, with its emphasis on polite behaviour and fastidious moral distinctions, plays a prominent role in the early novels where Conrad's usually sceptical and gloomy narrator often adopts the stance of an enlightened Victorian.

Conrad did not accept the late Victorian notion shared by the Fabians, Shaw, Cunninghame and Butler, that mankind was evolving into a higher creature or that Western civilisation was of superior quality to the more primitive kinds of human life. Conrad implies that the distinction between civilised white man and savage natives, a distinction which is taken as the essential premise of life by his Western European characters living in undeveloped areas, is fundamentally apocryphal. In the 1895 Author's Note to *Almayer's Folly*, Conrad stresses the common plight of all men:

> I am content to sympathize with common mortals, no matter where they live; in houses or in tents, in the streets under a fog, or in the forests. . . . For, their land—like ours—lies under the inscrutable eyes of the Most High. Their hearts—like ours—must endure the load of the gifts from Heaven: the curse of facts and the blessing of illusions, the bitterness of our wisdom and the deceptive consolation of our folly. (*AF*, p. viii)

In the early Malay novels it is Conrad's narrator, not Conrad's expatriates, as Lloyd Fernando argues, who is 'tantalized by the ideal of a true bond of humanity among all'.[8] His early works bitterly satirise imperialistic pretensions. In *Almayer's Folly*, *An Outcast of the Islands*, the stories comprising *Tales of Unrest*, and 'Heart of Darkness', white men and natives share similar passions and needs; both demonstrate the same potential for nobility and baseness. Almayer and Willems seek to exploit their racial position for economic gain. As Westerners who eschew hard work and seek a life of ease, they anticipate Kayerts and Carlier in 'An Outpost of Progress', the company men in 'Heart of Darkness', and the officers of the *Patna*. Conrad implies that what restrains Almayer and Willems from murder is not superior morality, but enervated instincts and atrophied will. In Conrad's Malay novels, as Fernando reminds us, Conrad's Europeans share the condition of exile with the major Malay characters—Babalatchi, Abdulla, Lakamba, Aissa.[9] Perhaps

Conrad blurs the line between cultures because in the 1890s he wanted to believe in the similarity between Poles and Englishmen. By emphasising the similarity between cultures, he eases both his psychic strain of being an expatriate writer for English audiences and his frustration in learning to speak the English language.

Conrad demystifies accepted late nineteenth-century distinctions between primitive and civilised by replicating in the Malay and Arab society the kind of social hierarchies that we mistakenly believe to be an implicit part of Western civilisation. He describes the Malay world in terms which his turn-of-the-century reader would have readily placed in the context of Edwardian England. Willems is a 'confidential clerk', Lakamba is a 'noble exile' and an 'ambitious nobleman', and Babalatchi is a 'sagacious statesman'. As a mysterious powerful figure whose reputation sustains him more than any action, Abdulla parallels Lingard. Conrad wants to imply that Sambir is analogous to Western civilisation, without going so far as saying so and thus risk offending his adopted country:

> It was one of the tolerated scandals of Sambir, disapproved
> and accepted, a manifestation of that base acquiescence in
> success, of that inexpressed and cowardly toleration of strength,
> that exists, infamous and irremediable, at the bottom of all
> hearts, in all societies; whenever men congregate; in bigger and
> more virtuous places than Sambir, and in Sambir also, where,
> as in other places, one man could steal a boat with impunity
> while another would have no right to look at a paddle. (*OI*, p.
> 309)

At times he suggests that Malay political life is the metaphorical vehicle for which English politics is the tenor. Can there be any doubt that English political pretensions are included in the following remark? 'The mind of the savage statesman, chastened by bereavement, felt for a moment the weight of his loneliness with keen perception worthy even of a sensibility exasperated by all the refinements of tender sentiment that a glorious civilization brings in its train, among other blessings and virtues, into this excellent world' (*OI*, pp. 214–15).

Despite the narrator's efforts to propose values and ideals, the first two novels posit a vision of mankind that emphasises mankind's powerlessness, his ineffectuality, his pettiness, his selfishness, and the ephemeral nature of the life he leads. Like Carlier and Kayerts in 'An

Outpost of Progress' and in 'Heart of Darkness', Almayer and Willems are men whose passions have been repressed and distorted by civilisation without a concomitant social development. With scathing irony, the narrator shows that the relationship between Almayer and Willems is marked by atavistic hatred: 'Those two specimens of the superior race glared at each other savagely . . .' (*OI*, p. 63). Yet, while Nina may conclude that, finally, the savages are preferable, the intrigues of Lakamba and Babalatchi do not lead the reader to that conclusion. Conrad attributes apparent differences in the political behaviour of whites and natives to the natives' relative weakness in relation to the white man's military power. For similar stimuli often evoke similar responses. Conrad recognises the need of men to communicate with one another as the basic impulse that draws them together. Both the native and white cultures rely on talk as a means of planning, reminiscing, and exchanging thoughts. Conrad's explanation of the uses and abuses of language anticipates a central theme of the three turn-of-the-century Marlow tales. For the natives, talk 'is their only accomplishment, their only superiority, their only amusement' (*OI*, p. 96). Lakamba depends on Babalatchi's talk to energise him; their exchanges contain abortive plots and insidious stratagems, but more than that their talk gives them the opportunity for friendship that neither seems to find elsewhere. Part of Almayer's problem is that he has no one in whom to confide; even before he retreats into autistic silence at the end of *Almayer's Folly*, the range of his verbal behaviour has atrophied and he uses speech only to give orders and to fence with his enemies. From the outset, when his wife's shrill cry disrupts his fantasy, language seems an enemy that threatens to intrude into the fictions that he weaves for himself. Almayer feels Taminah's urgings that he awake as 'the murmur of words that fell on his ears in a jumble of torturing sentences, the meaning of which escaped the utmost efforts of his brain' (*AF*, pp. 159–60).

Finally, Conrad's narrative structures and proleptic texture mirror a closed universe where man seems to be locked into a concatenation of events that he cannot control. In both novels, the Victorian humanism of the narrator is undermined by the dramatised action of the plot, and it is the pessimistic, morbid plot that reflects Conrad's own state of mind. Even while the narrator tries to establish a humanistic perspective, the plots of both novels dramatise the inevitable demise of a man who has debilitating moral flaws and the failure of human relationships among the rest of the major characters.

For example, Lingard's and Almayer's mutual failure to kill a fly unites in futility and frustration the seeming *übermensch*, Lingard, with the *untermensch* Willems: 'Lingard and Almayer [stood] face to face in the fresh silence of the young day, looking very puzzled and idle, arms hanging uselessly by their sides—like men disheartened by some portentous failure' (*OI*, p. 169). In *Almayer's Folly* each of the early chapters closes with significant codas which point to Almayer's demise: his wife's 'savage intrusion' concludes Chapter 2; his 'nameless fear', deriving from his suspicion that his daughter might want 'to be kidnapped' ends Chapter 3; the presence of Babalatchi juxtaposed to Almayer's unspoken and ineffectual threats closes Chapter 4; the river's violence climaxes Chapter 5; and the ironic juxtaposition of Verdi's *Il Trovatore* with Babalatchi's and Lakamba's plans to poison Almayer concludes Chapter 6. While the parabolic endings to chapters reinforce the dark vision of the plot, they may seem forced and anxious attempts by Conrad to transform nominalistic events into significant form. The collapse of the house of cards that Lingard builds to amuse Nina may be not only a metaphor for Lingard's failure to impose a structure upon the world, but a moment of self-irony on the part of the author who doubts whether he can get control of his imagined world. For as he wrote Edward Noble, while he was still completing *An Outcast*, '[Writing] is made up of doubt, or hesitation, of moments silent and anxious when one listens to the thoughts,—one's own thoughts,—speaking indistinctly, deep down somewhere, at the bottom of the heart' (17 July 1895; *LL*, vol. i, p. 175).

Whereas in *The Nigger of the 'Narcissus'* Conrad will *dramatise* the fellowship of an organic community and the virtues of self-reliance, resourcefulness, and fidelity to the ship and crew, the only affirmative values in the first two novels are in the telling. Conrad defines the narrator of the two early novels as a man who is morally and psychologically different from the protagonists, both of whom he not only patronises but despises. And yet Conrad reluctantly realises that Willems and Almayer, like Jim, must be regarded as 'one of us' and that all men share a kinship with the worst of men. Writing to Garnett of Aissa and Willems, he remarks: 'To me they are typical of mankind, where every individual wishes to assert his power, woman by sentiment, man by achievement of some sort—mostly base. I myself . . . have been ambitious to make it clear and have failed in that, as Willems fails in his effort to throw off the trammels of earth and of heaven' (24 Sept. 1895; *LL*, vol. i, p. 181). Royal Roussel speaks of the narrator's 'sympathetic' awareness of Almayer's world and his 'emotional involvement [with] and commitment' to all the characters of that novel.[10] But, on the contrary, what is remarkable is the compulsive *insistence* of Conrad's surrogate, the narrator, upon separating himself from his ineffectual protagonists. Almayer and Willems are fictional projections of self-doubt, weariness, and anxiety that Conrad desperately wishes to leave behind. The early novels are acts of initiation for the artistic self Conrad was trying to create and the casting off of the seaman identity with which he had achieved success and self-satisfaction.

NOTES

1. I use the abbreviations *AF* to indicate *Almayer's Folly* and *OI* to indicate *An Outcast of the Islands*. Although written first, *Almayer's Folly* takes place twenty years after *An Outcast of the Islands*. Conrad completed *Almayer's Folly* in 1894 and *An Outcast of the Islands* in 1895; the dates in parentheses are publication dates.

2. See G. Jean Aubry, *Joseph Conrad: Life and Letters*, 2 vols. (Garden City: Doubleday, Page and Company, 1927). Also John A. Gee and Paul J. Sturm, *Letters of Joseph Conrad to Marguerite Poradowska 1890–1920* (New Haven: Yale University Press, 1940); see for example, pp. 63, 82, 86, 88.

3. See Jocelyn Baines, *Joseph Conrad: A Critical Biography* (New York, McGraw Hill, 1960), p. 122.

4. For the original of Lingard, whom Conrad never met and only knew as a legend, see Norman Sherry, *Conrad's Eastern World* (Cambridge: Cambridge University Press, 1966), especially pp. 89–118.

5. John H. Hicks, 'Conrad's *Almayer's Folly*: Structure, Theme, and Critics', *Nineteenth-Century Fiction*, vol. xix (June 1964), pp. 17–31. See Royal Roussel, *The Metaphysics of Darkness* (Baltimore and London: The Johns Hopkins Press, 1971), pp. 28–50.

6. Hicks, p. 24.

7. Roussel, pp. 40–1.

8. See Lloyd Fernando, 'Conrad's Eastern Expatriates: A New Version of His Outcasts', *PMLA*, vol. xci (1976), p. 89.

9. *Ibid.*, pp. 78–90.

10. Roussel, pp. 49–50.

# 2 Unrest

I

A brief look at Conrad's state of mind soon after he started his writing career helps explain why Conrad began in his earliest stories to shift the focus from the tale to the teller. Although he has already published *Almayer's Folly* (1895) and *An Outcast of the Islands* was already completed and to be published in 1896, Conrad is plagued by anxiety and self-doubt about his new career. In an 1896 letter to Garnett he agonises: 'Everything seems so abominably stupid. You see the *belief* is not in me—and without the belief—the brazen thick headed, thick skinned, immovable belief nothing good can be done. . . . I doubt everything. The only certitude left to me is that I cannot work for the present' (5 Aug. 1896; *Garnett*, p. 65). The transition from seaman to author seems to have undermined Conrad's belief in the coherence and stability of his personality, a belief that he gradually acquired during his career as a seaman after a tumultuous and erratic youth:

> When once the truth is grasped that one's own personality is only a ridiculous and aimless masquerade of something hopelessly unknown the attainment of serenity is not very far off. Then there remains nothing but the surrender to one's impulses, the fidelity to passing emotions which is perhaps nearer to truth than any other philosophy of life. And why not? If we are 'ever becoming—never being' then I would be a fool if I tried to become this thing rather than that; for I know well that I never will be anything. (23 Mar. 1896; *Garnett*, p. 46)

The revealing shift in pronouns from 'we' to 'I' makes clear that Conrad is trying to generalise his own plight as if to convince himself that he is experiencing a representative rather than an idiosyncratic crisis. If man is constantly changing from moment to moment,

Conrad reasoned, how could anyone hope to have a consistent identity?

Conrad shares with many of the artists and intellectuals of the 1890s a belief that each man is enclosed in his private world, limited to his own perceptions, and quite separate and isolated from other men. Marlow's assertion in 'Heart of Darkness' that 'We live, as we dream—alone . . .' echoes a motif that appears in such diverse works as Hardy's *Jude the Obscure* (1895) and Wilde's *The Picture of Dorian Gray* (1890). Like most of his contemporaries, Conrad was familiar with Pater's *Marius the Epicurean* (1885), an influential book in the 1890s, that expresses the belief that each man is limited by his own sensations. (Marius reflects, 'All that is real in our experience [is] but a series of fleeting impressions: . . . given, that we are never to get beyond the walls of this closely shut cell of one's own personality. . . .')[1] In an 1895 letter to Edward Noble, Conrad asserts that each man experiences the world armed with the illusions which his psyche creates to sustain him: 'No man's light is good to any of his fellows. . . . All formulas, dogmas, and principles of other people's making . . . are only a web of illusions. . . . Another man's truth is only a dismal lie to me' (2 Nov. 1895; *LL*, vol. i, p. 184). Is it surprising that the need to be understood by another person, to complete oneself by finding a responsive consciousness, is a major theme of his early fiction? In the 1896–7 letters to his close friends, Cunninghame Graham and Garnett, one can feel Conrad's intellectual and emotional isolation as he strains to believe in the empathy of his friends. Just as the captain of 'The Secret Sharer' will later do with Leggatt, Conrad *creates* his alter ego by attributing to Garnett the qualities he felt himself lacking. Once his Uncle Thaddeus Bobrowski died in 1894 Conrad sought a father figure among his friends. In his 1896–7 letters, he alternately plays the role of ingenuous adolescent and agonising creative artist. While he did not follow his father's political quest, he did pursue his father's other career, that of a writer. Even after his marriage in 1896, he needed the intellectual and artistic support of his friends to sustain him. Conrad is never more revealing of his sense of inadequacy than in one 1897 letter to Garnett: 'For me you are the reality outside, the expressed thought, the living voice! And without you I would think myself alone in any empty universe' (20 Apr. 1897; *Garnett*, p. 97). Several months later, Conrad writes to Cunninghame Graham: 'Now I live so alone that often I fancy myself clinging stupidly to a derelict planet abandoned by its precious crew. Your voice is not a voice in the wilderness—it seems to come through the clean emptiness of space' (5 Aug. 1897; *Cunninghame Graham*, p. 46). His fiction provides him an imagined world to which he could escape from his frustrations in the real world. Although perhaps a shade too neat and simplified, Dr Bernard Meyer's explanation of Conrad's original motivation to write becomes compelling:

> It would appear then that in taking up his pen he was seeking to combat his loneliness by creating a world of fiction teeming with people and bursting with action. If his own existence seemed empty, devoid of purpose and direction, lacking in human companionship and fulfilled passion, through invented characters loving and raging in an invented world, the shy and lonely Joseph Conrad could enjoy vicariously a vibrant participation, achieving there a release of feeling and an unmasking of himself rarely permitted in his real life.[2]

Conrad's antidote for doubt and anxiety is not nihilism but humanism. Conrad's early artistic code, the 1897 Preface to *The Nigger of the 'Narcissus'*, is remarkable for its emphasis on creating a community of readers. Seen in the context of his own fear of loneliness and of not communicating, it reflects his decision that fiction will not only enable him to arrest the flux and turmoil within himself, but that it will relieve him of his sense of isolation. Conrad defines art 'as a single-minded attempt to render the highest kind of justice to the visible universe, by bringing to light the truth, manifold and one, underlying its every aspect' (*NN*, p. vii). The artist's *mission* is to reveal the experience that unites all men and, in particular, to make the reader aware of the common humanity each shares with mankind.

> The artist appeals to that part of our being which is not dependent on wisdom; to that in us which is a gift and not an acquisition—and, therefore, more permanently enduring. He speaks to our capacity for delight and wonder, to the sense of mystery surrounding our lives; to our sense of pity, and beauty, and pain; to the latent feeling of fellowship with all creation—and to the subtle but invincible conviction of solidarity that knits together the loneliness of innumerable hearts, to the solidarity in dreams, in joy, in sorrow, in aspirations, in illusions, in hope, in fear, which binds men to

each other, which binds together all humanity—the dead to the living and, the living to the unborn. (*NN*, p. viii)

Surely one reason that Conrad uses a voice—whether he be a first or third person speaker—who has a distinct personality and a character-istic speech pattern is to give his reader a figure with whom he can identify and establish a sense of solidarity. *The Nigger of the 'Narcissus'*, written after 'The Idiots', 'An Outpost to Progress', and 'The Lagoon', but before 'Karain: A Memory', is told in the form of the reminiscence of one of the ship's crew members. Although the speaker's voice is not completely distinct and, indeed, fluctuates from third to first person, the tale represents a crucial step towards the development of a self-dramatising speaker who is engaged in the process of understanding past events and finding an appropriate vocabulary for a crucial experience.

The 1897 Preface argues, as Avrom Fleishman remarks, that 'The artist's role . . . is to knit men together in a universal community based on their awareness of a common fate.'[3] The famous stress on solidarity in the Preface derives from Conrad's desire that his art close the gulf that he intensely felt divided each person from his fellows: 'Fiction—if it at all aspires to be art—appeals to temperament. And in truth it must be, like painting, like music, like all art, the appeal of one temperament to all the other innumerable temperaments whose subtle and resistless power endows passing events with their true meaning, and creates the moral, the emotional atmosphere of the place and time' (*NN*, p. ix). Conrad hopes for a community of responsive temperaments to verify the effectiveness of *his* creation; this hope may be behind the intensity of the famous but elusive assertion: 'My task which I am trying to achieve is, by the power of the written word, to make you hear, to make you feel—it is, before all, to make you *see*' (*NN*, p. x).

## II. 'THE IDIOTS' (1896) AND 'AN OUTPOST OF PROGRESS' (1897)

While hardly a masterpiece, 'The Idiots' is a penetrating study of emotional and moral idiocy and does not deserve the neglect and abuse it has received. Written in May 1896, while Conrad was living in Brittany with his recent bride, 'The Idiots' is his first published short story. Criticism has generally been content to pursue Conrad's retrospective comment in his Author's Note to *Tales of Unrest* that 'The Idiots' is 'an obviously derivative piece of work', and to discuss the influence of Flaubert, Maupassant, and Zola (p. ix). Few critics have disputed Albert Guerard's dismissal of 'The Idiots' as 'the product of an amateur's desperate search for a "subject"'.[4]

Yet 'The Idiots' is more than the naturalistic study of a couple, the Bacadous, who have a fateful propensity to produce severely retarded offspring. The blighted offspring are stark symbols of a community where family, clerical, and political structures are undermined by the hypocrisy, selfishness, and vanity of those in positions to provide moral leadership. The title refers not only to the children, but to the adults in Ploumar parish whose moral idiocy is the real subject. Within the rural parish, every human relationship is blighted: husband and wife, cleric and flock, aristocracy and peasants, parents and children. As in Conrad's first two novels, the insidious effects of greed and emotional self-indulgence are a major motif. Each character acts according to his own narrow interests in a world where survival of the fittest is a fact of both biological and moral life.

The first-person speaker becomes an omniscient voice who stands in judgement of Ploumar parish and whose values are a humanistic alternative to its pettiness and selfishness. Rather than dramatise the process by which the narrator learns the information on which his telling is based, as he will in his later tales, Conrad has his narrator rather clumsily explain that he pieced together the story until it stood as a unified 'tale formidable and simple'. As in the more polished 'Amy Foster', to which 'The Idiots' looks forward, village life is indicted as petty and mean, and piety is seen to be shallow in a society where Christianity exists in name only. The people accept a simple pecking order where idiots are reduced to animals and where human relationships are conducted without feeling. The political and religious structures under the aegis of the marquis are revealed as corrupt. In both 'The Idiots' and 'Amy Foster', Conrad indicts a rural community for failing to respond humanely. While in 'Amy Foster', an English village's parochialism and xenophobia are exposed by the appearance of a harmless stranger, in 'The Idiots', the community's lack of humanity is demonstrated by its failure to provide responsible care for the helpless children.[5]

Conrad's fascination with human decadence, begun in the Malay novels with Almayer and Willems and continued in 'The Idiots', is the subject of his next story, the powerful and underestimated 'An Outpost of Progress', which was written during an interlude from

*The Rescue*. Writing a story in which the moral distinctions were clear and in which he was in complete control of his materials was extremely important to him, because he was bogged down on *The Rescue*. Conrad's letter to Unwin makes clear that the story is in part an intense response to his 1890 Congo experience: 'All the bitterness of those days, all my puzzled wonder as to meaning of all I saw—all my indignation at *masquerading philanthropy* have been with me again while I wrote' (emphasis mine).[6]

In this story, Conrad examines his 1890 Congo journey—the source of 'Heart of Darkness'—for the first time. Although seemingly a return to the use of the omniscient convention of the Malay novels and 'The Idiots', 'An Outpost of Progress' actually represents a significant advance in Conrad's development of a distinctive drama-tised narrator. Conrad's self-assured surrogate, the narrator, is the major figure of the tale, alternating a lucid statement of his moral and intellectual values with a scathingly ironic view of two European traders, Kayerts and Carlier. We feel his presence in every paragraph. Rather than indict Conrad for ostentatious editorializing, we should understand that his insistence on expressing his disillusionment, bitterness, and outrage through the narrator is part of the story. As the pretensions of Kayerts and Carlier are exposed, and objective reality seems to dissolve into the intruding mist ('Things appeared and disappeared before their eyes in an unconnected and aimless kind of way' [p. 92]), the narrator's confident moral stance and self-control, demonstrated by the discipline and unity of the tale's structure, affirm the existence of an alternative and far more attractive concept of civilisation than the one espoused by the predatory colonialists.

The narrator anticipates his dramatic material with generalisations that are later demonstrated by the particulars of the plot. Clearly, he wants us to think of Kayerts and Carlier as representative figures of European civilisation; he gives them neither nationality nor unique personalities. They are the minor functionaries in the civil service and the military, but they could just as well have held routine jobs in industry. These men can only function within highly organised bureaucratic structures in which individuality has lost its meaning. That, as the narrator remarks, all but the exceptional person requires the 'irresistible force of [the crowd's] institutions' for his moral identity is a recurring motif in Conrad, most notably in 'Heart of Darkness', *The Secret Agent* and *Under Western Eyes* (p. 89). Kayerts and Carlier not only lack the emotional and intellectual tools to deal with an environment which offers new challenges, but they are morally unequipped to deal with the unique situations presented by their new environment.

Profoundly disillusioned by his experience in the Congo, Conrad stresses the phases of the two white men's degeneration. Despite their lip service to idealism, by the second day Kayerts and Carlier have already ceased trying to export their civil service version of European civilisation. In fact, the outpost of progress quickly becomes an outpost of savagery. Rather than being agents of change, these men are changed: like Kurtz, they gradually regress to savagery. But while Kurtz actually *renounces* civilised values and boldly practises 'unspeakable rites', Kayerts and Carlier forget their ideals and drift into anomie. If Eliot excluded Kurtz from his category of 'hollow men' because Kurtz chose evil, he could well have had Kayerts and Carlier in mind as the hollow men who did not will their fate. In progressive stages, the trappings of civilisation crumble. First, Kayerts and Carlier abandon their attempts to improve their outpost. Then, they abdicate the vestiges of their morality when they accede to Makola's trading of slaves for ivory.[7] Finally, they revert to complete savagery when Kayerts, after he thinks that Carlier intends to do the same to him, murders his companion.

## III. TOWARD A DRAMATISED SPEAKER: 'THE LAGOON' (1897) AND 'KARAIN: A MEMORY' (1897)

'The Lagoon' and 'Karain: A Memory' represent two important stages in the development of the introspective and meditative voice which Conrad created to render the subtleties of Marlow's consciousness. Written during his struggle with *The Rescue*, they reflect his need to discover a technique with which to render the self-consciousness, doubt, and anxiety that dominated his mind. Conrad's interest in the technical problem of perspective dates from his preoccupation with the idea that each of us perceives and experiences a different reality. As Conrad became acutely conscious that each man inhabits a world comprised of his own illusions, he feared that each man might be hermetically enclosed in his self-created universe. In an 1898 letter to Garnett, he excitedly recounts what he felt might be scientific support for his view that each man may inhabit a separate 'universe' isolated from other men:

The secret of the universe is in the existence of horizontal waves whose varied vibrations are at the bottom of all states of consciousness. If the waves were vertical the universe would be different. This is a truism. But, don't you see, there is nothing in the world to prevent the simultaneous existence of vertical waves, of waves at any angles; in fact there are mathematical reasons for believing that such waves do exist. Therefore it follows that two universes may exist in the same place and in the same time—and not only two universes but an infinity of different universes—if by universe we mean a set of states of consciousness. (29 Sept. 1898; *Garnett*, p. 143)

Written in 1896 immediately after 'An Outpost of Progress' but before *The Nigger of the 'Narcissus'*, 'The Lagoon' anticipates Conrad's later thematic and technical concerns. An omniscient narrator renders a white man's response to a native's tragedy; at times, the narrator uses 'seems' and 'appears' to indicate that the white man's perceptions are separate from his own. The anonymous narrator soon will merge with the engaged protagonist, such as Marlow, who introspectively meditates over a crucial experience. 'The Lagoon' juxtaposes two 'states of consciousness' to discover the similarities that bind the two cultures.

The thrust of the tale is to demonstrate that the basic ingredients of human life are the same; that the natives are not inferior beings; and that, despite differences in customs and the level of civilisation, mankind shares basic goals and dreams. Arsat's fantasy of escaping mortality through love is a universal human aspiration; his hope 'to find a country where death is forgotten—where death is unknown' is one to which the white man responds. Arsat says his people 'take what they want—like you whites' and speaks oracularly of qualities and behaviour common to all men. That the white man provides the gun which enables Arsat to run off with his beloved is Conrad's way of showing how each person is inexorably linked to the fate of his fellows and how our actions have completely unforeseen consequences. At the end, when the white man can sadly generalise Arsat's pathetic murmur, 'Tuan, I loved my brother,' into 'we all love *our* brothers', he is affirming the similarity between native and civilised men, and by implication, denying his earlier condescension (p. 202, emphasis mine). Arsat's hope for redemption, like his earlier hope for everlasting love in a land without death, is an illusion created to cope with the 'unquiet and mysterious country of inextinguishable desires and fears' that all men share.

Written in 1897 after *The Nigger of the 'Narcissus'*, the engrossing 'Karain: A Memory' represents another important stage in Conrad's shift of focus from the tale to the teller. It is one of the few tales in which two narrators are equally important; the focus is evenly divided between Karain's tortured soul and the English narrator's reaction to Karain. After the white man recreates the process of discovering that Karain's public personality masks a tortured private self, Karain himself becomes the teller. But the title insists upon the original speaker's consciousness as a subject of importance. Clearly the self-dramatising narrator is a step towards Conrad's development of the engaged narrator pondering over and struggling with the meaning of another's or his own experiences. The white man, who is trying to discover the source and meaning of Karain's vulnerability and 'unrest', is an early version of the narrator whose efforts to penetrate into the psyche of a complex character climax with growth in the narrator's self-knowledge. The speaker, in addition to performing the rhetorical role of 'placing' Karain in perspective and shaping our reactions to him, is a vital character. He is an acquaintance whom the troubled Karain seeks out as a sympathetic listener and, later, as a source for desperately needed emotional sustenance.

As in 'The Lagoon', the ideal, or illusion in Conradian terms, of lover-protector is incompatible with the ideal of friendship. Karain loyally devotes himself to helping avenge the honour of his closest friend, Pata Matara, whose sister has eloped with a Dutchman. He betrays this ideal by unconsciously surrendering himself to the roles of sexual lover and chivalric protector of a beautiful woman. By shooting Pata Matara he remains loyal to his ideal as her protector and her private lover in a world of his own creation. When the girl steps in front of the Dutchman to protect her lover against Pata Matara's physical attack, he in effect momentarily confuses his own identity and the Dutchman's. (That he can become so depersonalised as to lose virtually his identity and simultaneously adopt another's anticipates 'The Secret Sharer' and *Under Western Eyes*.) Once Pata Matara is shot, Karain's psyche immediately separates his identity from the Dutchman's, abandons his illusion of love, and becomes haunted by guilt and sorrow.

Repeating a major theme of the two early Malay novels and the prior short stories, 'Karain' blurs the distinction between Europeans and natives by showing that all men share common illusions. The crux of the story's irony is that both Karain and the white narrator mistakenly believe that the other is, for cultural reasons, fundamentally different. Until Karain tells his tale, the narrator could not imagine that a native could feel the same complex emotions of guilt and sorrow, of loyalty and hope, as a Western man. But Karain cannot be 'soothed' with the narrator's bromide to 'abide with your people', and he bitterly resents the insinuation that he *could* forget.

Finally, the narrator learns that all men share a common ground. The very telling of the imaginative narrative evoked by a newspaper article in London shows how far the narrator has come from his days as a gun smuggler. Subjective experience is now as valid to him as objective reality. London is the physical expression of the knitting machine, Conrad's image—cited in my introduction—for the mechanistic and amoral cosmos. The subjective life, with its commitment to values and ideals and its belief in imaginative expression, is an alternative to the knitting machine. The narrator has learned that Karain's private torment is at least as real as London. When he met Karain, the narrator was an adventurer, a gunrunner, immersed in *facts* and *things*. But his encounter with Karain makes him understand that illusions and imaginative experience are also part of human life. In retrospect, the speaker does not patronise the native chief, the 'obscure adventurer' who rules a tiny area of conquered land. Quite the contrary, he obviously appreciates that Karain's absolute control of 'an insignificant foothold' is an imaginative triumph over the external world.

## IV. 'THE RETURN' (1898)

Married little more than a year, Conrad found writing his next story 'The Return', with its grotesque marital relationship, a painful personal experience.[8] In the Author's Note to *Tales of Unrest*, written more than two decades after the story, he recalled 'how much the writing of that fantasy has cost me in sheer toil, in temper, and in disillusion'. A week later he wrote to Garnett, '[the tale] torments me like a memory of a bad action which you—friend—are trying to palliate. In vain. I am a prey to remorse. I should not have written that thing. It's criminal' (8 Oct. 1897; *Garnett*, p. 108). If he regarded 'The Return' as a bad action, it was because he could neither control his tone towards his characters nor clearly render his characters' psychology. Conrad was unusually explicit about how he wished the story to affect the reader:

I wanted to produce the effect of insincerity, of artificiality.
Yes! I wanted the reader to *see* [the husband] *think* and then to
hear him speak—and shudder. The whole point of the joke is
there. I wanted the truth to be first dimly seen through the
fabulous untruth of that man's convictions—of his idea of
life—and then to make its way out with a rush at the end.
(29 Sept. 1897; *Garnett*, p. 107)

Although, finally, an unsuccessful story, 'The Return' is an important
early experiment both in Conrad's quest to develop a highly refined
ironic omniscient voice and in his dealing with what Thomas Moser
has called 'the uncongenial subject' of heterosexual love.

While the inhumanity of the contemporary industrial city is a
major theme in *Tales of Unrest*, 'The Return' is Cornad's fullest satire
of people in the urban wasteland until *The Secret Agent*. Conrad
directs his satire at the wealthy managerial class who were almost
universally despised by Edwardian intellectuals. For example,
C. F. G. Masterman, describing the lives of the rich in *The Heart of the
Empire*, wrote: 'Tyrannised over by their own conventions, slaves to
their servants, frequently devoid of any real appreciation of the
beautiful, their lives are spent without knowledge of the highest
forms of happiness, with disastrous loss of energy, and opportunity—
a loss that falls on all.'[9] In a sense, Hervey is the late Victorian heir to
Dickens's Mr Podsnap, whom Conrad may well have had in mind as
a model. Each tries to convert others to his truths, and each enjoys
reciting his credo.

The tale oscillates erratically between social satire and psychological analysis. But the general satire of the wealthy and socially
prominent is supposed to be the context for the specific analysis of the
Herveys. The Hervey marriage crystallises the sterility of personal life
in the modern city. Hervey's wife leaves him, only to return because
she has no place to go. Both husband and wife are looking for
something to give a sense of wholeness, but each one's conviction of
his own superiority prevents his finding it in his mate. Until Mrs
Hervey's sudden flight disrupts their lives, their entire married life
had been veneer. Conrad becomes so indignant at Hervey's disloyal
wife that he seems to forget for a time that he is exposing the sterility
of Hervey's feelings.[10] When this occurs, he abandons his mocking
tone and alternatingly hyperbolic and undercutting language to
render sympathetically Hervey's consciousness, as if he felt Hervey's
plight as a rejected suitor and disappointed seeker for the 'gift'

deserved a different perspective. With an uncertain mixture of hostility and hesitant sympathy, Conrad renders Hervey's realisation of his needs and subsequent rejection by an equally emotionally self-indulgent woman. Yet the reader understands that merely because Hervey partially recognises his need for 'salvation' does not mean that he has the ability to find salvation.


V

The five stories that we have been discussing were collected in 1898 in *Tales of Unrest*. Throughout this first volume of tales, Conrad stresses that civilisation has not progressively evolved and that man inhabits, at best, an amoral universe. The natives in *Tales of Unrest*, despite their heroic potential, make the same ignoble choices as Almayer and Willems in Conrad's first two novels, *Almayer's Folly* and *An Outcast of the Islands*. While speaking somewhat ironically of Alan Hervey in 'The Return', the narrator defines the major theme of *Tales of Unrest*:

> There are in life events, contacts, glimpses that seem brutally
> to bring all the past to a close. There is a shock and a crash,
> as of a gate flung behind one by the perfidious hand of fate.
> Go and seek another paradise, fool or sage. There is a moment
> of dumb dismay, and the wandering must begin again; the
> painful explaining away of facts, the feverish raking up of
> illusions, the cultivation of a fresh crop of lies . . . (p. 134)

Each tale focuses on those moments when the protagonist's crucial illusions are shattered and he desperately seeks to create new ones. With the swordbearer's death, Karain can no longer believe that the old man exorcises his friend's ghost; Arsat's conception of a land without death is nullified by the death of his beloved; and Hervey's self-image is destroyed by his wife's departure. Kayerts and Carlier abandon their ideals when they accede to Makola's trade; and Bacadou cannot father a healthy child to perpetuate his relationship to the land.

   *Tales of Unrest* focuses on the narrator's quest for self-understanding. Conrad begins to transfer his personal search for values to a dramatised narrator. The intellectual and emotional responses of the observer become as much a focus as the tale. Beginning with 'The Idiots', we observe a gradual movement towards the dramatisation of the narrator's moral and mental life. Even in 'The Return' and 'An Outpost to Progress', at times the third person narrator is less the self-effacing and remote voice of the first two novels, than a prominent character in the tale whose action consists of creating the ironic context in which the events he describes are judged. In these two stories the narrator is an ironist and satirist who implicitly stands for sanity and integrity as he criticises exploitation and hypocrisy.

The phrase from 'The Lagoon' with which Conrad chose to end his first published volume of stories—'The darkness of a world of illusions'—punctuates the collection's tone of profound pessimism and despairing gloom. While 'The Lagoon' and 'Karain: A Memory'· contrast natives and Europeans, 'The Idiots', 'An Outpost of Progress', and 'The Return' satirically examine the mentalities of three socio-economic groups in contemporary Europe: the agrarian community, the colonial service, and the aristocracy. Cumulatively, *Tales of Unrest* implies a vision of Western society impelled toward self-destruction. Whatever their moral limitations, the natives (to whom the Europeans condescend) retain their instinct and vitality. The native tales, 'Karain: A Memory' and 'The Lagoon', imply that courage, loyalty, and passion may survive the vicissitudes of both tribal and modern civilisations.

## NOTES

1. Walter Pater, *Marius the Epicurean* (London: Macmillan, 1892), vol. i, p. 158; cited by C. T. Watts (ed.), *Joseph Conrad's Letters to R. B. Cunninghame Graham* (Cambridge: Cambridge University Press, 1969), p. 67.

2. Bernard C. Meyer, *Joseph Conrad: A Psychoanalytic Biography* (Princeton: Princeton University Press, 1967), p. 92.

3. Avrom Fleishman, *Conrad's Politics: Community and Anarchy in the Fiction of Joseph Conrad* (Baltimore: Johns Hopkins Press, 1967), p. 70.

4. See Milton Chaikin, 'Zola and Conrad's "The Idiots" ', *Studies in Philology*, vol. lii (July 1955), pp. 502–7. Albert Guerard, *Conrad the Novelist* (Cambridge: Harvard University Press, 1958), p. 95, speaks of the influence of Flaubert. Walter F. Wright, *Romance and Tragedy in the Fiction of Joseph Conrad* (Lincoln: Nebraska University Press, 1949), p. 169, asserts that the tale is in 'the style of Maupassant'.

5. For a more detailed study of 'The Idiots', see my 'Moral Bankruptcy in Ploumar Parish: A Study of Conrad's "The Idiots" ', *Conradiana*, vol. i (Summer 1969), pp. 113–17.

6. 1896 letter to Fisher T. Unwin, quoted by John Dozier Gordan, *Joseph Conrad:*

*The Making of a Novelist* (Cambridge: Harvard University Press, 1940), p. 242.

7. For an excellent discussion of Makola's role, see A. T. Tolley, 'Conrad's Favourite Story', *Studies in Short Fiction*, vol. iii (1966), pp. 314–320, especially p. 318

8. Conrad was not able to place 'The Return' in a periodical. In *Joseph Conrad: The Three Lives* (New York: Farrar, Straus and Giroux, 1979), Frederick Karl writes: 'As a "city tale" of marriage and infidelity, ['The Return's'] genre was unsuited for Conrad's kind of imagination, although it has biographical interest as an oddity within his canon' (p. 392).

9. C. F. G. Masterman, *The Heart of the Empire* (London: Fisher Unwin, 1901), p. vi; quoted by Samuel Hynes, *The Edwardian Turn of Mind* (Princeton: Princeton University Press, 1968), p. 60.

10. Given the tale's awkward narrative technique and the opacity of character motivation, one can see why Thomas Moser believes that while Conrad meant to satirise Hervey, he failed to 'judge and condemn Hervey's despair'. *Joseph Conrad: Achievement and Decline* (Cambridge: Harvard University Press, 1957), p. 73.

# 3 The necessary voyage: Voice and authorial presence in *The Nigger of the 'Narcissus'*

I

In the past three decades the influence of the New Criticism and Wayne Booth's seminal *The Rhetoric of Fiction* (1961) has made those fiction critics who rely on formalist methods reluctant and even embarrassed to speak of authorial presence within a text. But it is often necessary to understand the relationship between the artist and his creation if we are to understand the text. The author's personal circumstances may not only inform a text, but often become embodied within its plot, language, characterisation, and form. The intensity and importance of that presence vary from writer to writer and from work to work. Like *Sons and Lovers* and *A Portrait of the Artist as a Young Man, The Nigger of the 'Narcissus'* (1897) must be understood in terms of its creator's efforts to develop an authentic voice. In all three relatively early works, the author freed himself from past constraints and created a personal and artistic self which made future work possible. As a crucial passage in *A Personal Record* indicates, Conrad knew that an author's presence became embodied in the finished work of art.

> A novelist lives in his work. He stands there, the only reality in an invented world, among imaginary things, happenings, and people. Writing about them, he is only writing about himself. But the disclosure is not complete. He remains, to a certain extent, a figure behind the veil; a suspected rather than a seen presence—a movement and a voice behind the draperies of fiction. (*PR*, p. xv)

35

Prior to writing *The Nigger of the 'Narcissus'*, Conrad sought an appropriate plot structure and point of view with which to organise his subject matter. Agonising about his inability to make progress on 'The Rescuer', he wrote to Garnett: 'Now I've got all my people together I don't know what to do with them. The progressive episodes of the story *will* not emerge from the chaos of my sensations. I feel nothing clearly' (19 June 1896; *LL*, vol. i, p. 192).[1] He was bogged down with the early version of 'The Rescuer' after he had committed himself completely to literature ('Only literature remains to me as a means of existence'); the imagined voyage of the *Narcissus* became at once the material for a plot to examine ethical and political questions of fundamental importance to Conrad and a private metaphor for the process of creating significance (10 Mar. 1896; *LL*, vol. i, p. 185). The sea voyage—with its clearly defined beginning and ending, its movement through time towards a destination, its separation from other experience, and explicit requirements that must be fulfilled by the crewmen and officers—provided a correlative *within Conrad's own experience and imagination* for the kind of significant plot that he sought. The voyage of the *Narcissus* provided Conrad with an imaginative escape from his writing frustrations to the space and time of past success. Since he had actually sailed on a ship named the *Narcissus* in 1884, he could draw upon romantic memories of a successfully completed voyage at a time when his creative impulses were stifled by doubts.[2]

Significantly, Conrad spoke of the creation of *The Nigger of the 'Narcissus'* as a voyage with an inevitable destination: 'Of course nothing can alter the course of the *Nigger*. Let it be unpopular, it *must* be. . . . I am going on. Another 20 pages . . . will see the end. . . . Till it's over there's no watch below for me' (29 Nov. 1896; *LL*, vol. i, p. 197–8). The Preface indicates how at this time Conrad conceived his creative task in terms of a voyage or journey to be completed: 'The sincere endeavour to accomplish that creative task, to go as far on that road as his strength will carry him, to go undeterred by faltering, weariness or reproach, is the only justification for the worker in prose' (p. ix). Again, two pages later: 'Art is long and life is short, and success is very far off. And thus, doubtful of strength to travel so far, we talk a little about the aim—the aim of art, which, like life itself, is inspiring, difficult—obscured by mists' (p. xi). The voyage of the *Narcissus* reflects Conrad's attempt to impose order on recalcitrant materials. The *Narcissus*, seemingly self-enclosed and for a time independent of the rest of human life, is described as 'a fragment detached from the earth, [which] went on lonely and swift like a small planet. . . . She had her own future; she was alive with the lives of those beings who trod her decks; like that earth which had given her up to the sea, she had an intolerable load of regrets and hopes' (pp. 29–30). When we recall that he uses the theme of an isolated planet abandoned by his fellows to describe the hermetic nature of *his* loneliness, we begin to see how *The Nigger of the 'Narcissus'* reveals the figure behind the veil: 'I live so alone that I often found myself clinging stupidly to a derelict planet abandoned by its precious crew' (5 Aug. 1897; *LL*, vol. i, p. 208).

*The Nigger of the 'Narcissus'* shows a reductive dichotomy within Conrad's psyche between the evil land where he was terribly frustrated as he launched his new career and the sea where, as he remembered it, he had been fairly tested and had ultimately succeeded. Conrad may use his similes to create a fantasy of escape from pressures of the work: 'as if the unconscious ship, gliding gently through the great peace of the sea, had left behind and forever the foolish noise of turbulent mankind' (p. 126). Or he may idealise the sea in ways that minimise the very complications of life at sea that his narrative is illustrating: 'In the magnificence of the phantom rays the ship appeared pure like a vision of ideal beauty, illusive like a tender dream of serene peace' (p. 145). One could argue that Conrad expected the reader to notice that the crew member is narcissistically enclosing himself in lyrical evocations of the past; nevertheless, it is clear that Conrad is himself unconsciously seeking refuge in the language of his memories. The narrator's burlesque of life on land and jeremiad against urban life derive from Conrad's frustration with his relatively new mode of life in which it seemed that merit went unrewarded. Pejorative references reduce the narrator's conception of shore life to a cartoon: 'We made a chorus of affirmation to his wildest assertions, as though he had been a millionaire, a politician, or a reformer—and we were a crowd of ambitious lubbers' (p. 139). That Donkin succeeds on land while Singleton and Allistoun excel at sea illustrates the reductive division within Conrad's psyche.

The Preface shows how Conrad's developing interest in drama-tising the teller's discovery of significance derives from a fascination with the artist's creative process. The Preface was originally an afterword, a retrospective comment on a completed tale.[3] To the extent that Conrad's focus in the preface is on creation as a process of perception, rather than as a finished product or polished artifice, his concept of the artist places him not so much in the self-conscious

craftsman tradition of Flaubert and James as in the tradition of
European Romanticism which sees the artist as a lonely visionary.
Conrad's description of the artist's heroic effort to render 'the truth,
manifold and one, underlying . . . every aspect' is as applicable to the
narrator of *The Nigger of the 'Narcissus'* as it is to Marlow in 'Heart of
Darkness' and *Lord Jim*: 'The artist descends within himself, and in
that lonely region of stress and strife, if he be deserving and fortunate,
he finds the terms of his appeal' (pp. vii–viii). The parallel to the
hero's descent into hell indicates Conrad's own need, as he moved
from a life of action to a life of writing, to define the artist in terms of
the classical hero.

Conrad's sailor-tellor has also lived in stress and strife. The rapid
fluctuations between engagement and detachment dramatise the
speaker's inconsistent and uncertain response to his own complicit
role in undermining the ship's order. He has impulses both to speak of
his dereliction of duty and to evade it. He is a representative member
of the crew, differentiated from the others only by his articulated
energy and concomitant verbal facility. The speaker's focus on his
own personal experience alternates with his meditations on the
significance and value of the crew's voyage. The speaker's nostalgic
elegy for an earlier maritime age, of which Singleton is the last
vestige, and his scathing indictment of contemporary English
civilisation reveal that if he is a mere crew member, he is also a
persona whose range and complexity are not unlike the consciousness
of his creator. His values and attitudes often reveal him as a surrogate
for Conrad.

In the role of Conrad's surrogate, he is an omniscient narrator who
universalises the nominalistic experience of the tale, even while as
crew member he is trying to sort out the meaning of his own experience. As a dramatised character with a full range of emotion and
motivation, the crew member shows that he has grown morally since
he compromised himself by his sentimental response to Wait and
Donkin and his participation in an incipient mutiny. One could argue
that the crew member's meditations on the sea, his persistent similes,
his efforts to place the voyage within the great British maritime
tradition, his desire to see Donkin as representative of socialism
*dramatise* his urgent quest to discover universal meaning in his own
nominalistic experience. Finally, these aspects of the tale are incongruous with the speaker's experience. But they do fulfil Conrad's desire
to place his tale in a larger context, and his need to create a voice to do
so. And most of the time, the narrator's twin roles of authorial

spokesman and crew member create a richer text that shows the folly of dogmatic insistence upon a sharp distinction between omniscient narrator and the crew member's partially perceptive dramatic monologue. For the rapid shifts from third to first person, from singular to plural, from factual reminiscence to meditation upon values, reflect the crew member's groping for an appropriate attitude to events in which he has participated as well as Conrad's attempts to discover the necessary artifice for his tale.[4]

## II

Conrad has created two alter egos, two tentative doubles: the omniscient voice who is the perspicacious ideal self that Conrad wished to become; and the first person speaker, the crew member, who is the actual past self—the man of action that Conrad has not quite left behind. The voice is a Janus figure; the crew member's impulse is to look inward to the world of the voyage and the omniscient narrator's impulse is to look outward to his audience. Conrad's ideal self, his surrogate, uses an omniscient voice to provide both the philosophical remarks and intensifying similes that expand the journey's significance for the reader. He embodies the conservative ethos derived from Conrad's maritime experience. Conrad believed that this ethos with its strict conceptions of work, duty, responsibility, and fidelity was a viable alternative to the doctrines of the Fabians, utopians, and moral Darwinists. Yet the dramatised ingenousness of the crew member strains against these pretensions to authority. Perhaps the fallible sailor reflects both Conrad's fear that he might be found morally wanting when tested and his need to create a separate character to embody that fear. Later in his career Conrad probably would have divided the voice into two figures as in 'Youth', 'Heart of Darkness', and 'Amy Foster', where frame narrators objectify the participant's tale by making comments that extend the significance of the latter's nominalistic experience. Yet the very ambiguity in point of view gives added life to *The Nigger of the 'Narcissus'* because the reader experiences the process by which Conrad orders, evaluates, and discovers the significance of the raw material of his story.

In the novel the creation of a microcosm becomes as much the focus as the microcosm itself. Beginning with the disorder when the crew gathers for roll call, the hierarchal system, always presided over by Allistoun, checks and controls incipient turmoil. Conrad uses Allistoun as an ordering principle to contain the seeming fragmentation and barely controlled confusion of the narrator's opening scene. Threats to the order of the ship are simultaneously threats to the form of Conrad's tale. In the following passage the reader familiar with Conrad's self-doubt and gloom responds not only to the men on board, but to the author's own anxiety lest the *Narcissus*-narrative not reach completion (as the 'Rescuer'-narrative had not): 'And like the last vestige of a shattered creation she drifts, bearing an anguished remnant of sinful mankind, through the distress, tumult, and pain of an avenging terror' (p. 54). Within the mutinous night, when the men are milling and grumbling, the plot itself seems to hover on the brink of collapse. At this point the plot becomes more diffuse and less concentrated, and one feels that the scene is given more space than is required. Allistoun's struggle to master the men mirrors Conrad's effort to master his materials.

Like the artist, Allistoun uses his intelligence, his energy, and the force of his will to create order within the separate world of the ship: 'He seemed with his eyes to hold the ship up in a superhuman concentration of effort . . .' (p. 65). Defined by the crew member as 'the Master of our lives' (p. 61), the captain is as omniscient and ubiquitous as God—or as the artist himself must be if he is to fulfil what Stevens, in 'The Idea of Order at Key West', calls 'the maker's rage to order words of the sea': 'He was one of those commanders who speak little, seem to hear nothing, look at no one—and know everything, hear every whisper, see every fleeting shadow of their ship's life' (p. 125). As the captain must succeed in creating feelings of solidarity with the crew if the *Narcissus* is successfully to complete its voyage, the artist 'in a single-minded attempt . . . shall awaken in the hearts of the beholders that feeling of unavoidable solidarity; of the solidarity in mysterious origin, in toil, in joy, in hope, in uncertain fate, which binds men to each other and all mankind to the visible world' (p. x). The implicit comparison of a captain with an artist enabled Conrad to define himself as a writer and to establish a continuity between his two careers. In the Preface Conrad perceives the artist as another version of the Master. The artist's role is referred to five times as a 'task', a word which places art in the context of the world of labour in which Conrad felt comfortable. If the artist succeeds in his task, his audience will be rewarded according to their own deserts with 'encouragement, consolation, fear, charm—all you demand—and, perhaps, also [a] glimpse of truth' (p. x). Years later in the context of recalling former captains he knew, he writes in *The Mirror of the Sea* (1906): 'An artist is a man of action, whether he creates a personality, invents an expedient, or finds the issue of a complicated situation' (*MS*, p. 33). *The Mirror of the Sea* confirms the continuing dependence of Conrad's imaginative life upon his maritime career and shows how the sea provided him not only with a subject but an epistemology and semiology.

Among other things, the ship's name *Narcissus* indicates Conrad's realisation that in rendering the external world, he was really rendering himself. It also indicates his knowledge that the artist must strive to do this without succumbing to the temptations of self-indulgence and solipsism if he is to make his audience *see* in the sense of understanding. In *The Mirror of the Sea*, Conrad provides an important gloss on the Preface's famous definition of the artist's task as being 'to make you *see*': 'To see! to see!—this is the craving of the sailor, as of the rest of blind humanity. To have his path made clear for him is the aspiration of every human being in our beclouded and tempestuous existence' (*MS*, p. 87). Apparently 'to make one see' means to enable another to discover authentic direction and, by implication, the values that propel him in that direction. The Preface is an effort to define his artistic credo for both his readers and himself. Virtually every concept in the Preface has its personal as well as its public meaning. When Conrad refers to the subject of the written words as 'the rescued fragment' he may be referring unconsciously to the successful rescue of his frustrated and tormented career by means of creating *The Nigger of the 'Narcissus'* (p. x).

Conrad's 1914 Preface to the American edition makes clear that he meant the tale's focus to be on the crew's response to Wait: 'In the book [Wait] is nothing; he is merely the centre of the ship's collective psychology and the pivot of the action' (p. ix).[5] Sentimentalism is the peculiar form of egotism that preys upon the crew's response to Donkin's poverty at the outset and that causes the men to sacrifice their integrity in a desperate and pathetic effort to forestall Wait's inevitable death. Neither Wait nor Donkin has an identity independent of that conferred by the crew's sentimentalism; they flourish *because* the crew responds to them. '[Wait's] contempt [for us] was immense; it seemed to grow gradually large, as his body day by day shrank a little more' (p. 140). Wait is in a parasitic relationship with the crew: 'each, going out, seemed to leave behind a little of his own vitality, surrender some of his own strength, renew the assurance of life—the indestructible thing!' (pp. 147–8). Once the crew responds to Donkin with a 'wave of sentimental pity', 'the development of the destitute Donkin aroused interest' (pp. 12–13). When he responds to Wait and Donkin against his better judgement, the sailor-speaker embodies Conrad's own fear of sentimentalism. After he had completed *The Nigger* but before it had begun to appear in *The New Review*, Conrad wrote 'I feel horribly sentimental. . . . I want to rush into print whereby my sentimentalism, my incorrect attitude to life . . . shall be disclosed to the public gaze', (26 Mar. 1897; *LL*, vol. i, pp. 203–4). Just as the eternal truths of Singleton and Allistoun triumph over the 'temporary formulas' of Donkin and the crew's misguided sentimentalism, the fiction writer must eschew fashionable aesthetic philosophies: 'Realism, Romanticism, Naturalism, even the unofficial sentimentalism[,] . . . all these gods must . . . abandon him . . . to the stammerings of his conscience and to the outspoken consciousness of the difficulties of his work' (pp. x–xi).

*The Nigger of the 'Narcissus'* reflects Conrad's concern about the possibility of demagoguery and insincerity on the part of the artist. In the Preface, he speaks of the need of the writer to form sentences which by their suggestiveness will revitalise 'the commonplace surface of words: of the old, old words, worn thin, defaced by ages of careless usage' (p. ix). In early 1898, Conrad wrote to Cunninghame Graham: 'Half the words we use have no meaning whatever and of the other half each man understands each word after the fashion of his own folly and conceit' (14 Jan. 1898; *LL*, vol. i, p. 222). That Donkin is the master and exploiter of language, as Kurtz will be in 'Heart of Darkness', indicates Conrad's fretfulness about the potential immorality of language. Donkin, facetiously described as 'that consummate artist', represents a temptation that both artist and crew must overcome: 'He talked with ardour, despised and irrefutable. His picturesque and filthy loquacity flowed like a troubled stream from a poisoned source' (pp. 100–1). Donkin is Conrad's gross caricature of a political thinker; his demands typify 'the obstinate clamour of sages, demanding bliss and an empty heaven' (p. 90). The religious fanatic Podmore represents another narcissistic attitude towards language that must be avoided; although intense and sincere, his authentic self is subsumed by the incantatory language he speaks when he seeks to 'save' Wait; he becomes 'a voice—a fleshless and sublime thing. . . . Prayers vociferated like blasphemies and whispered curses [in] . . . an impassioned screeching babble where words pattered like hail' (pp. 116–17).

In response to a comment of Cunninghame Graham's, Conrad wrote:

> I think Singleton with an education is impossible. . . . If it is the knowledge of how to live, my man essentially possessed it. He was in perfect accord with his life. . . . Do you mean the kind of knowledge which would enable him to scheme, and lie, and intrigue his way to the forefront of a crowd no better than himself? . . . Then he would become conscious,—and much smaller,—and very unhappy. Now he is simple and great like an elemental force. (14 Dec. 1897; *LL*, vol. i, pp. 214–15)

Singleton embodies Conrad's own *fear* that verbal facility and self-conscious ratiocination might be at odds with his paradigmatic seaman—loyal, courageous, industrious, self-controlled. He is a tribute to the self that Conrad simultaneously wishes to be put behind him and to assimilate into the evolving creative self. Singleton and Allistoun are identified with the silence of the cosmos; during the storm 'all spoke at once in a thin babble' but 'the master's ardour, the cries of that silent man inspired us' and Singleton remains apart 'rigidly' steering (pp. 86, 88, 89). Singleton speaks only when he has something significant to say: 'The thoughts of all his lifetime could have been expressed in six words, but the stir of those things that were as much a part of his existence as his beating heart called up a gleam of alert understanding upon the sternness of his aged face' (p. 26). Loquacity is equated with corrupt worldiness that undermines man's integrity; 'If [the successors to Singleton's generation] have learned how to speak they have also learned how to whine' (p. 25). To the narrator, it seems as if the sea spoke through Singleton's lips: 'The wisdom of half a century spent in listening to the thunder of waves had spoken unconsciously through his old lips' (p. 24). The fulfillment of Singleton's prophecy that Wait will die in sight of land confirms the possibility of primitive kinds of knowledge which transcend the merely nominalistic and idiosyncratic.

## III

The crew member and Conrad's surrogate seek definition, clarity, and significance even while acknowledging the inevitable refraction of time on memory: 'All the first part of the voyage, the Indian Ocean on the other side of the Cape, all that was lost in a haze, like an ineradicable suspicion of some previous existence' (p. 100). For each voice the quest for meaning is in tension with the need to immerse oneself in the past as a means of forestalling the inevitability of death that continually suggests itself. The crew member has tried to propitiate death by making one of the dying into a totem. His proliferation of similes is peculiarly suitable for a tale in which the crew's confusion between the signified and the signifier is the central semiological action; unwilling to recognise that all men are dying throughout their lives, they take Wait's dying for death itself. Note the revealing shift from third to first person when the speaker recalls the effect of Wait on the crew: 'It was just what *they* had expected, and hated to hear, that idea of a stalking death. . . . [H]e paraded it unceasingly before *us* with an affectionate persistence that made its presence indubitable, and at the same time incredible. No man could be suspected of such monstrous friendship!' (p. 36; my emphases). The crew member, and possibly Conrad too, wants to believe that the crew's experience with Wait represents a confrontation with death. If the sailor were to lower the rhetorical ante, he would be left with his nominalistic adventure tale which boldly reveals his own mediocre behaviour. Sympathy with Wait almost caused the men, including the crew member, to refuse duty. Thus their catatonic fear of death evoked by the presence of Wait displaces the captain as master. '[Wait] overshadowed the ship. Invulnerable in his promise of speedy corruption he trampled on our self-respect, he demonstrated to us daily our want of moral courage; he tainted our lives. Had we been a miserable gang of wretched immortals, unhallowed alike by hope and fear, he could not have lorded it over us with a more pitiless assertion of his sublime privilege' (p. 47). Doesn't the following tell us less about Wait than about the fears of the crew, including the speaker? 'He seemed to hasten the retreat of departing light by his very presence; the setting sun dipped sharply, as though fleeing before our nigger; a black mist emanated from him; a subtle and dismal influence; a something cold and gloomy that floated out and settled on all the faces like a mourning veil' (p. 34).

The crew member-speaker faces death during the storm ('Every movement of her was ominous of the end of her agony and of the beginning of ours' [p. 71]) and during the subsequent calm when he is haunted by the spectre of starvation. Irrationally, the rescuers, including himself, throw the carpenter's equipment overboard as if to appease death and its apparent agent, the fury of the sea: 'We passed up our hats full of assorted nails to the boatswain, who, as if performing a mysterious and appeasing rite, cast them wide upon a raging sea' (p. 68). Although the men detest Wait as a possible malingerer, they irrationally equate preserving him with forestalling their own deaths: 'The secret and ardent desire of our hearts was the desire to beat him viciously with our fists about the head; and we handled him as tenderly as though he had been made of glass' (p. 73). They project their own fear of mortality on to Wait: 'The latent egoism of tenderness to suffering appeared in the developing anxiety not to see him die' (p. 138). While the crew is in servitude to Wait and his companion (death is his 'expected visitor', his 'hateful accomplice', his bosom friend', and, punning on death's usurpation of the captain's position, his 'masterful chum' [pp. 39, 41, 53, 73]), Singleton is in bondage to the sea and is parodoxically as free as a man can be. Unlike his younger peers, he knows no fear of death and disregards the ubiquitous threat of death as he performs his duty: 'He looked upon the immortal sea . . . and he saw an immensity tormented and blind, moaning and furious, that claimed all the days of his tenacious life, and, when life was over, would claim the worn-out body of its slave' (p. 99). Looking always to generalise, the crew member sees Wait's death as illustration that man's fictions are inevitably undermined by the facts that he tries to exclude: 'We did not know till then how much faith we had put in his delusions. We had taken his chances of life so much at his own valuation that his death, like the death of an old belief, shook the foundations of our society. . . . In going he took away with himself the gloomy and solemn shadow in which our folly had posed, with humane satisfaction, as a tender arbiter of fate' (pp. 155–6). As soon as Wait's body is cast out, 'the ship rolled as if relieved of an unfair burden' and, except for Belfast, the men, including the crew member himself, emotionally detach themselves from Wait's influence (p. 160).

The narrative simultaneously insists on death's presence and mocks the crew member's effort to discuss death and mortality only in terms of other men. Isn't it curious that the crew member eschews any final reflection about his own mortality? After all, *The Nigger of the 'Narcissus'* is a story about the impossibility of avoiding death, a story in which the mortality of Wait, Singleton, and *The Narcissus* is the subject, and a story in which images of graves and corpses are persistently interwoven into the tale. Is the crew member repeating the crew's futile and pathetic effort on board the ship to propitiate death? That Singleton discovers his own mortality at the centre of the story and at the climax of the crew's heroic and successful struggle to survive makes the crew member's failure to reflect upon his own mortality even more obvious. After his final reminiscence, his comment about Wait's use of memory seems ironically apropos to his own situation: 'He was very quiet and easy amongst his vivid reminiscences which he mistook joyfully for images of an undoubted future' (p. 149). Yet, even in his final lyric the crew member cannot evade death; the 'shadowy ship manned by a crew of Shades' suggests the spirits of the dead who inhabit Hades (p. 173).

Conrad maintains his distance from the crew member's monologue when the latter recalls how he and his fellows responded to Donkin. For a time Donkin stood for the possibility of a life of ease where every man's cup might be filled to the utmost. With embarrassment and bitterness, the crew member recalls how he had been temporarily hypnotised by the thought of creating a utopia on board: 'We were oppressed by the injustice of the world, surprised to perceive how long we had lived under its burden without realising our unfortunate state, annoyed by the uneasy suspicion of our undiscerning stupidity' (p. 102). As if recoiling in self-disgust, he suddenly changes from first to third person and mocks those who responded to Donkin:

> Our little world went on its curved and unswerving path
> carrying a discontented and aspiring population. They found
> comfort of a gloomy kind in an interminable and conscientious
> analysis of their unappreciated worth; and inspired by
> Donkin's hopeful doctrines they dreamed enthusiastically of
> the time when every lonely ship would travel over a serene
> sea, manned by a wealthy and well-fed crew of satisfied
> skippers. (p. 103)

Yet the crew member understands the folly of the ebullience and buoyancy that succeeded the storm and how in the headiness of their self-conceit, he and his fellows responded to Donkin's spurious arguments even while detesting themselves for doing so. The crew member is much less willing to acknowledge his own role when he narrates how the crewmen move from their own narcissistic self-appreciation to active mutiny. He uses the distancing third person perspective to separate himself from the grotesque behaviour to which the crew's narcissism led: 'They clustered round that moribund carcass, the fit emblem of their aspirations, and encouraging one another they swayed, they tramped on one spot, shouting that they would not be "put upon"' (p. 122). His use of the third person to depict how the officers reestablished control emphasises that his sympathies are unambiguously with the officers, as if he can hardly believe the enormity of what occurred.

As the boat returns home and the plot moves to its conclusion, Conrad's detached, philosophic voice briefly subsumes the crew member's voice. The comparison of England with a ship is meant to imply the applicability of the social and political struggle on board the *Narcissus*:

> Below its steady glow, the coast, stretching away straight and black, resembled the high side of an indestructible craft riding motionless upon the immortal and unresting sea. The dark land lay alone in the midst of waters, like a mighty ship bestarred with vigilant lights—a ship carrying the burden of millions of lives—a ship freighted with dross and with jewels, with gold and with steel. . . . A great ship! For ages had the ocean battered in vain her enduring sides; . . . A ship mother of fleets and nations! The great flagship of the race; stronger than the storms! and anchored in the open sea. (pp. 162–3)

This panegyric does not derive from the preceding narrative, but it simultaneously expresses the crew member's wish to establish himself as an heir to the British cultural tradition and to reaffirm his ties to England through its maritime tradition. The eulogy shows how Conrad's use of the epistemology and semiology of the sea enables him to order his telling. If Conrad can convince himself that the *Narcissus* is a metonymy for England, then his tale has the universal significance that he seeks.

The ending enables Conrad to vent his frustrations on land even while he completes his artistic voyage. Just as within the letters he perceives himself losing stature on land, both the *Narcissus* and the stature of the nation are reduced and contained by land which is personified as a living and breathing hostile leviathan:

> A low cloud hung before her—a great opalescent and tremulous cloud, that seemed to rise from the steaming brows of millions of men. Long drifts of smoky vapours soiled it with livid trails; it throbbed to the beat of millions of hearts, and

from it came an immense and lamentable murmur—the
murmur of millions of lips praying, cursing, sighing, jeering—
the undying murmur of folly, regret, and hope exhaled by the
crowds of the anxious earth. . . . Brick walls rose high above
the water—soulless walls, staring through hundreds of
windows as troubled and dull as the eyes of over-fed brutes.
(pp. 163–5)

The word 'crowd', the narrator's term for crew, sets up a comparison
between life on shore and life at sea. On land Allistoun is reduced to a
paymaster and Singleton to a pathetic drunkard, while Donkin
flourishes. But as we have seen, despite the reductive view of both
omniscient surrogate and crew member, baseness, cowardice, and
sloth are not restricted to the land. The speaker reflects Conrad's own
insecurity and feeling of alienation on land when, speaking more as
Conrad's surrogate than as a dramatised character, he perceives the
other crewmen in terms that emphasise their foreignness and
strangeness and the hostility of the environment in which they find
themselves:

Surrounded by the hurry and clamour of men, they
appeared to be creatures of another kind—lost, alone, forgetful,
and doomed; they were like castaways, like reckless and joyous
castaways, like mad castaways, making merry in the storm and
upon an insecure ledge of a treacherous rock. The roar of the
town resembled the roar of topping breakers, merciless and
strong, with a loud voice and cruel purpose. (p. 172)

Conrad uses the ending to establish his ironic distance towards his
speaker-sailor and thus to reassert his artistic control. In his narcissistic
conclusion the crew member stresses the crew's final solidarity in
order to imply that, after all, the voyage was a kind of triumph:

But at times the spring-flood of memory sets with force up the
dark River of the Nine Bends. Then on the waters of the
forlorn stream drifts a ship—a shadowy ship manned by a crew
of Shades. They pass and make a sign, in a shadowy hail.
Haven't we, together and upon the immortal sea, wrung out a
meaning from our sinful lives? Good-bye, brothers! You were
a good crowd. As good a crowd as ever fisted with wild cries

the beating canvas of a heavy foresail; or tossing aloft, invisible in the night, gave back yell for yell to a westerly gale. (p. 173)

Although the sailor eulogises the crew members, their real importance seems to be that they provided *him* with significance. Not only do they lose their individuality in his memory, but he has apparently not kept in touch with any of them. Perhaps his memory provides him with 'the illusion of splendour and poetry of life' that the rest of the crew sought in drink. Like the rest of the crew, like all men on land perhaps, he is 'lost, alone, forgetful, and doomed' (p. 172). While he seeks refuge in recollections of moments of solidarity, he is separate from his fellows. That once on land they seem vestiges of their former selves makes their existence as shadows ironically appropriate. Despite the crew member's final attempt to romanticise the crew's sea experience, the men have been divested of stature and identity. And, we recall that really they were not such a 'good crowd.' Collectively, they threatened mutiny, and individually several of them illustrated serious shortcomings as sailors. Knowles cut a piece of the ship's tackle to fasten himself during the storm; Belfast stole for Jimmy; the cook's religious frenzies were disruptive; someone abandoned the helm at a critical juncture; and Wait and Donkin were pernicious influences. Moreover, Allistoun's recollection of a 'real mutiny' undermines the narrator's nostalgic view of past generations of sailors.

## IV

Conrad discovered that the voyage experience of his sea career could free him from the debilitating restraints of shore life and be an ordering principle for his new career as a writer. Just as voyages must end, narratives must cease: 'The *Narcissus* came gently into her berth; the shadows of soulless walls fell upon her, the dust of all the continents leaped upon her deck, and a swarm of strange men, clambering up her sides, took possession of her in the name of the sordid earth. She had ceased to live' (p. 165). Like the passing of a period in a man's life, a ship's docking is a kind of prolepsis of her final death. But when Conrad presents his narrative to his readers, the created world and the self embodied in that world achieve a kind of immortality.

As Conrad acknowledged in the 1920 Author's Note to *The Rescue*, writing *The Nigger of the 'Narcissus'* released Conrad's creative energies and enabled him to develop his artistic potential: 'The finishing of 'The Nigger' brought to my troubled mind the comforting sense of an accomplished task, and the first consciousness of a certain sort of mastery which could accomplish something with the aid of propitious stars' (p. ix). In his next major work 'Youth', the ship has as much trouble beginning its voyage as the *Narcissus* had in finishing hers. But in 'Youth' Conrad is in command of the dramatisation of an incomplete voyage. Conrad can present Marlow as an independent personality whose consciousness may echo Conrad's but who is a separate and distinct character. During the actual voyage, Marlow confronts his own fear of death; during his reminiscence of past dangers, death is a continuous, intensive presence that cannot be confined to the past. That in 'Youth' Conrad completes the narrative without completing the imagined voyage of the *Judea* shows that while Conrad would use the voyage as the dominant experience, he did not require it to master his materials. That the captain is no longer an omniscient, ubiquitous figure, but a comic figure shows that Conrad no longer required an Allistoun as a thinly disguised ordering principle within his fiction.

The writing of *The Nigger of the 'Narcissus'* enabled Conrad to create an authentic identity as an artist, to discover the necessary angel for which he had been searching. Indeed, it is Stevens who best describes this process in 'Tea at the Palaz of Hoon': 'I was the world in which I walked, and what I saw / Or heard or felt came not but from myself; / And there I found myself more truly and more strange.' *The Nigger of the 'Narcissus'* enabled Conrad to become the master of his creative task, a master who could 'arrest, for the space of a breath, the hands busy about the work of the earth, and compel men entranced by the sight of distant goals, to glance for a moment at the surrounding vision . . . ' (p. xii).

NOTES

1. "The Rescuer" later became *The Rescue*.
2. See Jocelyn Baines, *Joseph Conrad: A Critical Biography* (New York: McGraw-Hill, 1960), pp. 75—7.
3. Ibid., p. 187.
4. In my judgement, the most interesting discussions of the point of view in *The Nigger of the 'Narcissus'* are those of Albert Guerard, *Conrad the Novelist*. (Cambridge, Mass.: Harvard University Press, 1958), pp. 100—25 and Ian Watt,

'Conrad Criticism and *The Nigger of the "Narcissus"* ', *Nineteenth-Century Fiction*, vol. xii (Mar. 1958), pp. 257–83. My discussion takes issue with Watt's ingenious argument that the philosophic comments suggest 'a plurality of voices' and resembles a Greek chorus; it also tries to be more specific and more speculative than Guerard in defining and explaining what he calls the 'waywardness in point of view'.

5. For this preface, I have consulted the Malay edition (Doubleday, Page: Garden City, New York, 1929).

# 4 Marlow's role in 'Youth' and 'Heart of Darkness'

I

Let us consider why Conrad created Marlow. As Conrad's 1894–1900 letters reveal, for him fiction writing is a self-conscious process in which he tests and explores his intellectual and moral identity. Except for brief moments of despair, Conrad believed in the essential value of self-knowledge and self-exploration. He created Marlow to explore himself. Conrad was also concerned with the dilemma of transforming the 'freedom' of living in a purposeless world from a condition into a value. And Marlow enabled him to examine this dilemma in "Youth" (1898), 'Heart of Darkness' (1899), and *Lord Jim* (1900).

By dramatising his own intellectual and moral problems in the mind of a fictional counterpart, Conrad creates a double who clarified and ordered the very problems that haunted him.[1] Marlow is a surrogate figure coping with versions of Conrad's own psychic turmoil and moral confusion. Thus he is a means by which Conrad orders his world. He is defining not only the form of the story but the relation between Conrad's past and present self. The younger Marlow was explicitly committed to the same conventional values of the British Merchant Marine to which Conrad had devoted his early adulthood, but the mature Marlow has had experiences which have caused him to re-evaluate completely his moral beliefs. That Marlow is a vessel for some of Conrad's doubts and anxieties and for defining the problems that made his own life difficult is clear not only from his 1890 Congo Diary and the 1890 correspondence with Mme Poradowska, but even more so from the letters of the 1897–9 period, selections from which have already been quoted. Take for example the following 1898 letter in which Conrad generalises his own self-conscious doubts and anxieties into abstract, theoretical statements about man's position in the universe:

Egoism is good, and altruism is good, and fidelity to nature
would be the best of all, and systems could be built, and rules
could be made—if we could only get rid of consciousness.
What makes mankind tragic is not that they are victims of
nature, it is that they are conscious of it. To be part of the
animal kingdom under the conditions of this earth is very
well—but as soon as you know of your slavery the pain, the
anger, the strife—the tragedy begins. We can't return to
nature, since we can't change our place in it. Our refuge is in
stupidity, in drunkenness of all kinds, in lies, in beliefs, in
murder, thieving, reforming—in negation, in contempt—each
man according to the promptings of his particular devil. There
is no morality, no knowledge and no hope; there is only the
consciousness of ourselves which drives us about a world that
whether seen in a convex or a concave mirror is always but a
vain and fleeting appearance. (31 Jan. 1898; *Cunninghame
Graham*, pp. 70–1)

Man is cursed not because he lives within an amoral cosmos, but
because he is conscious of both his position and his inability to change
his status.

At times Conrad despaired of communication in such a world. In
an 1898 letter to Henley, Conrad writes: 'Were I to write and talk till
Doomsday you would never really know what it all means to
me . . . because you never had just the same experience' (Pierpont
Morgan Library, 18 Oct. 1898).[2] He transfers to Marlow his doubts
about the effectuality of language as a means of communication.
Usually, he believed in the act of telling as a means of sharing one's
subjectivity with a responsive soul. Marlow's quest for a responsive
mind—whether it be for Kurtz or Jim in the original experience or
the present effort to communicate with an audience—is usually
motivated either by a feeling of excruciating loneliness or a need to
share the burden of consciousness. As Marlow concludes his telling,
the reader becomes aware that the inevitable lapse of the questing
consciousness into silence and stasis is not only a movement back
towards isolation, but a foreshadowing of death. Yet that the
introductory speaker retells the story dramatises that Marlow has
discovered a responsive temperament and has made someone 'see'.

In the 1898–1900 Marlow tales Conrad exploited the advantages
of limited point of view. As Susanne K. Langer has written: 'The
character in question is not telling a tale, but is experiencing the

events, so that they all take on the appearance they would have for that person. Filtering them all through the mind assures, of course, their conception in terms of personal feeling and encounter, gives to the whole work—action, setting, speech and all—the natural unity of a perspective.'[3] The richness of these stories depends in part on the confrontation between the present self and the past self.[4] As Marlow reveals his present identity, his memory presents versions of his past self prior to, during, and after the crucial events of the narrative.

## II. 'YOUTH' (1898)

'Youth', the first short story after *Tales of Unrest* was completed, addresses the dour view of European life presented in *Tales of Unrest*. Marlow is the heir of the white men of 'The Lagoon' and 'Karain: A Memory', those sensitive, if disillusioned men, who neither live passionately like the natives nor believe in any sustaining ideals. The Marlow of 'Youth' is trying to find meaning in the evanescent world described in an 1898 letter to R. B. Cunninghame Graham:

> Life knows us not and we do not know life—we don't know even our own thoughts. Half the words we use have no meaning whatever and of the other half each man understands each word after the fashion of his own folly and conceit. Faith is a myth and beliefs shift like mists on the shore; thoughts vanish; words, once pronounced, die; and the memory of yesterday is as shadowy as the hope of tomorrow—only the string of my platitudes seems to have no end. (14 Jan. 1898; *LL*, vol. i, p. 222)

Marlow's secular meditation in 'Youth' represents one method of dealing with ennui and despair. The contemplation of the significant moments of one's past is one way to suspend temporarily passing time. By means of intensely focusing on the past, Marlow's narrative is an unconscious effort to seal himself within the present and thus forestall the future.

'Youth' is about Marlow's efforts to create a significant yesterday so that his life will not seem a meaningless concatenation of durational events. His narrative reflects Marlow's need 'to arrest' time and pre-empt the future. Somewhere past the middle of his life, Marlow attempts to discover a symbolic meaning in the past voyage of the

*Judea*. He wishes to believe that his first journey to the East was one of 'those voyages that seem ordered for the illustration of life, that might stand for a symbol of existence' (pp. 3 – 4). As Marlow recalls his great adventure, he discovers that, in spite of the voyage's failure, it not only contains great significance for him, but enables him to recapture on occasion his feeling of youthful energy.

Conrad takes a good-natured ironical view of the supposedly mature Marlow's attempts to expose his own youthful illusions. While he purports to take an objective and detached view of a meaningful experience of his youth, mature Marlow is revealed as a romantic sentimentalist. Conrad shows us that reality is partly subjective and that our illusions and oversimplifications are as real as so-called objective facts. Marlow, while admitting that youth is the time of illusion and romance, nevertheless invites his listeners to agree that one's subjective reaction to experience is paramount: 'Wasn't that the best time, that time when we were young at sea; young and had nothing, on the sea that gives nothing, except hard knocks—and sometimes a chance to feel your strength—that only—what you all regret?' (p. 42). And his listeners, all successful men, confirm Marlow's view that the subjective contrast between meaningful and unmeaningful experience is as important as the 'objective' distinction between romance and reality. 'Youth' depends upon multiple perspectives: (1) young Marlow's original experience and young Marlow's limited reactions to that experience; (2) mature Marlow's perspective on young Marlow's experience which begins as if it were to be a mature view but becomes gradually less and less detached and ironic; (3) the response of an audience of peers to Marlow's tale; (4) Conrad's perspective which, even while acknowledging the legitimacy of how both old Marlow and his younger self deal with experience, emphasises the futility of man's efforts to forestall mutability.[5]

Marlow originally tries ironically to recount his youthful exploits within the perspective of his present maturity, but increasingly this process gives way to the urgency of his intense efforts to recapture his youth. The voyage of Marlow's youth contains the presence of death, age, and experience. The act of telling is a desperate attempt to suppress the knowledge of experience in a song of innocence. Not only has the *Judea* met her death, but death is the inevitable destiny that awaits the old Captain and his ageing mate, Mahon. T. S. Eliot wrote in 'East Coker': 'In my beginning is my end'; Marlow's beginning contains the seed of his own mortality, and his triumphal first voyage contains mortality for others: 'The mysterious East faced me, perfumed like a flower, silent like death, dark like a grave' (p. 38). If the voyage demonstrates the feeling of strength that derives from a trial of life, the destination with its symbolic trappings of death suggests the inevitability of mortality. The introductory narrator's concluding paean about the value of experiencing the 'glamour' and 'strength' of youth recoils from the gloomy implications of Marlow's narrative. Gradually the empirical impulse gives way to the romantic one as Marlow's psychic need to create a sustaining myth asserts itself. But the perfected world that emerges in the vision of his own heroism is threatened by the inevitability of change and the ubiquitous presence of death. Ironically, he cannot escape the objective world. The impressionistic verbal texture of Marlow's narrative belies his efforts to impose stasis upon his past. His language, fraught with similes, dramatises a process of astonishing—almost phantasmagoric—flux. The boat, always evolving, becomes match-wood; Abraham is transformed into 'an animal that won't leave the stable' and then into a package that is 'pitched down the cabin companion': and the turbulent sea is described as 'white like a sheet of foam, like a cauldron of boiling milk' (p. 11).

Beginning his reminiscence in a tone of good-natured urbanity, Marlow implies that the meaning of the voyage seems to be that it shows man's inability to deal with the natural forces that confront him:

> You fight, work, sweat, nearly kill yourself, sometimes do kill yourself trying to accomplish something—and you can't. Not from any fault of yours. You simply can do nothing, neither great nor little—not a thing in the world—not even marry an old maid, or get a wretched 600-ton cargo of coal to its port of destination. (p. 4)

He begins in unexcited, lucid, straightforward prose, dispassionately setting the stage: 'It was altogether a memorable affair. It was my first voyage to the East, and my first voyage as second mate; it was also my skipper's first command' (p. 4). What is not said at this point is significant. Not yet emotionally involved in his reminiscences, he says nothing about *his* first command. Nor does he mention the scope of his heroic activities, or intimate that his subject is more the voyage's personal meaning to him than that which the voyage itself illustrates.

But it is soon apparent that mature Marlow, the supposedly worldly realist, is rarely endangering the impression of young Marlow as 'heroic'. While modestly admitting Jermyn was probably right that he 'knew very little then', and *intellectually* believing it, old Marlow's narration of young Marlow's heroics belies his acceptance of Jermyn's judgement. (For no other reason than this opinion delivered years ago, he still resents Jermyn 'to this day' [p. 6].) As Marlow remembers his role, he is the vital figure in every crisis. He is the one who notices the approaching steamer, who reacts urbanely when he is the first officer to discover the smoke ('I answered negligently, "It's good for the health they say"' [p. 19]), who first sees the revived fire, and who is the only officer not malingering when the boat should be abandoned. Even where he is most ironical about his own conduct, when he leaps down to save the cook, he is really giving testimony to his own heroic behaviour. He invites us to smile with him at his impetuous heroism and his rescue by a 'chain-hook tied to a broom handle'. In the facetious understatement that follows, he shows himself as a sympathetic figure who can laugh at his own quixotic zeal. ('I did not offer to go and fetch up my shovel, which was left down below' [p. 21]. )

The supposedly urbane older Marlow does little to divest his youthful heroics of epic significance. To be sure, he does contrast his 'subjective' reality with what he knows to be the 'objective' situation. He recalls how 'the' old bark lumbered on, heavy with her age and the burden of her cargo, while I lived the life of youth in ignorance and hope', and he attributes his patience to his youthful expectation and self-satisfaction (p. 18). The evocation of legendary Elizabethan predecessors and the references to Nemesis and Erebus represent Marlow's effort to place his journey in an archetypal pattern. As the reader realises, these allusions to cultural antecedents which begin as part of his urbane irony gradually become one of a piece with his tendency to magnify the importance of his youthful voyage. Old Marlow may be ironical when he first remembers how he had thought of his spiritual heirs, 'who, centuries ago, went that road in ships that sailed not better' (p. 18). But recollecting his arrival in the East, he enthusiastically recalls how he had '[exulted] like a conqueror' as he arrived at the 'East of the ancient navigators' (pp. 38, 41).

When old Marlow's monologue reaches his recollection of abandoning the ship and his subsequent arrival in the East, his rhetoric tends to broad generalisation, vague abstraction, and impressionistic oversimplification. Morton Zabel's unhappiness with this language does not take into account the point of view.[6] Old Marlow's tendency to rhapsodise increases as he becomes more and more involved in and infatuated with his own experience. The remove between older Marlow and young Marlow completely breaks down in his excitement. He forgets to ask for the bottle (although he has drunk enough perhaps so that his increasingly uncontrolled verbal rhapsodies can be partially attributed to claret) and his apostrophes to youth become less controlled, more intense, and more frequent. Typical of Marlow's later rhetoric is his glib comparison of the glamour of youth with the flames of the ship (p. 30). To the sentimental, garrulous old Marlow, the flames to be quenched may suggest how the vitality of youth is exhausted by time. But the perceptive reader, while feeling the pulsation of old Marlow's enthusiasm, nevertheless realises that the dramatic story—as opposed to Marlow's statement—does not sustain this rather romantic and hyperbolic metaphor. Once Marlow's monologue reaches his leaving the ship, his sentimentalism sweeps away all pretences to self-irony.

Earlier, as we have seen, he could laugh at his futile attempt at heroism or his bathetic encounter with a saucepan, even while taking himself seriously. Now the lyric element predominates, and the ability to see the humour of his behaviour and to look at himself good-naturedly disappears. Subjective impressions and illusions do not depend entirely on objective reality. Even though Marlow, sometimes unknowingly but often quite knowingly, shows us that his youthful conduct had not always been exemplary, this does not affect *his* emotional feelings about his youthful conduct. By and large, he is much readier to see the humour of his captain's or helmsman's behaviour than his own. The scenes in which the captain and helmsman are separated from their ship are narrated with a levity of tone that he rarely applies to himself except in the comic rescue scene. Yet the bathetic reduction of his abortive rescue and his self-ridicule at catching saucepans as a means of discovering the cook's peril do qualify our impression of Marlow's youthful experience. Until the ship is abandoned, old Marlow does have a capacity for seeing the humour in his glamorous voyage which young Marlow had apparently lacked. For example, he can smile at excited young Marlow's expectations that the elements would empathise with his experience; after the explosion, young Marlow apparently expected the sea and sky to be 'convulsed with horror' (p. 24).

Early in the narrative when Marlow still maintains some semblance

of objectivity toward his youth, he qualifies the attitudes of his youth
by positing them in such terms as 'one would think' or 'it seemed' or
'I felt as though', all terms which suggest that perhaps his youthful
feelings were exaggerated: for example, he says:

> *One would think* that the sole purpose of that fiendish gale had
> been to make a lunatic of that poor devil of a mulatto.
> (p. 14);

or,

> *It seemed as though* we have been forgotten by the world,
> belonged to nobody, would get nowhere . . . (p. 16);

and, the pumping

> *seemed* to last for months, for years, for all eternity, *as though*
> we had been dead and gone to a hell for sailors. (pp. 11–12;
> emphasis mine in the above passages)

In these examples, the relativity and control of 'seemed' are partly
undermined by the enthusiasm—marked by appositives and by
increased stresses—with which Marlow speaks. Later, almost all
qualifications disappear. If old Marlow partially recognises and mocks
the egocentricity of his emotions—as with his youthful response of
'By Jove! This is the deuce of an adventure' (p. 12)—he nevertheless
savours the emotional satisfaction and comfort that his recollections
momentarily provide.

Old Marlow has a variety of self-serving devices for disguising his
own youthful fears and anxieties. He attributes madness to the
captain's controlled reaction to the explosion. Or he transforms a
personal response into a generalisation; for example, he says 'This was
disheartening' for 'I was disheartened' (p. 20). He sometimes reveals
his fears in the form of similes which expose his anxieties. Thus he
recalls how boards protruded overboard after the explosion 'like
a gangway leading upon nothing, like a gangway leading over the
deep sea, leading to death—as if inviting us to walk the plank at once
and be done with our *ridiculous* troubles' (p. 26, emphasis mine).
Realising that he may have aroused doubts about his courage,
Marlow abruptly changes his tone to introduce the bathetic incident
of the helmsman who jumps overboard deliberately. The elder

Marlow instinctively senses whenever he is revealing more than he wishes about his youthful emotions. So in the above quotation, he uses a word like 'ridiculous' to force a comic perspective on situations which might reveal his youthful fears to both his audience and himself.

The presence of death and mutability is everywhere. The old skipper 'looked as though he would never wake'; Mahon appeared 'as though he had been shot where he sat at the tiller' (p. 41). The tired men 'slept thrown across the thwarts, curled on bottom-boards in the careless attitudes of death' (p. 41). As in Kafka's *The Metamorphosis*, there seems to be a principle of conservation of life substance at work. If one man thrives, it is seemingly at the expense of others. Even while mature Marlow sees the flames of the ship as a symbol of the mutability of youth, we realise that it is a funeral pyre for the voyage, the boat, the aged captain, and the old first mate: 'Oh, the glamour of youth! Oh, the fire of it, more dazzling than the flames of the burning ship, throwing a magic light on the wide earth, leaping audaciously to the sky, presently to be quenched by time, more cruel, more pitiless, more bitter than the sea—and like the flames of the burning ship surrounded by an impenetrable night' (p. 30). The syntactical progress from contemplation of youth to its consequences is a verbal action that confirms the impossibility of isolating a period of time. Youth is a voyage to age, disillusionment, and experience: 'I remember my youth and . . . the feeling that I could last forever, outlast the sea, the earth, and all men; the deceitful feeling that lures us on to joys, to perils, to love, to vain effort—to death; the triumphant conviction of strength, the heat of life in the handful of dust, the glow in the heart that with every year grows dim, grows cold, grows small, and expires—and expires, too soon, too soon—before life itself' (pp. 36–7). He cannot now sustain his rhapsody about 'the feeling that I could last forever' because the recognition of his fallibility and mortality can never be more than momentarily suppressed. Given Conrad's knowledge of Shakespeare, it becomes possible that Sonnet 73 was an inspiration for 'Youth': 'In me thou see'st the glowing of such fire / That on the ashes of his youth doth lie, / As the deathbed whereon it must expire, / Consum'd with that which it was nourish'd by.' In the sonnet and in 'Youth', youth consumes man's vitality and strength and leaves the remnants for old age.

Marlow's paean to youth is in fact the psychic gesture of a man escaping from the ravages of age and the disillusionment of experience. However, the story reveals that the journey cannot be isolated as a moment out of time, but has a temporal dimension: 'I have seen the [East's] mysterious shores, the still water, the lands of brown nations, where a stealthy Nemesis lies in wait, pursues, overtakes so many of the conquering race, who are proud of their wisdom, of their knowledge, of their strength' (pp. 41–2). He reflexively recoils from the implications of this discovery: 'But for me all the East is contained in that vision of my youth. It is all in that moment.' Marlow's thoughts dissolve into an incantational lyric in an effort to exorcise the presence of death: 'And this is all that is left of it! Only a moment; a moment of strength, of romance, of glamour—of youth! . . . A flick of sunshine upon a strange shore, the time to remember, the time for a sigh, and—good-bye—Night—Good-bye . . . ! (p. 42). For Marlow, language becomes the only reality. His non-syntactical language is psychic gesture, an effort to replace the temporal dimension of language, syntax, with an ecstatic chant, whose repetitions defy movement. 'Ah! the good old time—the good old time. Youth and the sea. Glamour and the sea! The good, strong sea, the salt, bitter sea, that could whisper to you and roar at you and knock your breath out of you' (p. 42). Although Marlow's nostalgic, lyrical recollection dissolves into an escapist ecstasy, it differs from the Romantic ecstasies of the early nineteenth century. In *Journey Through Despair 1880–1914*, John A. Lester helpfully differentiates between earlier nineteenth-century ecstasies and those of this period: 'The difference in late-century ecstasy is that it was more emotional, less purposefully energetic, and it lacked the insistent upward surge of aspiration; there was more escapism in it, and more willful, even blind, immersement in sensation.'[7] He attributes the quest for a moment of illumination when one is transported out of one's sense of space and time to a number of factors including 'the collapse of all belief in the transcendent': 'the contemporary disillusionment with the intellect'; and 'the new relativism, the growing conviction among scientists and all thinking men that the world is not fully intelligible to human reason'.[8]

Marlow's style reflects the emotional self-indulgence of his narration. Gradually the self-irony dissolves in his efforts to impose a myth on his voyage. Marlow's character is revealed by the evolution of his style: vague generalisations and abstractions unsupported by specifics, repetitions that do not clarify the sense, and references to an epic past that his adventures only burlesque. The themes of solipsism and narcissism recur in British fiction of the 1890s; they derive from the period's pervasive belief that each man was hermetically sealed in his own perceptions and that there was neither an omniscient God nor an objective reality. As we have seen, *The Nigger of the 'Narcissus'* concludes with a reaching towards celebration which is belied by what precedes. While the narrator desperately tries to impose a significance upon the disintegrating crew by means of his final reductive fantasy, the tale refutes the narrator's recollection as a narcissistic wish-fulfilment and makes us understand that the narrator, as much as Wait, belongs to the *Narcissus*.

Marlow's monologue provides him with a memory of romance and innocence which remains to sustain him, even after he has become somewhat disillusioned by time and age. This remembrance of time past is part of him now. And his attempts to take an ironical objective view, now that the 'triumphant conviction of strength' has faded, dissolve into a nostalgic lyric to a time when he felt differently. Marlow fails to dispel his own youthful illusions, but his very failure makes him realise their personal value. For mature Marlow, the fact that he could not move a '600-ton cargo of coal to its port of destination' becomes, finally, irrelevant. What matters to him is that the past feeling of his own physical and moral strength still contributes to his present emotional life. Marlow's monologue implies the need for a romantic view of reality in which the mind creates experience to supplement empirical experience. Conrad universalises this theme by having his audience, men of varied endeavours but united by common background, endorse Marlow's view that the *memory* of how one felt towards events is *as important* as what actually happened:

> And we all nodded at him: the man of finance, the man of accounts, the man of law, we all nodded at him over the polished table that like a still sheet of brown water reflected our faces, lined, wrinkled; our faces marked by toil, by deceptions, by success, by love; our weary eyes looking still, looking always, looking anxiously for something out of life, that while it is expected is already gone—has passed unseen, in a sigh, in a flash—together with the youth, with the strength, with the romance of illusions. (p. 42)

The members of the audience, also ageing and unable to recapture their youth, endorse the mythmaking process. They participate in his vision, even while the inevitable progress of the speaker's syntax imitates the passing of 'the something unseen', until nothing remains but silence for the audience and blankness for the reader; the mythos of youth has been enclosed by duration.

## III. 'HEART OF DARKNESS' (1899)

The subject of 'Heart of Darkness' is primarily Marlow, but the presence of Conrad is deeply engraved on every scene.[9] Marlow's effort to come to terms with the Congo experience, especially Kurtz, is the crucial activity that engaged Conrad's imagination. Marlow's consciousness is the arena of the tale, and the interaction between his verbal behaviour—his effort to find the appropriate words—and his memory is as much the agon as his Congo journey. Both the epistemological quest for a context or perspective with which to interpret the experience and the semiological quest to discover the signs and symbols which make the experience intelligible are central to the tale.

Conrad dramatised Marlow's efforts to narrate his experience at a time when he himself was anxious that he might not be able to fulfil his artistic credo of making other men see. In November 1898, he had written to Ford: 'How fine it could be if the thought did not escape—if the expression did not hide underground, if the idea had a substance and words a magic power, if the invisible could be snared into a shape. And it is sad to think that even if all this came to pass— even then it could never be so fine to anybody as it is fine to me now, lurking in the blank pages, in an intensity of existence without voice, without form—but without blemish.'[10] Conrad transfers to Marlow the agonising self-doubt about his ability to transform personal impressions into a significant tale.

The Congo experience had plunged Marlow into doubt and confusion. Sitting 'apart, indistinct, and silent' in his ascetic Buddha pose, Marlow is deliberately trying to separate himself from the cynicism and hypocrisy that he associates with Europeans. As in 'Youth', while Marlow is telling the story he arrests the future, places his back against the present, and becomes part of the created world of his own imagination. The tale Marlow tells becomes not only a version of, but an epistemological quest into, 'the culminating point of my experience' (p. 51). The experience proves recalcitrant to Marlow's efforts to understand it. Marlow's probing mind cannot impose an interpretation on Kurtz: 'The thing was to know what he belonged to, how many powers of darkness claimed him for their own. That was the reflection that made you creepy all over. It was impossible—it was not good for one either—trying to imagine' (p. 116). Part of his hostility to his audience derives from his own frustrated desire to discover the language that will make his experience comprehensible to himself. Marlow's is the voice of a man desperately trying to create meaning; unlike Kurtz who 'could get himself to believe anything', Marlow's problem is convincing himself that there is the possibility of belief (p. 154). Marlow's narration is a quest for the symbols and signs to explain the darkness that still haunts his imagination.[11]

Marlow's experience in the Congo invalidated his belief that civilisation equalled progress. While Kurtz, the man who seemed to embody all the accomplishments of civilisation, has reverted to savagery, the cannibals have some semblance of the 'restraint' that makes civilisation possible. Kurtz is a poet, painter, musician, journalist, potential political leader, a 'universal genius' of Europe, and yet once he travelled to a place where the earliest beginnings of the world still survived, the wilderness awakened 'brutal instincts' and 'monstrous passions'.

Kurtz haunts Marlow's memory. When Marlow visited the Intended, he first learned that Kurtz was not like other memories of dead men: 'I had a vision of him on the stretcher, opening his mouth voraciously, as if to devour all the earth with all its mankind. He lived then before me; he lived as much as he had ever lived . . .' (p. 155). As much as he would like to, Marlow cannot separate himself from Kurtz, cannot 'surrender personally all that remained of him with me to that oblivion which is the last word of our common fate' (p. 155). He is a recurring part of Marlow's present. One aspect of the 'darkness' of the title that Marlow must perpetually face is the knowledge that civilised man's potential includes the possibilities of Kurtz's behaviour.

Marlow begins as if he were recollecting a spiritual voyage of self-discovery: 'It seemed somehow to throw a kind of light on everything about me—and into my thoughts. It was sombre enough too—and pitiful—not extraordinary in any way—not very clear either. No, not very clear. And yet it seemed to throw a kind of light' (p. 51). As Marlow engages in an introspective monologue, the catalyst for which is his recognition that the Thames, too, contained the same potential darkness for the Romans as the Congo does for him, he recalls how he had discovered the pretensions of European civilisations. At first, his morality and point of view are one-dimensional. He relies on conventional Victorian conceptions of honour, integrity, discipline, and the intrinsic value of hard work, and glibly indicts those who fails to live up to these abstract conceptions.

Although every event is informed by his present attitudes, Marlow's meditation follows the order of the original experience until he reaches the circumstances surrounding his first meeting with Kurtz. He desperately wants to believe that his journey into the atavistic Congo and his climactic encounter with Kurtz have broken down his personality only to prepare him for a new, broader integration and a deeper understanding of his relationship with and responsibility to other people. Marlow defers recounting the meeting with Kurtz in order to leap ahead to his meeting with the Intended, to comment on Kurtz's megalomania, and to relate how he saw the shrunken heads. He has difficulty recollecting his impression of the more gruesome details of his experience. Except for the shrunken heads, he contents himself with merely alluding to 'subtle horrors' and 'unspeakable rites'. He claims he had almost expected to discover symptoms of atavistic behaviour in his journey 'back to the earliest beginnings of the world'. (He specifically says, 'I was not so shocked as you may think' [p. 130].) Yet, now that Marlow is back within the civilised world, he recoils from the grotesque memories.

Marlow's journey from Europe to the Congo helped prepare him to sympathise with Kurtz. From the outset he was offended by the standards and perspectives of the European imperialists, and gradually, he began to sympathise with the natives against the predatory colonialists. As an idle passenger on a boat taking him to the Congo, he caught glimpses of the inanity which he later encountered as an involved participant. Even then, he saw the fatuity of the 'civilised' French man-of-war's shelling the bush: 'Pop, would go one of the six-inch guns; a small flame would dart and vanish, a little white smoke would disappear, a tiny projectile would give a feeble screech—and nothing happened' (p. 62).

Soon, more than his Calvinistic belief in the redemptive powers of purposeful labour was offended. He viewed the company's outer station from an ironic standpoint, noticing the neglected machinery, lying like an animal 'carcass'; the 'objectless blasting'; and the native workers, their rags resembling tails, chained together as if they were a team of mules. He mocked the folly of those who put out fires with buckets that have holes in the bottom and who considered diseased and starving men 'enemies' and 'criminals'. His original epistemological stance, dependent not upon a naive idealised conception of the trading company's commercial ventures, but simply upon his belief that European civilisation represents a tradition of humane values, was shaken. He began to realise that this version of civilisation is not an 'emissary of light', but an instance of exploitative imperialism at its worst. After arriving at the Central Station, Marlow's quest soon focused on discovering an alternative to the amoral pragmatism and cynicism illustrated by the manager and his uncle. The manager's only objection to Kurtz's abominations is that the results were unsatisfactory: 'The district is closed to us for a time. Deplorable! Upon the whole, the trade will suffer' (p. 137).

The manager's cynical materialism impelled Marlow to turn to Kurtz. Speaking of the origins of Marlow's commitment to Kurtz, Albert Guerard remarks:

> Marlow commits himself to the yet unseen agent partly because Kurtz 'had come out equipped with moral ideas of some sort.' Anything would seem preferable to the demoralized greed and total cynicism of the others, 'the flabby devil' of the Central Station.[12]

Gradually, as the people he despised maligned Kurtz, he became interested in meeting him. Thus, contrary to his own sense of integrity and dislike of lying or dissembling, he allowed the 'brickmaker', who really was a spy, to believe that he did have influence in Europe. Marlow, desperate to retain his illusions, wanted to meet a man reputed to be an 'emissary of pity, and science, and progress' (p. 79). The next he heard of Kurtz was in the dialogue between the manager and his uncle when he learned that Kurtz had come three hundred miles up the river only to turn back. When he imagined Kurtz 'setting his face towards the depths of the wilderness', Marlow tried to put the best possible interpretation on his motives: 'Perhaps he was simply a fine fellow who stuck to his work for its own sake' (p. 90).

The more he became disillusioned, the more Kurtz became the goal of his quest: 'The approach to this Kurtz grubbing for ivory in the wretched bush was beset by as many dangers as though he had been an enchanted princess sleeping in a fabulous castle' (p. 106). Conrad describes the quest in romance terms to suggest ironically Marlow's kinship with folk and legendary heroes who also search for miracles and magicians to solve their problems and relieve their anxieties. Standing in the blood of his helmsman, Marlow could only think that Kurtz was dead and would never talk to him. It was as if he were frustrated in a journey to consult an oracle. After discovering that Kurtz had 'taken a high seat among the devils of the land', he did not renounce his existential commitment to Kurtz as 'the nightmare of my choice'; Kurtz still seemed preferable to the hypocrisy and malignity of the Europeans who have deprived language of its meaning, civilisation of its ideals, and life of its purpose. Marlow, formerly a representative of European civilisation, desperately identified with a man he knew to be ostracised by that civilisation. Ironically, Marlow turned only to a different form of greed and egotism; Kurtz's atavistic impulses have a magnitude and purity that contrast with the pettiness and niggling greed of the imperialists.

We do not know how perceptive Marlow was when he met Kurtz, but Marlow *now* knows that Kurtz was without the restraint that even the helmsman and other cannibals had: 'Mr. Kurtz lacked restraint in the gratification of his various lusts . . .[;] there was something wanting in him—some small matter which, when the pressing need arose, could not be found under his magnificent eloquence' (p. 131). Earlier in his narration, Marlow seemed to be preparing to extenuate Kurtz. Marlow had asserted that the 'idea' behind an action can be redemptive for the committed individual:

> The conquest of the earth, which mostly means the taking it
> away from those who have a different complexion or slightly
> flatter noses than ourselves, is not a pretty thing when you
> look into it too much. What redeems it is the idea only. An
> idea at the back of it; not a sentimental pretence but an idea;
> and an unselfish belief in the idea—something you can set up,
> and bow down before, and offer a sacrifice to . . . (pp. 50–1)

However, his narrative discredits this view that the ultimate test of an action is the sincerity of the concept that motivates it. Originally, Kurtz had 'set up and [bowed] down before' a benevolent idea, but when the wilderness had 'sealed his soul to its own by the inconceivable ceremonies of some devilish initiation', Kurtz's idea became its own solipsistic parody: 'My intended, my ivory, my station, my river, my—' (pp. 115, 116).

For Marlow piloting the steamer is an important psychic buffer with which to keep the inner darkness at bay: 'When you have to attend . . . to the mere incidents of the surface, the reality—the reality, I tell you—fades. The inner truth is hidden—luckily, luckily. But I felt it all the same; I felt often its mysterious stillness watching me at my monkey tricks, just as it watches you fellows performing on your respective tightropes . . .' (pp. 93–4).[13] But the man aware of his place in an indifferent cosmos must commit himself to some ideals beyond himself.

> The earth for us is a place to live in, where we must put up with sights, with sounds, with smells, too, by Jove!—breathe dead hippo, so to speak and not be contaminated. And there, don't you see? your strength comes in, the faith in your ability for the digging of unostentatious holes to bury the stuff in— your power of devotion, not to yourself, but to an obscure, back-breathing business. (p. 117)

The commitments of innumerable individuals to their respective responsibilities make it possible for mankind to cope collectively with the indifferent objective world. While the surrender of self to function has its dehumanising aspects, civilisation depends on the countless souls who seem to exist for and be defined by their tasks. The helmsman illustrates the beneficial effects of work: 'He ought to have been clapping his hands and stamping his feet on the bank, instead of which he was hard at work, a thrall to strange witchcraft, full of improving knowledge' (p. 97). Marlow gradually learned that once he leaves the surface, there is no epistemological map for the 'inner truth'. Well before he met Kurtz, he discovered that conventional standards had not prepared him for understanding man's complex antecedents and potential for evil. While Marlow could deal with the manager, the persistent presence of the wilderness overwhelmed him with its 'lurking death', 'hidden evil' and 'profound darkness of its heart' (p. 92).

In the young Russian motivated by 'glamour' and the 'spirit of adventure' Marlow met a version of the younger self that had sailed the *Judea* in 'Youth'. The Russian's response to Kurtz contrasted with Marlow's multidimensional reaction. For a time, the Russian apotheosised Kurtz, claiming that Kurtz had 'enlarged my mind'. But although Marlow refused to suspend completely his judgement of Kurtz, he does commit himself to preserving the memory of a man whose solipsism he despises, because for a brief time he had, or *believed he had*, discovered a 'rent' in the veil of the 'impenetrable darkness' of Kurtz's soul, and had gone 'through the ordeal of looking into

[Kurtz's soul] myself' (p. 145). However, the real reason for his commitment is that Kurtz has been the catalyst for Marlow's looking into his own soul and learning fundamental things about himself and mankind.

Marlow invests Kurtz with values which fulfil his own need to embody his threat of the jungle in one tangible creature. If Kurtz is considered the centre of the 'heart of darkness', the business of following Kurtz and winning the 'struggle' enables Marlow to believe that he had conquered a symbol of the atavistic, debilitating effects of the jungle. This belief is central to his interpretation of the journey's significance. For Marlow, capturing Kurtz after he escapes symbolises a personal victory over darkness. Increasingly, he had been attracted to the jungle by the urge to go ashore for 'a howl and a dance'. Having given in to his primitive urges, Kurtz appropriately crawls away on all fours. Marlow recalls how he, too, was tempted by savage impulses and confused his heartbeat with the beat of the natives' drums. Uncharacteristically, he thought of giving Kurtz a 'drubbing'. He was 'strangely cocksure of himself' and enjoyed stalking his prey. His assertion that 'he left the track' indicates that he, too, is in danger now that he is alone in the jungle; he thinks that he might never get back. But when Marlow confronts Kurtz, he recalls, 'I seemed to come to my senses, I saw the danger in its right proportion' (p. 143). To him, the confrontation represents coming to terms with the dark potential within himself against the background of primitive and unspeakable rites. But he does not surrender to the appeal of the wilderness precisely because he has internalised the restraints imposed by civilisation.

That Kurtz has achieved a 'moral victory' may very well be a necessary illusion for Marlow. But did Kurtz pronounce a verdict on his reversion to primitivism and achieve the 'supreme moment of complete knowledge' (p. 149)? Or is this what Marlow desperately wants to believe? Coming from a man who 'could get himself to believe anything', how credible is Marlow's interpretation that 'The horror! The horror!' is 'an affirmation, a moral victory paid for by innumerable defeats, by abominable terrors, by abominable satisfactions' (p. 151)? When Kurtz had enigmatically muttered, 'Live rightly, die, die . . .', Marlow had wondered 'Was he rehearsing some speech in his sleep, or was it a fragment of a phrase from some newspaper article?' (p. 148). Marlow had just remarked that Kurtz's voice 'survived his strength to hide in the magnificent folds of eloquence the barren darkness of his heart' (p. 147). If Kurtz had kicked himself loose of the earth, how can Kurtz pronounce a verdict on his ignominious return to civilisation or an exclamation elicited from a vision of his own imminent death? For the reader, Kurtz remains a symbol of how the human ego can expand infinitely to the point where it tries to will its own apotheosis.

The lie to the Intended is another crucial moment of self-definition. Marlow's return to his homeland as something of a misanthrope suggests Gulliver's return from the land of the Houyhnhnms.[14] Disappointed and resentful, he actually detested the people of the 'sepulchral city' scurrying about

> . . . to dream their insignificant and silly dreams. They trespassed upon my thoughts. They were intruders whose knowledge of life was to me an irritating pretence, because I felt so sure they could not possibly know the things I knew. (p. 152)

But he brought himself to participate in the 'silly dreams' in order to protect the Intended's sensibilities. Knowing that the lie hurts no one, he allows the Intended to believe in Kurtz. Marlow consciously adjusted his morality to suit the needs of others, and he deliberately took part in a scene which required not only absolute self-control, but the use of the disingenuous tactics he despised. The ability to function morally within the complexities of 'civilized' life was the final test of his personal development. Walter F. Wright puts it well: 'If he had told the girls the simple facts, he would have acknowledged that the pilgrims in their cynicism had the truth, that goodness and faith were the unrealities.'[15] Marlow's lie to the Intended, allowing her to sustain her faith, is paradoxically a rejection of indifference and cynicism; as he acknowledges, to tell the truth 'would have been too dark—too dark altogether'. Marlow has journeyed back from the inner reality to the surface world where illusions are essential. He recognised the place in a civilised community of both relative morality and humane responses to the needs of others.

The introductory narrator has warned us that Marlow's narratives do not *mean* in the usual sense: 'To him the meaning of an episode was not inside like a kernel but outside, enveloping the tale which brought it out only as a glow brings out a haze . . .' (p. 48). And indeed the first narrator has learned from the tale that the world is enclosed in an 'immense darkness', with neither purpose nor meaning. Marlow returns from his journey with no inner truth, no symbolic light to clarify the darkness. The equation of the Roman voyage up the Thames and Marlow's up the Congo suggests an important parallel. That Marlow says 'this also has been'—not 'this also was'—'one of the dark places on the earth' denies the idea of humanity's progressive evolution, still a widely held view in the 1890s, by showing that the manifestation of barbaric impulses is a continuous possibility. The essential nature of Europeans and natives is the same: 'The mind is capable of anything—because everything is in it, all the past as well as all the future' (p. 96). Conrad stresses that illusions are not only a defence against reversion to primitive life, but the basis of civilisation.

John A. Lester succinctly summarises one aspect of the spiritual and intellectual milieu in which Conrad lived: '(1) There was no room for any lasting and higher significance for man's life whatsoever, and (2) man was granted consciousness to be aware that such was the case.'[16] That self-fulfilment and a limited self-knowledge are ultimate goals in a world in which there is a disjunction between subjective and objective is acknowledged by Marlow: 'Droll thing life is—that mysterious arrangement of merciless logic for a futile purpose. The most you can hope from it is some knowledge of yourself—that comes too late—a crop of unextinguishable regrets' (p. 150). In this *Zeitgeist*, man cannot discover absolute values; discovering 'principles' won't do; what he searches for is a sustaining illusion, a 'deliberate belief' (p. 97). In a famous letter to Garnett, written a few months after Conrad finished 'Heart of Darkness', Conrad complained:

> I am like a man who has lost his gods. My efforts seem unrelated to anything in heaven and everything under heaven is impalpable to the touch like shapes of mist.
>
> Even writing to a friend . . . does not give me a sense of reality. All is illusion—the words written, the mind at which they are aimed, the truth they are intended to express, the hands that will hold the paper, the eyes that will glance at the lines. Every image floats vaguely in a sea of doubt—and the doubt itself is lost in an unexplored universe of incertitudes.
> (16 Sept. 1899; *Garnett*, p. 155)

Marlow echoes Conrad's despair with the ability of language to communicate his subjective world: 'Do you see him? Do you see the story? Do you see anything? It seems to me I am trying to tell you a dream—making a vain attempt, because no relation of a dream can convey the dream-sensation, that commingling of absurdity, surprise, and bewilderment in a tremor of struggling revolt, that notion of being captured by the incredible which is of the very essence of dreams . . .' (p. 82). Marlow concludes this passage by generalising his solitude: 'We live, as we dream—alone.' The meanings of words like 'civilized', 'workers', 'criminals', 'enemies', and 'rebels' have been blurred as if the gift of language itself had been corrupted by civilisation.

Yet paradoxically Kurtz's effect on Marlow illustrates the power of language. Kurtz is àt first presented as a master of language. The hypnotic effect of Kurtz's voice has a kinship with the incantations of the savages rather than the syntactical patterns of ordinary discourse. Eloquence is Kurtz's gift, and his report is 'a beautiful piece of writing' whose peroration makes Marlow 'tingle with enthusiasm': 'This was the unbounded power of eloquence—of words—of burning noble words' (p. 118). Anticipating Jim on Patusan, Kurtz's fiction becomes his life; but unlike Jim who models the standards of his imaginative world upon the home world, Kurtz's world takes shape from forbidden dreams of being worshipped and from libidinous needs that brook no restraint. In transforming his imaginative world into reality, Kurtz 'had kicked himself loose of the earth. . . . He had kicked the very earth to pieces. He was alone . . .' (p. 144). For a moment Marlow lived in Kurtz's world, only to have had the 'magic current of phrases' interrupted by the grotesque appendix, 'Exterminate all the brutes!' However pernicious, the appendix does communicate and belies the idea that language is solipsistic, even if Kurtz, the demonic artist, is appropriating language to his own uses. Kurtz's words, Marlow recalls, 'were common everyday words—the familiar, vague sounds exchanged on every waking day of life . . . [but] they had behind them, to my mind, the terrific suggestiveness of words heard in dreams, of phrases spoken in nightmares' (p. 144). It is from this point that the narrative includes the gestures of the savage mistress and the Intended; the beating of the drums, the shrill cry of the sorrowing savages; and the development of Kurtz into Marlow's own symbol of moral darkness and atavistic reversion. Marlow's recurring nightmare begins not only to compete with his effort to use language discursively and mimetically, but to establish a separate, more powerful telling. This more inclusive tale, not so much told as revealed by Marlow as he strains for the signs and symbols which will make his experience intelligible, transcends his more conventional discourse. Conrad shows that these instinctive and passionate outbursts, taking the form of gestures, chants, and litany, represent a tradition, a core of experience, that civilised man has debased. In a brilliant surrealistic touch, Conrad makes Marlow's consciousness an echo chamber for the haunting sounds of his 'culminating' experience. After recalling that Kurtz 'was little more than a voice', the past rushes in to disrupt the present effort to give shape and meaning to his narrative: 'And I heard him—it—this voice—other voices—all of them were so little more than voices— and the memory of that time itself lingers around me, impalpable, *like* a dying vibration of one immense jabber, silly, atrocious, sordid, savage, or simply mean, without any kind of sense. Voices, voices— even the girl herself—now—' (p. 115, emphasis mine). The temporary breakdown of Marlow's syntax in the passage dramatises the resistance of his experience to ordinary discourse, even as the simile comparing Kurtz's voice to an 'immense jabber' reveals the challenge of his nightmare to language.

Yet Marlow's decision to narrate his experience is predicated upon at least a tentative faith that language is the vehicle of order, reason, and symbolic light which would serve as his intellectual guide to explore the mystery and darkness of the human soul. Marlow's tale deeply affects the nameless listener who becomes our narrator: 'I raised my head. The offing was barred by a black bank of clouds, and the tranquil waterway leading to the uttermost ends of the earth flowed sombre under an overcast sky—seemed to lead into the heart of an immense darkness' (p. 162). Since the nameless narrator recreates his original process of learning the tale, we can assume that his comment about Marlow's inconclusive tales occurs *before* he has heard Marlow's tale and parallels Marlow's ingenuous assertion that he was like 'a silly little bird' (p. 52). The tale shatters the first speaker's innocence which we have seen in his evocation of the greatness of England's epic past. As he listens, he becomes as fascinated with Marlow's voice as Marlow had been with Kurtz's voice, and turns to Marlow as if he were oracular:

> The others might have been asleep, but I was awake. I listened, I listened on the watch for the sentence, for the word, that would give me a clue to the faint uneasiness inspired by this narrative that seemed to shape itself without human lips in the heavy night-air of the river. (p. 83)

The adaptation of Marlow's brooding tone and style of expression indicates that Marlow had communicated something of his experience. That Marlow communicates demonstrates that man does not live completely alone as he had claimed, and implies that language can establish the 'fellowship' and 'solidarity' that both Marlow and his creator seek.

## NOTES

1. For important discussions of Marlow's general function, see John Palmer, *Joseph Conrad's Fiction: A Study in Literary Growth* (Ithaca: Cornell University Press, 1968), Chap. 1; and John Oliver Perry, 'Action, Vision, or Voice: The Moral Dilemmas in Conrad's Tale-telling', *Modern Fiction Studies*, vol. x (Spring 1964), pp. 3—14.

2. Quoted in Jocelyn Baines, *Joseph Conrad: A Critical Biography* (New York: McGraw Hill, 1960), p. 219.

3. Susanne K. Langer, *Feeling and Form* (New York: Scribner's, 1953), p. 292.

4. Edward Said, *Joseph Conrad and the Fiction of Autobiography* (Cambridge: Harvard University Press, 1966), has written: 'The past, requiring the illumination of slow reflection on former thoughtless impulses, is exposed to the present; the present demanding that "desired unrest" without which it must remain mute and paralyzed is exposed to the past' (p. 93).

5. For penetrating remarks on Marlow's role in 'Youth', see W. Y. Tindall 'Apology for Marlow', in R. C. Rathburn and M. Steinmann, jun. (eds.), *From Jane Austen to Joseph Conrad* (Minneapolis: University of Minnesota Press, 1959), reprinted in Bruce Harkness (ed.), *Conrad's 'Heart of Darkness' and the Critics* (Belmont, California: Wadsworth, 1960), pp. 123—331.

6. Morton Dauwen Zabel, Introduction to *The Portable Conrad* (New York: Viking, 1947), p. 17, speaks of 'cloying lyrical verbalism', but such a style is deliberately assigned to old Marlow as part of Conrad's dramatisation of his speaker.

7. John A. Lester, jun., *Journey Through Despair 1880—1914: Transformations in British Literary Culture* (Princeton: Princeton University Press, 1968), p. 173.

8. Ibid., pp. 172—4.

9. My discussion of 'Heart of Darkness' has been especially influenced by Guerard, *Conrad the Novelist* (Cambridge: Harvard University Press, 1958) pp. 33—48; J. Hillis Miller, *Poets of Reality: Six Twentieth Century Writers* (Cambridge: The Belknap Press of Harvard University Press, 1965), pp. 13—29; James Guetti, *The Limits of Metaphor: A Study of Melville, Conrad, and Faulkner* (Ithaca: Cornell University Press, 1967), pp. 46—68. The selections in the following anthologies have also played an important role in my thinking: Robert Kimbrough, '*Heart of Darkness*': *Text, Sources, Criticism*, rev. ed. (New York: Norton, 1971); Bruch Harkness (ed.), *Conrad's 'Heart of Darkness' and the Critics* (Belmont, California: Wadsworth, 1960).

10. Quoted in Baines, p. 223.

11. Ernest Cassirer, *The Logic of the Humanities*, trans. Clarence Smith Howe (New Haven: Yale University Press, 1961), provides a helpful gloss: 'The possibility and necessity of . . . a "breaking free" of the limitations of individuality emerges

nowhere so clearly and indubitably as in the phenomenon of speech. The spoken *word* never originates in the mere sound or utterance. For a word is an intended meaning. It is construed within the organic whole of a "communication", and communication "exists" only when the word passes from one person to another . . .' (p. 58).

12. Guerard, pp. 35–6.
13. Commenting upon the disjunction between the objective and the subjective within the late Victorian and Edwardian periods, John A. Lester Jnr. has written:

> Materialistic monism rendered all phenomena *objective*; indeed, it eliminated the *subjective* altogether. In the later years of the period, when renewed emphasis was being put on man's inner life, the groping, rootless world of the subjective still seemed to have lost its relationship with the objective. In both phases the spiritual world was cast away from the material, the world of appearance from the world of 'reality' . . . (p. 135).

14. See Harkness, p. 173.
15. Walter Wright, 'Ingress to the Heart of Darkness', from his *Romance and Tragedy in Joseph Conrad* (Lincoln: University of Nebraska Press, 1948), reprinted in Harkness, p. 154.
16. Lester, p. 60.

# 5 The journey to Patusan: The education of Jim and Marlow in *Lord Jim*

Inevitably, the attempt to isolate a significant incident, dialogue, or minor character in the most complex and subtle novels leads to oversimplification and distortion. Rather than review the considerable literature that reduces the extraordinary structure of *Lord Jim* to the significance of a few of its parts, let me begin this chapter by clarifying one of my critical premises. The meaning of a work of fiction inheres in our perception of the gradually developing and continuously changing pattern as it emerges through the process of reading, as well as in our apprehension of the completed pattern that clarifies the preceding flux. The criticism of fiction has tended to be more comfortable with addressing the completed 'event', as if a novel could be perceived in its totality like a painting or sculpture. But fiction is the most linear of art forms and exists for the reader primarily within the duration required to complete the act of reading; the memory of the infinitely detailed fictive world fades as the reader's consciousness is invaded by other experiences. It is not enough to discuss a novel in its moment of stability after its ending has apocalyptically clarified every preceding detail with proleptic (and prophetic) meaning. If we are to do justice to the complexity of a novel, we must 'report' on the crucial process between reader and novel during which tentative patterns of meaning are proposed, tested, transformed, and/or discarded.

At first, *Lord Jim* explores the response to the objective world by two seemingly diametrically opposed men: Jim, the captive of his own imagination, and Marlow, the rational empiricist who speaks for the very values that Jim has implicitly, by the nature of his deeds, renounced when he jumped from the *Patna*. Then the novel dramatises the gradual movement of Jim towards Marlow's original position and the counter-movement of Marlow towards Jim's. Finally, Marlow's epistemological quest culminates with the blurring of the distinction between objective and subjective experience and with the disconfirmation of his belief that only a 'few simple notions' are required to meet the world outside oneself. On Patusan, Jim shapes his dreams and fantasies according to the values that Marlow originally represented: those 'home values' that were for Marlow and are for the recipient of Marlow's privileged information, 'the ethical code which enables men to live together through trust of each other, and which, in so binding them, gives them self-respect'.[1] Patusan fulfils the vision of Jim's fantasies by seemingly providing a realm that is outside of time and space and immune to the mutability and relativism that haunted Jim's life in the 'home' world. But the impossibility of permanently vacating one's past, of escaping the pattern of one's life, is demonstrated by Gentleman Brown's emergence. As when Jim's ship collided with the submerged derelict, his intrinsic character is brought out by external circumstances over which he had no control. Even the oracular Stein cannot impose form and order on his own life, as his resignation to mutability in the final paragraph and his inability to maintain certitude while speaking to Marlow make clear.

## II

If there is a crystallising image in *Lord Jim*, it is the omniscient narrator's image for Jim's imprisonment by the *facts* of the *Patna* case. Because of his belief that 'visible' and 'tangible' facts cannot convey the 'directing spirit of perdition' that gives life to the facts, Jim despises the facts that the court demands:

> He wanted to go on talking for truth's sake, perhaps for his own sake also; and while his utterance was deliberate, his mind positively flew round and round the serried circle of facts that had surged up all about him to cut him off from the rest of his kind; it was like a creature that, finding itself imprisoned within an enclosure of high stakes, dashes round and round, distracted in the night, trying to find a weak spot, a crevice, a place to scale, some opening through which it may squeeze itself and escape. This awful activity of mind made him hesitate at times in his speech . . . . (p. 31)

The man for whom the actual phenomenon of a gale is a 'pretense' becomes a captive of facts. Even before the *Patna*, Jim lived apart in a world of his imagination. When his fantasies conflict with the demands of the objective world, he responds to his own dreams. Faced with a chance to perform a rescue while he is on the training ship, his visions of heroism distract him. His fantasy that he is the storm's special target causes a crucial moment of paralysis: 'There was a fierce purpose in the gale, a furious earnestness in the screech of the wind, in the brutal tumult of earth and sky, that seemed directed at him, and made him hold his breath in awe. He stood still. It seemed to him he was whirled around' (p. 7). Because he imagines what will happen to the natives on the *Patna*, he rationalises that there is no point in warning them. The intensity of his imagination gives the possible death of the passengers the validity of a completed event: 'He stood still looking at these recumbent bodies, a doomed man aware of his fate, surveying the silent company of the dead. They *were* dead! Nothing could save them!' (p. 86, emphasis Conrad's). Even amidst his first excruciating interview with Marlow, Jim can forget the actuality of his situation and lose himself completely in visions of heroic accomplishment that are momentarily oblivious to the imprisonment of facts:

> I could see in his glance darted into the night all his inner
> being carried on, projected headlong into the fanciful realm of
> recklessly heroic aspirations. He had no leisure to regret what
> he had lost, he was so wholly and naturally concerned for what
> he had failed to obtain. . . . With every instant he was
> penetrating deeper into the impossible world of romantic
> achievements. He got to the heart of it at last! (p. 83)

That Jim, after the *Patna*, can no longer elude the world of facts for more than an instant is indicated by his memorable response to the gratuitous use of the word 'cur'. The facts of his desertion become a perpetually living past, even contributing to his slightly idiosyncratic appearance and peculiar manner:

> He was an inch, perhaps two, under six feet, powerfully built,
> and he advanced straight at you with a slight stoop of the
> shoulders, head forward, and a fixed from-under stare which
> made you think of a charging bull. His voice was deep, loud,
> and his manner displayed a kind of dogged self-assertion which

had nothing aggressive in it. It seemed a necessity, and it was
directed apparently as much at himself as at anybody else.
(p. 3)

The facts become haunting personal furies not only shaping Marlow's
response to him, but his response to himself. Jim's memory of failure
and the psychic needs created by that failure shape his perceptions to
every situation, from the various positions he briefly holds between
the *Patna* and Patusan to the encounter with Gentleman Brown. As
much as the injury to his leg, these facts are responsible for the
'invisible halt of [Jim's] gait.' Seemingly dormant, they contain the
potential—like the submerged wreck—to manifest themselves when
least expected.

Conrad perceived Jim as having an artist's imagination. Like Jukes
and Decoud, Jim's cowardice exemplifies the incompatibility of the
imaginative life with the life of action and responsibility. Often
Conrad has Marlow speak of Jim in language that suggests Jim's
identity as an artist: 'You must remember he was a finished artist in
that peculiar way, he was a gifted poor devil with the faculty of swift
and forestalling vision' (p. 96). Later Marlow, obviously drawing
upon his own experience as listener, notes the efficacy of Jim's
rhetoric: 'It's extraordinary how he could cast upon you the spirit of
his illusion' (p. 109). Patusan fulfils the needs of a man for whom
'dreams and the success of his imaginary achievements' were 'the best
parts of life, its secret truth, its hidden reality. They had a gorgeous
virility, the charm of vagueness, they passed before him with an
heroic tread; they carried his soul away with them and made it drunk
with the divine philtre of an unbounded confidence in itself' (p. 20).
When Marlow departs, he recalls how Patusan

> dropped out of my sight bodily with its colour, its design
> and its meaning, like a picture created by fancy on a canvas,
> upon which, after long contemplation, you turn your back for
> the last time. It remains in the memory motionless, unfaded,
> with its life arrested, in an unchanging light. There are the
> ambitions, the fears, the hate, the hopes, and they remain in
> my mind just as I had seen them—intense and as if for ever
> suspended in their expression. (p. 330)

Conrad was sympathetic to the dilemma of the imaginative man who,
he believed, was always vulnerable to the seduction of his own

fantasies and to the 'creative terrors of his imagination'. Just as 'in his own image' the novelist seeks to 'create for himself a world, great or little, in which he honestly can believe', Jim's imagination and energy shape the raw material of Patusan into a fulfilment of his dreams of conquest, fame, love, and sexual fulfilment (*NLL*, p. 6). Jim's imagination enables him to penetrate the invisible wall of facts and to construct a realm that fulfils his psychic needs. In Patusan Conrad combines Jim's earlier dreams of heroism with his later dreams of a second chance. Jim's vision is a vatic one, a kind of utopian version of Kurtz's megalomania, with himself imagined as the combined shaman and political leader of a primitive tribal structure.

For a time Patusan combines the fantasy of heroic dominance accompanied by adulation with the fulfilment of the wish to escape the acculturation that civilisation requires. Almost magically, Jim's presence soon transforms Patusan into a world that fulfils his fantasies of accomplishment and dominance. Patusan is a not-home world in which all of us participate. It represents a kind of permanent vacation that relieves us from the 'home' world that defines and limits us. Because it re-enacts the triumph of primitive man over his antagonists and nature, Patusan is the kind of fiction that enriches both our childhood play and adult fantasising. (The appeal of this fiction is inherent in the stereotyped Hollywood westerns and in the Tarzan stories.) Patusan lacks the objective standards and orderly political structures of the civilisation that Jim leaves behind, but it offers him a beautiful and sensitive mate, the adoration of the people whom he rules and, most importantly to him, the raw material to impose moral standards that fulfil his own psychic needs. Like Kubla Khan and Prospero, Jim all but rules the elements: 'He had regulated so many things in Patusan! Things that would have appeared as much beyond his control as the motions of the moon and stars' (p. 221). Although to Marlow, Patusan seems to be a static and aesthetic realm from which he is excluded, Jim discovers that he cannot permanently wish himself outside the processes of life, because, unlike Yeats's old man in 'Sailing to Byzantium' he must take his 'bodily form' from 'natural things'. The other people of Patusan may exist for Marlow as part of an aesthetic structure 'as if under an enchanter's wand. But the figure round which all these are grouped—that one lives, and I am not certain of him. No magician's wand can immobilise him under my eyes. He is one of us' (pp. 330–1).

It does appear that the physical leap through Tunku Allang's imprisoning fortress is a leap through the imprisoning wall of facts and an undoing of the first jump. Jim first perceives 'a horrible cold, shiny heap of slime. . . . It seemed to him that he was burying himself alive, and then he struck out madly, scattering the mud with his fists' (p. 254). But the man whose underdeveloped superego exposes him as a moral anachronism according to Marlow's standards recreates the major phases of human history. Overcoming the oozing mud of primordial life, he organises Patusan's atavistic social and political structures, and finally becomes a messianic figure.

When Marlow visits Patusan and finds that Jim's fantasy of heroism has become the central fact of existence in Patusan, he is clearly overwhelmed: 'Immense! No doubt it was immense; the seal of success upon his words, the conquered ground for the soles of his feet, the blind trust of men, the belief in himself snatched from the fire, the solitude of his achievement' (p. 272). The ontological basis for Patusan's political and moral system seems to be Jim's psychic need for a redemptive second chance and his memory of his experience in the world that he has left behind. But Jim's triumph proves evanescent; to impose a static pattern on life is impossible because the disparate instances of the present are always merging into a developing future pattern which soon becomes the irrevocable past. Jim shares with Dorian Gray and Jude Fawley, those other great fictive characters of the 1890s, the dream of hermetically sealing himself in an immutable state unaffected by the vicissitudes of an unknown future. In the late nineteenth century it seemed to many intellectuals that each man is enclosed in his private world, a world separate and distinct from that of other men.[2] The notion that each man creates his own reality is implicit in F. H. Bradley's remark: 'My external sensations are no less private to myself than are my thoughts or my feelings. In either case my experience falls within my own circle, a circle closed on the outside. . . . In brief . . . the whole world for each is peculiar and private to that soul.'[3]

Speaking of Bulstrode, another character who cannot escape his consciousness of the past, George Eliot writes: 'A man's past is not simply a dead history, an outworn preparation of the present; it is not a repented error shaken loose from life: It is a still quivering part of himself.'[4] Marlow perceives that part of the reason Jim is a captive even in Patusan is that he does not believe in the redemptive power of the 'Jim-myth': 'The land, the people, the forests were [Jewel's] accomplices guarding him with vigilant accord, with an air of seclusion, of mystery, of invincible possession. There was no appeal, as it were; he was imprisoned within the very freedom of his power . . .' (p. 283). While the natives accept Jim's every word as truth ('their creed, his truth' [p. 393]), Jim cannot believe that Patusan is as real as the world he left behind: ' "Upon my soul and conscience . . . if such a thing can be forgotten, then I think I have a right to dismiss it from my mind. . . . If you ask them who is brave—who is true—who is just—who is it they would trust with their lives?—they would say, Tuan Jim. And yet they can never know the *real, real truth*. . . ." ' (p. 305, emphasis mine). More than anyone else, Jim feels that his accomplishments are apocryphal, that beneath the surface can be found 'the secret truth of his pretences'. Even in triumph, the successes of his achievements do not provide the solace that his dreams of accomplishment had once provided. Because Patusan is not the same level of reality for Jim, and because Jim is inextricably bound to Marlow's moral code and unlike the captain of the *Patna* cannot disappear, Jim is one of us. He judges his accomplishments not ontologically but referentially, using as touchstone the very standards by which he has once failed: the notion of the benevolent white man taking upon himself the responsibility of a 'social fabric of orderly, peaceful life where every man was sure of tomorrow'; inculcating a 'belief in the stability of earthly institutions'; and convincing the natives that he, the white lord, 'had no thought but for the people's good' (pp. 387, 389).

Paradoxically, it is Jim's imaginative response to Gentleman Brown that intrudes flux into Jim's aesthetic realm. Marlow alludes to this when he writes to his former listener: 'There is to my mind a sort of profound logic in [Jim's story], as if it were our imagination alone that could set loose upon us the might of an overwhelming destiny. The imprudence of our thoughts recoils upon our heads; who toys with the sword shall perish by the sword' (p. 342). Like the submerged wreck, Gentleman Brown seems to connive with Jim's latent psychic needs to discover the latter's nature and destiny. He presents the lower, darker side that Jim has purged from the world that fulfils his fantasies. Once Jim recognises a mirror image in Gentleman Brown, the social fabric that he has woven on Patusan collapses. The world he has internalised within his imagination disappears, to be replaced by cosmic emptiness, and its creator willingly embraces what he perceives as his final collision with his destiny. For Marlow, Jim's death completes the 'Jim-myth' with apocalyptic finality: 'He goes away from a living woman to celebrate his pitiless wedding with a shadowy ideal of conduct' (p. 416).

Discussing *Crime and Punishment*, R. P. Blackmur remarked that coincidental and fatal encounters are 'the artist's way of representing those forces in us not ourselves.' Such encounters 'create our sense of that other self within us that we can neither quite escape nor quite meet up with'.[5] But that other self is really another version of ourselves brought out by a confluence of personality at a specific spatial-temporal locus. Gentleman Brown insinuates himself into Jim's conscience and undercuts his credo in a way that deliberately echoes how Jim affects Marlow and, even more radically, Brierly. In their brief exchange, Gentleman Brown parodies the desperate insinuations and defensive innuendoes with which Jim had engaged Marlow's sensibilities:

> 'I made him wince,' boasted Brown to me. 'He very soon left off coming the righteous over me. He just stood there with nothing to say, and looking as black as thunder—not at me—on the ground.' He asked Jim whether he had nothing fishy in his life to remember that he was so damnedly hard upon a man trying to get out of a deadly hole by the first means that came to hand—and so on, and so on. And there ran through the rough talk a vein of subtle reference to their common blood, an assumption of common experience; a sickening suggestion of common guilt, of secret knowledge that was like a bond of their minds and of their hearts. (p. 387)

Jim's response to Gentleman Brown is similar to Brierly's response to him; it is a completely empathetic response that derives from the catalytic effects that words can have on latent impulses and motivations. Gentleman Brown, although a separate person, penetrates the protective shield that Patusan has erected around Jim, the psychological shield that enables Jim to become finally '*in his own eyes* the equal of the impeccable men who never fall out of the ranks' (p. 393, emphases mine).


III


Jim can transform Patusan, but finally cannot arrest the individual instances of his life and weave them into a permanent pattern. Nor can Marlow, himself *developing* through the novel's time and space, arrest Jim or his relationship with Jim within a coherent pattern. Jim survives Marlow's original monologue and experiences a future which qualifies and redefines Marlow's verdict. Seeing Jim as symbolic and static and imagining Patusan as an aesthetic realm separate and distinct from 'the world where events move, men change, light flickers, [and] life flows in a clear stream' are convenient fictions for Marlow who desperately wants to distance Jim before going home. Hence, although Marlow originally establishes Jim's 'symbolic identity' and perceives him 'like a figure set up on a pedestal, to represent in his persistent youth the power, and perhaps the virtues, of races that never grow old, that have emerged from the gloom', Jim's encounter with Gentleman Brown, with that darker side of his destiny, insists upon re-evaluation from us and from Marlow (p. 265). For Marlow, Patusan is claustrophobic and static because it lacks the presence of standards that support and define him. Leaving is a welcome relief from a world where he felt inexplicably morally adrift, where—for reasons which he cannot articulate—the restraints on which he depends seem to dissolve. Marlow needs to feel spatial distance between himself and Jim: 'The shadow of the impending separation had already put an immense space between us, and when we spoke it was with an effort, as if to force our low voices across a vast and increasing distance' (p. 331). He needs a sense of open space which he can occupy and define as his own, separate and distinct from the one inhabited by Jim, whose past never completely disappears from Marlow's unconscious response to him:

> I breathed deeply, I revelled in the vastness of the opened
> horizon, in the different atmosphere that seemed to vibrate
> with a toil of life, with the energy of an impeccable world.
> This sky and this sea were open to me. . . . I let my eyes
> roam through space, like a man released from bonds who
> stretches his cramped limbs, runs, leaps, responds to the
> inspiring elation of freedom. (pp. 331–2)

We must distinguish between Marlow's past attitudes and present attitudes to understand the results of his epistemological journey. It must be remembered that Marlow's telling takes place on two separate occasions: The first is his monologue to a group of listeners at the height of Jim's triumph, and the second is the epistolary section that takes place after Jim's death. At the time of his encounter with Jim, Marlow's standards approximate those of the man he later chooses to receive the packet. Marlow too believed in the 'order, the morality, of an ethical progress', and had felt 'its justice and necessity' as a shaping force of his life. Reflecting upon his original interest, Marlow reveals both his beleif in the necessity of a 'standard of conduct' and the doubt that Jim insinuated into his moral sensibility:

> Why I longed to go grubbing into the deplorable details of an occurrence which, after all, concerned me no more than as a member of an obscure body of men held together by a community of inglorious toil and by fidelity to a certain standard of conduct, I can't explain. You may call it an unhealthy curiosity if you like; but I have a distinct notion I wished to find something. Perhaps, unconsciously, I hoped I would find that something, some profound and redeeming cause, some merciful explanation, some convincing shadow of an excuse. I see well enough now that I hoped for the impossible—for the laying of what is the most obstinate ghost of man's creation, of the uneasy doubt uprising like a mist, secret and gnawing like a worm, and more chilling than the certitude of death—the doubt of the sovereign power enthroned in a fixed standard of conduct. . . . Was it for my own sake that I wished to find some shadow of an excuse for that young fellow, whom I had never seen before, but whose appearance alone added a touch of personal concern to the thoughts suggested by the knowledge of his weakness—made it a thing of mystery and terror—like a hint of a destructive fate ready for us all whose youth—in its day—had resembled his youth? (pp. 50-1)

Only at the end of this long meditative passage do we learn the real reason for his interest is that he sees Jim as a younger version of himself. Jim not only makes Marlow doubt whether his own life has been the result of ability or of merely fortuitous circumstances, but raises the larger problem of whether any human being, given certain circumstances, is immune to deviation from the values he espouses.

What troubled Marlow was his inability to separate himself from 'a man who has been found out, not in a crime but in a more than criminal weakness' (p. 42). Marlow's initial response to Jim reveals his original epistemology which was rational, logical, and derived from a belief in the value of 'a few simple notions' to regulate man's conduct;

> I liked his appearance; I knew his appearance; he came from the right place; he was one of us. He stood there for all the

parentage of his kind, for men and women by no means clever
or amusing, but whose very existence is based upon honest
faith, and upon the instinct of courage. I don't mean military
courage, or civil courage, or any special kind of courage. I
mean just that inborn ability to look temptations straight in the
face—a readiness unintellectual enough, goodness knows, but
without pose—a power of resistance, don't you see, ungracious
if you like, but priceless—an unthinking and blessed stiffness
before the outward and inward terrors, before the might of
nature, and the seductive corruption of men—backed by a faith
invulnerable to the strength of facts, to the contagion of
example, to the solicitation of ideas. Hang ideas! They are
tramps, vagabonds, knocking at the back door of your mind,
each taking a little of your substance, each carrying away some
crumb of that belief in a few simple notions you must cling to
if you want to live decently and would like to die easy! (p. 43)

(By the time of the narration, Marlow nostalgically longs for such
simple notions). The first sentence implies the essence of Marlow's
epistemology and cosmology at the time he met Jim. The movement
from one assertion to another, the faith in the logic of that procedure,
the precision and control of the closed predicates speak eloquently for
Marlow's mid-Victorian faith in a fixed standard of conduct and for
his belief in his own power of resistance.

A confession is a shared experience between the man who confesses
and the man who listens. By his willingness to listen, the man who
hears the confession enters into a special relationship with the man
who chooses to speak. (The complexities and ambiguities of this
relationship are involved in Haldin's mistaking Razumov's
willingness to listen for sympathy in *Under Western Eyes*.) It is not
unusual for Marlow to be the 'receptacle of confession' for men 'with
soft spots, with hard spots, with hidden plague spots' (p. 34). That
Marlow's original empathetic response is to an ostracised coward,
who is a total stranger to him, tells us something about Marlow. The
role of confessor and surrogate father answers Marlow's psychic
needs. He seems to derive positional assurance from demonstrating
his moral posture, as if he needs to convince himself that there is not a
drop of 'alloy' in his own moral make-up. Brierly's response to Jim is
a parody of Marlow's. Brierly identifies so completely with Jim that
he sees Jim's destructive soft spot as his own. As Marlow listens to
Jim's tale and later as his relationship to Jim develops, he himself

becomes prone to this radical empathy where one sees another man as the objectification of part of oneself.[6]

The effect of his first interview with Jim is to involve inextricably Marlow's ego: 'If he had not enlisted my sympathies he had done better for himself—he had gone to the very fount and origin of that sentiment, he had reached the secret sensibility of my egoism' (p. 152). Jim imposes himself upon Marlow by making Marlow feel that he is needed as a sympathetic listener. Relatively early in the Malabar interview, Marlow notes: 'He was not speaking to me, he was only speaking before me, in a dispute with an invisible personality, an antagonistic and inseparable partner of his existence—another possessor of his soul. These were issues beyond the competency of a court of inquiry: it was a subtle and momentous quarrel as to the true essence of life, and did not want a judge. He wanted an ally, a helper, an accomplice' (p. 93). Jim's persistent inquiries about how Marlow would have behaved evoke the shadow of self-doubt in Marlow. His response to Jim reflects an element of the sham sentimentalism that is responsible for the crew's behaviour in *The Nigger of the 'Narcissus'*: just as the crew of the *Narcissus* 'totemized' Wait as a reflection of its own sense of inadequacy, Marlow imputes value to the man he has charged himself with saving and to whom he has made an emotional commitment. The ritual of preserving a person to whom one has attributed value derives from moral and psychic needs. Retrospectively, Marlow understands some of these complex reasons:

I was made to look at the convention that lurks in all truth and on the essential sincerity of falsehood. He appealed to all sides at once—to the side turned perpetually to the light of day, and *to that side of us which, like the other hemisphere of the moon, exists* stealthily in perpetual darkness, with only a fearful ashy light falling at times on the edge. He swayed me. I own to it, I own up. The occasion was obscure, insignificant—what you will: a lost youngster, one in a million—but then he was one of us; an incident as completely devoid of importance as the flooding of an ant-heap, and yet the mystery of his attitude got hold of me as though he had been an individual in the forefront of his kind, as if the obscure truth involved were momentous enough to affect mankind's conception of itself . . . (p. 93, emphasis mine)

Marlow now understands that if Jim is one of us, it works both ways and we are all part Jim, just as Jim is part Cornelius and part Stein. Marlow recognises the complexity of human motives; seeing the existence of that side of us that exists in perpetual darkness makes him respond empathetically to Jim's needs. At the time of his monologue Marlow no longer believes in his own vulnerability, and the terms in which he presents his understanding of the fallibility of all men suggest that Jim has played an important role in his change of heart: 'Which of us here has not observed this, or maybe experienced something of that feeling in his own person—this extreme weariness of emotions, the vanity of effort, the yearning for rest? Those striving with unreasonable forces know it well—the shipwrecked castaways in boats, wanderers lost in a desert, men battling against the unthinking might of nature, or the stupid brutality of crowds' (p. 88). Explaining, even partially justifying, Jim's immobility in the face of danger, Marlow affirms his belief that we are all prone to the passivity and ennui that paralysed Jim.

Marlow's snide comments and seemingly unprovoked nastiness during his first interview with Jim at the Malabar result from his instinctive discomfort with the moral ambiguity of Jim's situation and his realisation that his developing empathy with Jim presents an insidious threat to his standards. Abusing Jim seems to convince Marlow that a moral distance divides them. Responding to Jim's ecstatic vision of heroism that follows his exclamation, 'Ah! What a chance missed!', Marlow recalls that he 'whisked him back by saying, "If you had stuck to the ship, you mean!"', and he recalls adding, 'with every unkind intention', 'It is unfortunate you didn't know beforehand!' (pp. 83–84).

Three separate situations teach Marlow something about his own vulnerability and fallibility, and make him realise the precarious nature of his belief that a vast moral gulf divides him from Jim. The first occurs when he proffers Brierly's plan of evasion not only to avoid disgrace to the reputation of the merchant marine for professional decency but to spare himself the pain and anxiety of a challenge to his own self-confidence. Like Brierly, he sees the trial as a trial of his own standards and his belief in those standards, and tacitly accepts the premise that a trial of 'one of us' becomes a trial for all of us. Previously, Marlow had found that the most admirable aspect of Jim was his willingness to face the judgement of his peers. Retrospectively, Marlow understands the immorality of proposing Brierly's plan:

> In this transaction, to speak grossly and precisely, I was the
> irreproachable man; but the subtle intentions of my immorality
> were defeated by the moral simplicity of the criminal. No
> doubt he was selfish too, but his selfishness had a higher
> origin, a more lofty aim. I discovered that, say what I
> would, he was eager to go through the ceremony of ex-
> ecution; . . . he believed where I had already ceased to
> doubt. (p. 153)

At this point, Jim was willing to act in accordance with the rules and
conventions of civilised life, while Marlow was departing from his
fixed standard of conduct. Marlow admits that he had 'lost all
confidence in myself; and it was as if he, too, had given me up . . .'
(p. 154).

The second instance of fallibility is his motivation for sending Jim
to Patusan. But this time Marlow feels inextricably involved: 'It
seemed to me that the less I understood the more I was bound to him
in the name of *that doubt* which is the inseparable part of our
knowledge. I did not know so much more about myself' (p. 221,
emphasis mine). Doubt for Marlow is emptiness, an intellectual and
moral void that must be filled with meaning. To 'dispose' of Jim is to
find a convenient definition. Sending Jim permanently away gives the
necessary spatial dimension to Marlow's need to believe that an
unbridgeable distance divides Jim from Marlow. While Marlow
believes his main purpose is to give Jim a second chance, he
retrospectively understands that self-interest probably played a
significant role: 'I was about to go home for a time; and it may be I
desired, more than I was aware of myself, to dispose of him—to
dispose of him, you understand—before I left' (p. 221). Marlow
derives his standards from the implicit and explicit ethical code of the
merchant marine and British imperialism. For Marlow, the only
possibility to assuage the agonising doubt that Jim continually
impresses upon his mind is his return to home where one meets 'the
spirit that dwells within the land, under its sky, in its air, in its valleys,
and on its rises, in its fields, in its waters and its trees—a mute friend,
judge, and inspirer. Say what you like, to get its joy, to breathe its
peace, to face its truth, one must return with a clear consciousness'
(p. 222). The spirit of the land is one important source of Marlow's
essential values. He speaks in religious diction of those who
understand best the spirit's 'severity, its saving power, the grace of its
secular right to our fidelity, to our obedience' (p. 222). Marlow's

apotheosising of the spirit of the land is a means of trying to control
his emerging anxiety and dubiety.

Thus Marlow responds to the 'home' ethos when he goes to Stein
with Jim's dilemma. Even while mocking the notion that the spirit of
the land will inquire about 'my very young brother', Marlow shows
his consciousness of the conventional Victorian Christian ideal that
each man is his brother's keeper. However ironic they are, Marlow's
allusions to Jim as his brother do reveal how his sense of responsibility
to Jim has developed. Inherent in the Jim—Marlow relationship is a
version of the Cain—Abel myth. Saving Jim is a gratuitous act that
makes Marlow his brother's keeper, but his motives for disposing of
Jim contain a strongly selfish element. He instinctively fears that Jim
as a kind of lower self will confront him in the form of a drunken
loafer and that his failure to protect Jim from himself will result in a
discomforting face-to-face encounter. The same ambivalence of
motive defines Jim as both Cain and Abel when he responds to
Gentleman Brown. Because the charity to Gentleman Brown as Abel
becomes betrayal of his mistress, his best friend, and his people, he
takes on a Cain identity. As in 'The Secret Sharer', charity and self-
preservation are often incongruous ethical positions, but each man's
actions may be motivated by a subtle combination of these. In Stein's
words, '[Man] wants to be a saint, and he wants to be a devil—and
every time he shuts his eyes he sees himself as a very fine fellow—so
fine as he can never be. . . . In a dream. . . . ' (p. 213). Man shuts his
eyes to his darker possibilities and lives in a fictive world that only
accounts for his impulses towards selflessness; but his baser, more
selfish impulses remain to be aroused.

Marlow's most crucial demonstration of his own fallibility takes
place during his interview with Jewel. Marlow's indiscreet loss of
control is in sharp contrast to the controlled, but discomforting, lie to
the Intended in 'Heart of Darkness'. When recalling this incident,
Marlow is less than rigorous in evaluating his conduct. Self-justifyingly
he inquires of his audience about how one deals with a
spectre of fear, even while recalling how he insisted to Jewel that Jim
would not leave. As he spoke for 'my brother', he gradually lost
control, and he became animated by an 'inexplicable ardour' to
convince her, until his 'dogged fierceness' gave way to 'rage' and
'brutality'. As Jim's superego is inadequate to the complete solitude of
the *Patna*, since he feels separated from the white men and the natives
at the crucial moment, Marlow, too, responds to a desperate need to
fill silence with sound, emptiness with meaning. Before he lost his

self-control and brutally shouted, the dialogue had stopped and he
had noticed the silence of Patusan: 'The silence over Patusan was
profound, and the feeble dry sound of a paddle striking the side of a
canoe somewhere in the middle of the river seemed to make it
infinite' (p. 318). His loss of control is a direct response to this
silence and recalls Decoud's suicidal response to silence in *Nostromo*: 'I
felt that sort of *rage* one feels during a hard tussle . . . you want to
know [why the world did not want him]? I asked in a fury. "Yes" she
cried. "Because he is not good enough," I said *brutally*' (p. 318,
emphases mine). The absence of moral restraints and the stress of
silence provoke Marlow to needless cruelty. In retrospect, Marlow's
whole conduct is hardly explicable to him: 'I remember with wonder
the sort of dogged fierceness I displayed. I had the illusion of having
got the spectre by the throat at last. Indeed the whole real thing has
left behind the detailed and amazing impression of a dream' (p. 318).
Yet his explanation shows how imaginative Marlow has become and
how circumstances have forced him to depart from his fixed
standards. He now understands that one's life includes spectres of fear,
spirits of the land, and other fictions which shape our conduct. To
realise this is to acknowledge tacitly that Jim's behaviour on the *Patna*
is *not* the simple breach of faith with mankind that Marlow once saw
so clearly it was, but the complex response of a man who instinctively
and irrationally answered the all too human, but uncontrollable,
demands of his psyche: 'If the spirits evoked by our fears and our
unrest have ever to vouch for each other's constancy before the
forlorn magicians that we are, then I—I alone of us dwellers in the
flesh—have shuddered in the hopeless chill of such a task' (p. 315).


IV


If a man's destiny is conceived as a slow accretion of defining
situations and encounters which gradually emerge from the future
into the present, then Marlow's destiny, the pattern of his experience,
is triggered by his continuing and developing imaginative response
to Jim. The cry to 'jump', the disappearance of the ship's light, the
certainty of disaster, all give credence to Dorothy Van Ghent's view
that Jim's acts externalise the destiny that he carries within him, a
destiny which becomes externalised by events beyond his control.[7]
The collision of the *Patna* with a sunken wreck is a radical version of

the limiting and defining nature of interpenetration with the objective, not-I world. Just as the *Patna* elicited the hidden part of Jim's character, Jim represents for Marlow a collision between his own soul and the circumstances beyond his control that inevitably have a stake in shaping his destiny. Once Marlow had accidentally encountered Jim by a ludicrous misunderstanding, Jim becomes part of the pattern of imprisoning facts for Marlow and vice versa. With unconscious deftness and subtlety, Jim plays upon Marlow's sensibilities and psychic and moral needs as surely as the *Patna* connived with his own personality to shape his destiny.

Language for Marlow is a means of ordering his perceptions and creating the illusion of understanding. But during his interview with Jewel, Marlow loses his psychic bearings:

> 'The tears fell from her eyes—and then she died,' concluded the girl in an imperturbable monotone, which more than anything else, . . . more than mere words could do, troubled my mind profoundly with the passive, irremediable horror of the scene. It had the power to drive me out of my conception of existence, out of that shelter each of us makes for himself to creep under in moments of danger as a tortoise withdraws within its shell. For a moment I had a view of a world that seemed to wear a vast and dismal aspect of disorder, while, in truth, thanks to our unwearied efforts, it is as sunny an arrangement of small conveniences as the mind of man can conceive. But still—it was only a moment: I went back into my shell directly. One *must*—don't you know?—though I seemed to have lost all my words in the chaos of dark thoughts I had contemplated for a second or two beyond the pale. These came back, too, very soon, for *words also belong to the sheltering conception of light and order* which is our refuge. (p. 313, emphasis mine, except for 'must')

Language is part of the shelter because by imposing a pattern on consciousness, it provides the illusion of order and control that man desperately needs, Marlow retrospectively realises that we are all imprisoned by our conception of light and order, our subjective ordering of a chaotic world that we organise to fit our needs. But this vision informs his doubts about the ultimate efficacy of communicating to his audience. He is frustrated with words that seem no more than an artificial ordering which makes of life 'an arrangement of small conveniences', a refuge in which man shuts his eyes to that dark side he wishes neither to understand nor to acknowledge.

Marlow understands that language weaves patterns that seem to control the chaotic flux of experience, if only by bringing to consciousness and imposing form on the contents of the mind, and that, in a sense, each of us uses language to weave his own comfortable shelters. Marlow realizes that because his listeners are as safely entrenched within the refuge of their own illusions as he had been before encountering Jim, they cannot fully understand him: 'My last words about Jim shall be few. I affirm he had achieved greatness; but the thing would be dwarfed in the telling, or rather in the hearing. Frankly, it is not my words that I mistrust but your minds. I could be eloquent were I not afraid you fellows had starved your imaginations to feed your bodies' (p. 225). But for Jim, words can never be a means of ordering his interior world because he cannot separate them from the not-I world where they are potential weapons capable of destroying the fictions of his imagination. Indeed, the comfort and security that others find in language are forever lost to Jim; once he responds to the cry 'jump', he leaps into an abyss where the belief in the innocence of language as an ordering principle in a fundamentally hostile world is no longer possible. He cannot form a message for Marlow to deliver when the latter returns from Patusan; nor can he communicate the significance of—or even a simple narrative about—Gentleman Brown's treachery.

Marlow learns that his nastiness to Jim, his motives for sending Jim away, and his loss of control with Jewel demonstrate the kinship of all mankind. Marlow's grimly ironic retrospective remark about the 'wisdom of life' tacitly recognises that every man is capable of what one man does: 'To bury him would have been such an easy kindness! It would have been so much in accordance with the wisdom of life, which consists in putting out of sight all the reminders of our folly, or our weakness, or our mortality; all that makes against our efficiency—the memory of our failures, the hints of our undying fears, the bodies of our dead friends' (p. 174). Near the end of his epistle, Marlow acknowledges some kinship with Gentleman Brown who, he realises, illustrates 'some obscure and awful attribute of *our* nature which, I am afraid, is not so very far under the surface as we like to think' (p. 404, emphasis mine). Marlow understands that man is composed of noble desires that he willingly acknowledges and those other needs—dark, unacknowledged, embarrassing and misunderstood—that he is unable to recognise as his own. Marlow is now concerned with responding to Jim's psychic needs and understanding his consciousness, rather than with measuring Jim by fixed standards shared by a community: 'He had seen a broad gulf that neither eye nor voice could span. I can understand this. He was overwhelmed by the inexplicable; he was overwhelmed by his own personality—the gift of destiny which he had done his best to master' (p. 341). Marlow, like his creator, suggests the possibility of creating a community of understanding which he believes is the only possible replacement for a community based on moral standards.

NOTES

1. Dorothy Van Ghent, 'On *Lord Jim*', in her *The English Novel: Form and Function* (New York: Harper Torchbooks, 1961 [orig. ed. 1953]), p. 238.
2. See John A. Lester, jun, 'The Challenge', in his *Journey Through Despair 1880–1914: Transformations in British Literary Culture* (Princeton: Princeton University Press, 1968), chap. 2, pp. 19–52.
3. F. H. Bradley, *Appearance and Reality: a Metaphysical Essay*, 2nd ed. (London, 1908), p. 346. Cited in Lester, p. 34.
4. George Eliot, *Middlemarch: A Study of Provincial Life*, ed. Quentin Anderson (New York: Collier Books, 1962), p. 569.
5. R. P. Blackmur, *Eleven Essays in the European Novel* (New York: A Harbinger Book, 1954), p. 126.
6. Perhaps the most striking example of this phenomenon is when the captain in 'The Secret Sharer' imagines the sun beating down on *his own head* rather than Leggatt's as he envisions the latter wandering through Cochin-China.
7. See Van Ghent, pp. 234–5.

# 6 Conrad's shorter fiction: 1901 — 1902

I

In the 1901—2 period Conrad wrote five stories, including two of his great tales, 'Typhoon' and 'The End of the Tether'. While the former was published with 'Falk: A Reminiscence', 'Amy Foster', and 'Tomorrow' in *Typhoon* (1903), the latter appeared with 'Youth' and 'Heart of Darkness' in *Youth* (1902). 'Falk: A Reminiscence' and 'Amy Foster' reflect Conrad's continuing interest in the epistemological quest of a dramatised first person narrator. But the other tales are significant departures in their exploration of the possibilities of the omniscient voice. When Conrad discovered that he did not want to dramatise exclusively subjective states of mind, he turned again to the omniscient narrator. Although Conrad had used a primitive version of that voice in his first two novels and in a few of his early stories, he now learned in these stories how to control the readers' responses by means of subtle modulations of tone, changing perspectives, deft withholding of crucial information, and manipulation of chronology. Conrad originally experimented with these techniques when writing his Marlow tales. But he still had to adopt them to the omniscient voice that he preferred when he was examining a panoramic situation or when he knew exactly what he thought about the central dramatic situation of a work. As we shall see, much of the art of the next two novels, *Nostromo* and *The Secret Agent*, depends upon the subtlety and control of the omniscient voice.

Before turning to the omniscient tales, let us examine the two stories in which dramatised narrators are, like Marlow, characters in the tale's action.

## II. 'FALK: A REMINISCENCE' (1903)

Although 'Falk: A Reminiscence' is the title in every edition that I
have seen, critics usually refer to the tale simply as 'Falk'. But the
original title intimates that the story's focus is meant to be upon the
narrator's recollection of his encounter with Falk.[1] More importantly, the Author's Note, written eighteen years after the tale's
composition in 1901, gives us reason to believe that the narrator was
very much on Conrad's mind:

> But what is the subject of 'Falk'? I personally do not feel so
> very certain about it. He who reads must find out for himself.
> My intention in writing 'Falk' was not to shock anybody. *As
> in most of my writings I insist not on the events but on their effect
> upon the persons in the tale.* (emphasis mine)[2]

The tale's principal focus of interest is the middle-aged narrator's
struggle to come to terms with and communicate the meaning of a
crucial experience of his youth.

To recollect a psychic journey on which he embarks from the
'civilized', rational values of Hermann's world and discovers the
primitive, instinctive values of Falk's world, the narrator's telling
must partially repeat the journey. Thus after failing to mention his
title character at all for thirteen pages of his reminiscence, the narrator
begins by introducing Hermann as his friend and Falk as his enemy,
and postpones the telling of Falk's macabre secret because he wants to
repress it. Indeed, the narrator implies why he has trouble telling the
tale 'of primitive passion' when he explains his original difficulty in
coming to terms with Falk's experience:

> Remembering the things one reads of it was difficult to
> realize the true meaning of his answers. I ought to have seen at
> once—but I did not; so difficult is it for our minds,
> remembering so much, instructed so much, informed of so
> much, to get in touch with the real actuality at our elbow.
> (p. 226)

And this process 'of getting in touch with the real actuality' is
repeated in the telling. To revive Falk's experience as a living reality,
the narrator must again find the elusive 'true meaning', and to do so
he must overcome considerable unconscious reluctance. He must

struggle to get to the dark side of his reminiscence because it means going back to man's savage origins and seeing man's primitive needs as the source of his civilised social relationships. To help him 'get in touch', the narrator recalls various facets of Falk which set him apart from other men: his characteristic gesture of drawing his hands over his face while giving an 'almost imperceptible shudder', his Herculean aspect, and his resemblance to natural forces.

With its emphasis on coming to terms with someone who had stripped himself of civilisation's restraints and returned to man's temporal and emotional origins, 'Falk: A Reminiscence' bears an obvious similarity to 'Heart of Darkness'. But in the responsibility it thrusts on the reader to distinguish between the captain-narrator's original attitudes and those he takes in the retelling, the tale strikingly resembles 'Youth'. As in 'Youth', telling becomes a means of partially knowing; and, despite the increased perspicacity that time and experience have brought to the narrator, areas remain in which the retrospective speaker is guilty of self-deception. As we have seen, the Marlow of 'Heart of Darkness', unlike the Marlow of 'Youth', has the insight to see himself in a larger perspective and to objectify his subjective experience. Sitting apart in his 'ascetic posture', Marlow clearly differentiates himself not only from Kurtz, but from his original attitudes before embarking on his journey into the Congo. However, in both 'Youth' and 'Falk: A Reminiscence', Conrad depends upon his reader to see that the narrator is unable to be objective about certain aspects of his private experience. In these tales, Conrad reveals the discrepancy between the significance of the event as it appeared to a vulnerable and impressionable young man and the retrospective significance of the same event when the speaker is more mature and self-confident. And he also points up the discrepancy between the narrator's necessarily subjective view, conditioned by his own emotional and intellectual needs, and the more dispassionate one which is accessible to the reader. As in the case of the mature Marlow in 'Youth', the narrator of 'Falk: A Reminiscence' uses humour to distance uncomfortable events and self-consciously justifies some aspects of his youthful behaviour to his audience of peers. But the narrator of 'Falk: A Reminiscence' is far more introspective than his counterpart in 'Youth' and does not share his relish for telling about his experience. If in 'Youth' Marlow's early attempts at irony and dispassionate objectivity dissolve into sentimentalism, in 'Falk: A Reminiscence' the narrator proceeds in the direction of increased, if still incomplete, perceptiveness.

Conrad provides both an introductory speaker to set the stage for the mature captain's reminiscence and an ironic setting which merges the civilised and the primitive: The 'river-hostelry', 'stuck out over the mud of the shore like a lacustrine dwelling', anticipates the union between Hermann's 'civilized' niece who instinctively responds to Falk's interest and 'instinctive' Falk who circumspectly courts her (p. 145).

Because the narrator's own 'artless tale of experience' is composed of the same ingredients, the tale reveals that 'civilized' man carries within himself a latent primitive version of self that is never far from the surface. John A. Lester speaks of the 'dark response to Darwinism' in the late nineteenth century, citing *Jude the Obscure* as one example: 'Man was now thought of as the helpless pawn of Malthusian biological drives of sex and hunger and caught up . . . in a 'reality' utterly inhuman and wholly unresponsive to his spiritual or imaginative aspirations.'[3] Conrad hardly would have accepted the Neo-Lamarckian view that inherited characteristics (sometimes with the help of a 'Life Force') were propelling man to a higher quality of life. Conrad, like Hardy, did not believe that time represented progress; nor did he believe that mankind evolved into finer, more sensitive organisms. In 'Falk: A Reminiscence', 'An Outpost of Progress', and 'Heart of Darkness', Conrad implies that Western civilisation has perverted the instincts and passions of mankind's primitive heritage.

The telling of the tale is a difficult task for the narrator because it confronts him with memories of his own inadequacy. Recalling his experience with Falk means remembering his own self-doubt concerning his fitness for command: 'I would discover at odd times (generally about midnight) that I was totally inexperienced, greatly ignorant of business, and hopelessly unfit for any sort of command . . .' (p. 155). Had he failed to bring the boat and crew safely out to sea, his career would have been severely jeopardised. Yet he had inherited a command that had been mishandled by his predecessor; the first mate was disgruntled and the second was unintelligent; and the ship was beset by illness. The narrator's feelings of inadequacy and demoralisation were increased by the theft of his thirty-two sovereigns. As for most of us, challenges overcome seem uncomplicated, and the mature captain underplays how upset he had been. He confesses that he 'could not bear . . . the long lonely evenings' and was 'agitated' by the mate's snoring which made 'gross and revolting noises' (p. 156). We understand that a man who cannot remain alone and is upset by another's snoring is in a precarious emotional condition. Reflecting that 'even the command of a nice little barque, may be a delusion and a snare for the unwary spirit of pride in man', he sought escape on what seemed to be the idyllic *Diana* (p. 156).

At first, as we have noted, the narrator introduces the personae of the tale as 'my enemy Falk, and my friend Hermann' (p. 147). Yet the telling of the tale turns the epithets inside out as the narrator reveals that he admires and identifies with Falk while he despises Hermann's values. As the captain loses himself in the memory of his 'absurd experience', he again comes to see the pettiness and hypocrisy of the supposedly civilised Hermann and the 'qualities of classic heroism' in Falk's apparent savagery (p. 234). Originally the *Diana* is recalled as a 'saintly retreat' removed from the world's iniquities and untouched by the 'scandals' and 'iron necessity' of the sea. But the smugness with which he had been distancing the embarrassing 'episode' breaks down and he begins to recall the bankrupt sentimentality of Hermann and his family. Not only does he remember Nicholas's cold ruffianly leer and Lena's perpetual sorrowing over her rag doll, but he comes to recognise these qualities at their source and to see Hermann as a repulsive looking and predatory specimen. Gradually he remembers that Hermann perverted his instinct for self-preservation into an insidious moral cannibalism which is a parody of Falk's pitiless resolution and which expressed itself by measuring everything in terms of monetary value. Hermann resented paying passage for his niece and knowingly exploited her by employing her as a governess for his children. Far more than with her happiness or the sensibilities of Falk or the narrator, his concern was with being repaid for the damage to his ship.

If the captain does not even now understand why Falk considered him as a rival for Hermann's niece, the reader gets a clue from his enjoyment in recalling her. His enthusiasm for describing her charms belies his denial of all interest. His rather opaque schoolboy romanticism transforms her into a kind of mythic figure. For example, he says that he thought of the niece as an 'allegoric statue of the Earth'. As far as he is concerned, the niece seemed quite appropriate to the ship's name, *Diana*, even if the prolific Hermann family did not.

Of course the main reasons that Falk mistook the captain for a rival were Hermann's deception and the captain's behaving to the girl in a manner which resembled his own. The captain also carried on a similar silent courtship and, for that reason, was unable to see the 'symptoms' of Falk's adoration. He, too, came to Hermann's boat and noticed and admired the niece while he kept company with Hermann. He admits that he had 'cast eyes' on her, and his implied indifference is clearly false. There is even a hint that Hermann considered him as a possible alternative for Falk. But even in retrospect the captain does not want to admit why he had become the object of Falk's single-minded instinct for self-preservation. After all, he believes that the need for companionship, rather than an impulse to look at Hermann's niece or his own sense of inadequacy, was the cause of his 'assiduous' visits to the *Diana*.

Contact with the sordid Eastern seaport was crucial to the alteration of the captain's attitude towards Falk and Hermann. The search for the missing Johnson to pilot the narrator's boat provided a macabre prolepsis to the narrator's discovery of the purity of Falk's instincts. The grotesque odyssey through the city displayed the crude level to which man's primitive instincts have been warped by his social organisation. The Hussar became the captain's guide through a surrealistic urban inferno where horrors were piled on horrors and where objects took on animate identities of their own ('An empty Australian beef tin bounded cheerily before the toe of my boot,' the captain recalls [p. 191].) Significantly, the narrator shrinks from describing this humiliating adventure: 'But why dwell on the wretchedness, the breathlessness, the degradation, the senselessness, the weariness, the ridicule and humiliation and—and—the perspiration, of these moments?' (p. 193).

The retrospective narrator justifies his 'diplomatic' behaviour—his having become Falk's marriage broker to get his ship out of port—in oversimplified terms, attributing it to 'my youth, my inexperience, my very real concern for the health of my crew' (p. 195). From his present vantage point, forgetting the full dimensions of his former self-doubt and despair, he can justify his behaviour. But even now the older narrator is *defensive*. He explains his conduct by generalisation and abstraction. When a captain has a 'sickly crew', he argues,

. . . a skipper *would* be justified in going to any length, short of absolute crime. He *should* put his pride in his pocket; . . . he *ought* to conceal his horror and other emotions, and, if the fate of a human being, and that human being a magnificent young girl, is strangely involved—why, he *should* contemplate that fate . . . without turning a hair. (p. 196, emphases mine)

But this kind of sententiousness, disguised as moral delicacy, seems to result from his need to assure his listeners and himself of his own scruples. He concludes that 'nobody, not even Hermann's niece, I believe, need throw stones at me now' (p. 196). In fact, he *still* feels uncomfortable about his diplomacy and perhaps suspects that his *realpolitik* is the method of Hermann, the man whom the narrator increasingly disavows, rather than Falk with whom he increasingly identifies.

After recalling how he had taken the role of Falk's representative, the narrator becomes far more sympathetic to Falk. Time has confirmed Falk's assumption that the narrator, as a fellow sailor and as a 'man of experience', was in a position to sympathise with his desperate behaviour. When he compares Hermann's changeability with Falk's fanatical urge to survive and to marry the woman to whom he was passionately attracted, the captain comes to see the superficiality of those who 'did not seem to be able to retain an impression for a whole twelve hours' (p. 238). Yet, because Falk was not quite indifferent to conventional values, because if he had one foot in the mythic world, another foot was in the human world, Falk's cannibalism deeply disturbs the narrator. Falk's concern with respectability and his need for companionship make him enough 'like everybody else' to frighten the captain. The narrator finds it comfortable to describe Falk in similes and allusions which make Falk's physical appearance different from that of other men. As if literal, objective descriptions were not adequate to comprehend Falk and Hermann's niece, the captain uses magnifying contexts. The narrator's analogies transform Falk into an heroic figure, an heir to the Greek heroes and demiurges. Thus he recalls that Falk has 'an anchorite's bony head fitted with a Capuchin's beard and adjusted to a herculean body' (p. 201). And he remembers how Falk's face resembled the face of a mountain, and speaks of the 'extraordinary breadth of the high cheek-bones, the perpendicular style of the features, the massive forehead, steep like a cliff, denuded at the top' (p. 200). His last recollection of Falk is as a mythic figure, a fusion of Ulyssean and Herculean qualities, merged with Hermann's Olympian niece. He believes Falk and the man he killed displayed 'pitiless resolution, endurance, cunning, and courage' (p. 234). Falk's law is not a Mosaic or Christian one, but a credo based on preservation of his own physical being. The essence of Falk's character is revealed by his attitude to his cannabilistic experience:

'But it's a great misfortune *for me*. But it's a great misfortune *for me*' (p. 219, emphases mine).

What the captain learned from his confrontation with Falk and his recollection of that experience is that man's civilised relationships have their source in man's primitive origins. His commitment to self-preservation and his passionate desire to live and love have a kind of pristine purity that the seemingly civilised Hermann lacks. The standards Hermann evoked to judge Falk are those of a fastidious society in an age of manners: 'He wanted to know from Falk how *dared* he to come and tell him this? Did he think himself a *proper* person to be sitting in this cabin where his wife and children lived? Tell his niece! Expected him to tell his niece! His own brother's daughter! *Shameless!*' (pp. 218–19, emphases mine). But the narrator understands that the splendour and magnitude of Falk's unrestrained instincts—as demonstrated by the expression of his physical desire for Hermann's niece and his unbridled instinct for self-preservation—are attractive in comparison to the fastidiousness of conventional standards. His simile, comparing Falk's 'gigantic' instinct to live with a 'child's naive and uncontrolled desire' (p. 224), perceptively intimates that Falk's atavistic energy is part of man which civilised adults are supposed to repress if not disavow. Falk is a 'child' because he represents a supposedly less developed stage of mankind; yet to the speaker, he is a mythic figure, a 'dark navigator', who has a magnitude civilised man lacks. As in 'Heart of Darkness', Conrad wants to show us that instincts underlie civilised man's so-called refined behaviour and that no man can be sure of his potential when put into a situation in which life is dependent on his animal instincts.

The narrator, then, recollects the process of disenchantment with Hermann's world and the growth of his realisation that the Falk world is part of us whether we would willingly acknowledge it or not. He, too, had journeyed into darkness, widened his range of experience, and emerged with a different view of the so-called civilised world. He had used the means of civilisation, with its duplicity and diplomacy, to learn about the instinctive base of our social behaviour from Falk. Perhaps in his willingness to embrace a desperate course to preserve his identity, he shows his instinct for self-preservation. In his *retelling* of this critical incident, the mature narrator retraces the steps by which he discovered that the seminal relationship of civilised society—the conjugal relationship between man and woman—is derived from our primitive needs and that civilised behaviour may only be a veneer for a perversion of man's atavistic impulses. If cannibalism results aboard the *Borgmester Dahl* when the captain who should be the apostle of order and decorum is ineffectual, a more tepid reversion to savagery occurs aboard the *Diana*. Hermann threatens mayhem against those who displease him, and Mrs Hermann's courtesy is apparently limited to those who accept her standards. When the narrator repeats Falk's view that the best man had survived, he is adopting Falk's epistemology. His narrative becomes his personal tribute to purity of passion in a world infested by duplicity and hypocrisy.

While Conrad structures the events and rhetoric of the narrator's 'reminiscence' to show that the vantage point of several decades vastly increases one's understanding of events, he nevertheless points up the incompleteness of the captain's self-knowledge. Even now the older captain will not acknowledge the extent of his infatuation with Hermann's niece, nor consequently why Falk considers him a rival. Nor does his self-knowledge extend to recognising that Falk's experience includes a lesson about the necessity for effective command which pertains to his own leadership crisis. More importantly, the mature captain does not realise that even to tell of his encounter with Falk required an emotional effort to again break down his comfortable preconceived attitudes of what is right and wrong. Although certainly not equal to the original shock to his sensibilities, his recollection of Falk challenges anew his distinction between civilisation and barbarism.

## III. 'AMY FOSTER' (1901)

Perhaps in part reflecting frustration with the parochialism of his neighbours in Kent, Conrad wrote in 1901–2 'Amy Foster' and 'Tomorrow', two stories about the provincialism of English village life. These stories recall 'The Idiots', his prior depiction of narrow and mean behaviour in a rural French village. In 'Amy Foster', Conrad dramatises the process by which Dr Kennedy, a well-meaning, sensitive physician tries to come to terms with the senseless cruelty that an English village inflicts upon the emigrant, Yanko. It is the poignant story of how a lonely, yet vital man, falls victim to xenophobia and parochialism, culminating with the desertion by his dull-witted wife, the title character. The first narrator presents Dr Kennedy as a paradoxical figure, a scientist who would use the methods of science to philosophise on the nature of man: 'The penetrating power of his mind, acting like a corrosive fluid, had destroyed his ambition, I fancy. His intelligence is of a scientific order, of an investigating habit, and of that unappeasable curiosity which believes that there is a particle of a general truth in every mystery' (p. 106). Kennedy's tale alternates between specific details of Yanko's demise and vague speculations which desperately try to place Yanko within a comprehensible intellectual framework. As he retells the story, Dr Kennedy gropes for the effective language that will satisfy his psychic and intellectual demands for generalisation and order. He is concerned not only with specific problems of Yanko's treatment by the local denizens and the alteration in Amy Foster's attitude, but with the significance of Yanko's tragedy.

Dr Kennedy deeply feels for Yanko as a pathetic example of man's potential for mistreating his fellows. Although the doctor has come to the Eastbay area by choice, he separates himself from the values of the local folk. As a fellow alien, a former friend, and the physician for a patient whose needless death he might possibly have prevented, Dr Kennedy is a narrator whose every word is shaped by personal involvement in the narrative. Kennedy tends to exaggerate his guilt.[4] He blames himself for overlooking the deteriorating domestic situation between Yanko and Amy when he paid his penultimate medical call on Yanko. He holds himself responsible for not preventing the crucifixion of an innocent man. Perhaps he is troubled by the ambiguity of Yanko's final cry. The epithet 'Merciful!' may have been meant in praise of the doctor's attendance during his illness after his wife has fled. But more likely it is the supplication of a believer to his god that he be rescued from further earthly trials. (The doctor takes it not only in this sense, but interprets it as a personal rebuke.)

Kennedy's impressions of Yanko implicitly comment upon those of the rural folk who scorn his differences. To Smith, Yanko is an 'apparition'; to Kennedy, he is a special innocent adventurer who has left a simple world where men live in an idyllic relationship to the soil in contrast to the warped society of Brenzett. To Smith, Yanko is a madman and a menacing wild beast whom he views, at one point, as a 'nondescript and miry creature . . . swinging itself to and fro like a bear in a cage' (p. 120); to Kennedy, Yanko is a deeply religious and passionate man. Kennedy alternately mocks and berates his fellow residents while recalling their approach to Yanko and how they behaved to him. Swaffer alone treated Yanko humanely, and this was because Yanko rescued his granddaughter from drowning. By recounting the various points of view of the townspeople to Yanko, Kennedy hoists them on their own petard. Mr Bradley bragged how he lashed 'his whip at a hairy sort of gypsy fellow. . . . He caught him a good one, too, right over the face . . . that made him drop down in the mud a jolly sight quicker than he had jumped up' (pp. 118–19). Three boys confessed to throwing stones at a 'drunk'. Kennedy resorts to facetiousness to make his points as when he tells us how Mrs Finn hit Yanko 'courageously' with her umbrella because his 'babbling . . . was enough to make one die of fright' (p. 119). Ironically, Smith remained convinced of Yanko's 'essential insanity to this very day', although Yanko, in his own language, addressed him as 'gracious lord' and 'adjured [him] in God's name'.

Yanko's passionate nature and his enjoyment of dance and song contrast with the stolid English personality of the villagers. And his deeply religious nature is contrasted with the professing Christians of Eastbay whose only concern is to convert him to High Church. Yanko sees Amy as 'angelic' and 'divine' because she treats him well, but his apparent redeemer turns into his destroyer when she deserts him as she had abandoned the parrot that had once fascinated her. Kennedy clearly hints that disappointment and despair cause Yanko's 'heart failure'. But is it surprising that, given Amy's passivity and lack of intelligence, she became innoculated with the community's pervasive fear of differences among people? Parenthood apparently had a similar effect on her father who once had the imagination and vitality to elope, but now is as myopic as everyone else.

Kennedy resents the treatment Yanko received and goes to considerable lengths to develop the tale into a parable of man's potential meanness to his fellow man. But the inconsistency of the doctor's allusions shows how he is engaged in a search for the context that will make Yanko's history comprehensible to *himself*.[5] Kennedy views Yanko's fate as the most 'simply tragic' fate suffered by 'the *most* innocent' of men (p. 113, emphasis mine). He sees Yanko as a man 'plainly in the toils of his obscure and *touching* destiny' and speaks of a 'net of fate' closing on him (p. 119, emphasis mine). Another pattern of allusions establishes Yanko—who communes with earth, and sky—as a traditional pastoral figure, linking Pan, the nature god, and Christ, the innocent. The deeply religious Yanko was 'full of goodwill' and attracted the love of the meek and outcast Amy who loved him as if he were a strange god. Yet, as in many pastoral eclogues, the naive rustic dies broken-hearted after he is abandoned by his lover.

The first narrator has two interrelated functions: he plays a choral role—intensifying the reader's emotional reactions, and creating the moral atmosphere in which the reader first makes tentative and then final judgements—and he provides an objective view of Kennedy's character prior to the telling. As we have seen, in the 1898–1902 period, from the Marlow tales through 'Falk', Conrad favoured the use of introductory speakers to present data about his principal speakers, data which become essential to any interpretation of the speaker's character. In this case, the nameless narrator emphasises how the Eastbay area is a physical wasteland which has, by implication, created the weariness and despair of its citizens. At the outset, he follows Kennedy's introduction of Yanko's tragedy with a description of the physical setting, which is actually his impressionistic, subjective responses to the landscape:

> The uniform brownness of the harrowed field glowed with a rose tinge, as though the powdered clods had sweated out in minute pearls of blood the toil of uncounted ploughmen. From the edge of a copse a waggon with two horses was rolling gently along the ridge. Raised above our heads upon the skyline, it loomed up against the red sun, triumphantly big, enormous, like a chariot of giants drawn by two slow-stepping steeds of legendary proportions. And the clumsy figure of the man plodding at the head of the leading horse projected itself on the background of the Infinite with a heroic uncouthness. The end of his carter's whip quivered high up in the blue.
> (p. 108)

The contrast between the carter's first appearance and the corrected impression, between the 'chariot of giants' and the clumsy, plodding carter who is heroic only in his 'uncouthness', undercuts mankind's pretensions of grandeur. A few pages later, the narrator's remarks demonstrate the destructive relationship between the physical wasteland and the people who live there: 'A sense of penetrating sadness, like that inspired by a grave strain of music, disengaged itself from the silence of the fields. The men we met walked past, slow, unsmiling, with downcast eyes, as if the melancholy of an over-burdened earth had weighted their feet, bowed their shoulders, borne down their glances' (p. 110). These people, bent and burdened by their endless struggle to eke out a livelihood, are utterly incapable of responding to Yanko's spontaneity. Although a transient uninvolved visitor, the nameless narrator has begun to speak with a brooding tone similar to the one that conveys the doctor's profound disappointment.

The nameless narrator develops the sea into a symbol of the indifferent, amoral cosmos which thwarts man's aspirations. Looking toward the sea which had inexplicably claimed the lives of Yanko's fellow emigrants and the crew, the nameless narrator saw 'the frigid splendour of a hazy sea lying motionless under the moon. Not a whisper, not a splash, not a stir of the shingle, not a footstep, not a sigh came up from the earth below—never a sign of life but the scent of climbing jasmine; and Kennedy's voice, speaking behind me, passed through the wide casement, to vanish outside in a chill and sumptuous stillness' (p. 113). When the narrator first looks to the sea, he notices that 'the light blur of smoke, from an invisible steamer, faded on the great clearness of the horizon like the mist of a breath on a mirror' (p. 111). The vastness and emptiness of the sea subsume the results of human life: the steamer's smoke 'fades', Kennedy's words 'vanish', and people and ships are destroyed. Innocence, malice, Yanko's Catholicism, and Dr Kennedy's efforts to comprehend all seem irrelevant in the face of the sea's permanence. Not only the sea, but all nature is indifferent to man. When Yanko cried out 'Why?' 'in the penetrating and indignant voice of a man calling to a responsible Maker', he is answered by 'a gust of wind and a swish of rain'. Near the conclusion of his tale, the doctor comes to the window and looks out 'at the frigid splendour of the sea, immense in the haze, as if enclosing all the earth with all the hearts lost among the passions of love and fear' (p. 138). This perception of a 'frigid splendour' enclosing the earth suggests mankind's helplessness in an indifferent, amoral cosmos. The evanescence of human life and man's inability to create structures to order his life radiate throughout the tale: men do not control their destinies; a lighthouse cannot prevent shipwrecks; and Yanko's difficulties in making himself understood show that the ability to speak does not insure communication. Upon his return to Yanko's house one morning following Amy's flight, it seemed to Dr Kennedy that his voice lost 'itself in the *emptiness* of this tiny house as if I had cried in a desert' (p. 140, emphasis mine).

Yet even in this most pessimistic story, Conrad has his character- istic humanistic qualification. To balance partially the gloom, he has the tale's structure move outward in concentric circles toward control and comprehension. The xenophobic inhumanity to Yanko is 'framed' by the conscientious doctor's interest which, in turn, is 'enclosed' by the narrator's sympathy with the subtleties of Dr

Kennedy's response and his poetic generalisation of Yanko's tragedy.

## IV. SPOKESMAN FOR VALUES: REDISCOVERING THE OMNISCIENT VOICE

Conrad's conception of the artist changed since the 1897 Preface to *The Nigger of the 'Narcissus'*. In the Preface, we might recall, he speaks movingly of his attempt to awaken the 'unavoidable solidarity' which 'binds men to each other, and to all mankind'. (Recall: 'The artist descends within himself, and in that lonely region of stress, and strife, if he be deserving and fortunate, he finds the terms of his appeal' [*NN*, p. viii].) The 1898– 1900 Marlow tales are based on the implicit assumption that others will identify with the narrator's complex state of consciousness and his moral and emotional dilemmas.

Gradually Conrad put behind him the self-conscious stress on the illusion of values and the difficulty of communication. In the 1905 essay entitled 'Books', literary activity is defined as a kind of action. Its value depends on how well it depicts the variety of human behaviour, not merely the artist's own experience:

Literary creation being only one of the legitimate forms of human activity has no value but on the condition of not excluding the fullest recognition of all the more distinct forms of action. This condition is sometimes forgotten by the man of letters, who often, especially in his youth, is inclined to lay a claim of exclusive superiority for his own amongst all the other tasks of the human mind. (*NLL*, p. 7)

Conrad may very well be thinking of his own former emphasis on the artist's lonely agony.

When he chooses an omniscient voice, Conrad does not write of his own moral initiation or search for values. His narrator is not an individual consciousness for whom the tale was an occasion for introspective self-analysis. In an 1898 essay, Conrad had criticised Daudet for intruding his opinions into his fictions. But he now knew that 'A writer of imaginative prose (even more than any other sort of artist) stands confessed in his works. His conscience, his deeper sense of things, gives him his attitude before the world' (*PR*, p. 95). In the tales that follow, Conrad's narrator is his surrogate conscience who defines the ethical significance of the narrative. Before the telling begins, the experimental underbrush has been cleared and cities of values have risen. Mostly by implication—his selection and arrangement of incidents, his imagery, his tonality—and occasionally by explicit comments, the narrator creates the standards by which the characters should be judged by the readers.

If in the Preface to *The Nigger of the 'Narcissus'* he desperately sought an audience of responsive temperaments, in the 1905 James essay he writes rather condescendingly of the 'multitude' who 'cry, "Take me out of myself!"' (*NLL*, p. 13). Now he stressed the way that the artist can teach and persuade. In a 1908 letter he wrote: 'A good book is a good action. It has more than the force of good example. And if the moralist will say that it has less merit—let him. Indeed we are not writing for the salvation of our own soul' (6 Oct. 1908; *LL*, vol. ii, p. 89).

The writer of fiction becomes a moral historian who 'in his calling of interpreter' writes 'for the edification of mankind' (*NLL*, pp. 13, 14). *A Personal Record* (1908–9) contains an eloquent testimony for using literature to persuade an audience:

He who wants to persuade should put his trust not in the right
argument, but in the right word. The power of sound has
always been greater than the power of sense. I don't say this by
way of disparagement. It is better for mankind to be
impressionable than reflective. . . . On the other hand, you
cannot fail to see the power of mere words; such words as
Glory, for instance, or Pity. I won't mention any more. They
are not far to seek. Shouted with perseverance, with ardour,
with conviction, these two by their sound alone have set whole
nations in motion and upheaved the dry, hard ground on
which rests our whole social fabric. . . . Give me the right
word and the right accent and I will move the world. (*PR*,
pp. xiii–xiv)

Conrad used an omniscient voice when he had relatively few doubts about what constituted ethical behaviour. In the early chapters of *Lord Jim*, Conrad uses an omniscient narrator to demonstrate by reference to Jim's previous conduct that Jim's jump is a characteristic rather than a gratuitous action; the anonymous narrator's original, quite rigid indictment provides an important touchstone to which Conrad expected the reader to refer. Like the early part of *Lord Jim*,

'Typhoon' and 'The End of the Tether' are maritime tales to which Conrad could apply precise standards; 'To-morrow' concerns the obvious exploitation of a young woman by three separate men.

If we are to accept a narrator's judgements—whether he is a first-person or omniscient narrator—then the narrator must implicitly distinguish himself from the other characters in most or all of the following: superior intellect, perspicacity, emotional maturity, and, most importantly, moral sensitivity. As Conrad becomes more confident of his ability to confront and judge the major intellectual and historical trends of the twentieth century, he uses an omniscient speaker to articulate subtle alternatives to moral and political anarchy. In *The Secret Agent*, the seemingly anonymous narrator is a subtle, self-dramatising satirist who, on occasion, not only speaks in the first person, but who conveys a definite alternative to the world he depicts. The language teacher of *Under Western Eyes* gives the appearance of a rather ludicrous figure, but gradually grows in stature into a viable illustration of—as well as an explicit and implicit spokesman for—decency, friendship, tolerance, and tact.

The use of an omniscient narrator implies an objectivity and finality with which Conrad never feels completely comfortable. Conrad's complex vision, expressed not only in the dramatic action but in the structure and texture, strains against the narrator's judgements. His impulse is to dramatise the process by which the narrator's opinions evolve, as if it were simultaneously necessary to justify his views to his readers and to reassure himself that he was not simply deluding himself into arbitrary judgements. At times the technically 'omniscient' voice is torn between sympathy for his characters and commitment to his ostensible values. (This is characteristic of the turn-of-the century novel. In *Jude the Obscure* the omniscient voice becomes an empathetic spokesman, if not apologist, for the protagonist's action.)[6] Except when he feels absolutely certain of his judgements, such as his indictment or urban civilisation in *The Secret Agent*, or of pretentions imperialism in 'An Outpost of Progress', Conrad's omniscient tales contain elements of the Marlow tales in which an active mind grapples with complex experience. Nor, if we recall *A Personal Record*, will this surprise us. In a typical qualification, no sooner does Conrad tell us that 'In order to move others deeply we must deliberately allow ourselves to be carried away beyond the bounds of our normal sensibility,' than he warns us in the next sentence of a writer's 'becoming the victim of his own exaggeration, losing the exact notion of sincerity, and in the end coming to despise truth itself as something too cold, too blunt for his purpose—as, in fact, not good enough for his insistent emotion' (*PR*, pp. xix–xx). That he returns to a complex first person narrator for most of his major work after *The Secret Agent* shows his reluctance to dramatise omniscience. *Under Western Eyes*, 'The Secret Sharer', *Chance* and *The Shadow-Line* all involve a speaker's discovery of the meaning of events.

## V. 'TYPHOON' (1902)

'Typhoon', the work following *Lord Jim*, juxtaposes MacWhirr, a stolid, dependable, and responsible captain, with Jukes, his imaginative and impulsive first mate. Completed in January 1901, the tale shows that in times of severe stress, simple courage and diligent performance of duty count for everything, and that in situations of life and death, the man regarded as more intelligent according to ordinary standards may be found wanting. The story renders a multitude of different viewpoints, from Jukes and MacWhirr to those of several minor characters, such as Bun Hin's clerk and the boatswain. The purpose of rendering a wide range of behaviour during the crisis is to provide a yardstick against which we may measure Jukes and MacWhirr. Most of the crew are even more disoriented than Jukes until MacWhirr impels him to provide the necessary leadership. But, with the exception of the contemptible second mate, the rest of the *officers* perform their duties competently and with instinctive courage. John Howard Wills argues that Jukes undergoes a 'spiritual regeneration' comparable to that of the captains of 'The Secret Sharer' and *The Shadow-Line*, but it is more accurate to say that the mate proves his competence as a seaman *without* undergoing profound change.[7] While there is little danger of his relapsing into psychic apathy in the face of another crisis, he does not develop the judgement and sense of fairness that mark the captain's brand of leadership. The high-spirited irony of Jukes's final letter belies the notion that his experience has fundamentally affected his character.

Conrad's omniscient voice creates the process of discovering the value of MacWhirr's one-minded service to a code and the shortcomings of Jukes's aesthetic imagination when confronted with a situation requiring instinctive reactions. He places the ingenuous reader in the position of misunderstanding MacWhirr and Jukes prior

to the crisis, and then gradually awakens him to the actual value of the
two characters. At first, MacWhirr is presented as a rather unimpos-
ing, even slightly ludicrous figure:

> Captain MacWhirr, of the steamer *Nan-Shan*, had a
> phsysiognomy that, in the order of material appearances, was
> the exact counterpart of his mind: it presented no marked
> characteristics of firmness or stupidity; it had no pronounced
> characteristics whatever; it was simply ordinary, irresponsive,
> and unruffled. (p. 3)

The one-dimensional irony and chaffing wit resemble the tone of
Jukes's letters. But occasionally the narrator speaks in a more tolerant
voice that prepares the reader to change his mind:

> Having just enough imagination to carry him through each
> successive day, and no more, he was tranquilly sure of himself;
> and from the very same cause he was not in the least conceited.
> It is your imaginative superior who is touchy, overbearing,
> and difficult to please; but every ship Captain MacWhirr
> commanded was the floating abode of harmony and peace.
> (p. 4)

Even within the early unfavourable impression can be found the seeds
of MacWhirr's efficacy and reputation with shipowners: his minute
attention to detail, his dedication to duty, and his essential integrity.
But Mr Juke's impulsiveness and expansiveness seem more attractive; he writes his friend 'out of the fulness of his heart and the
liveliness of his fancy' (p. 18).

In Chapter 2, as the crisis approaches, the narrator presents
MacWhirr with a flippancy that is very similar to Jukes's attitude:

> Had he been informed by an indisputable authority that the
> end of the world was to be finally accomplished by a
> catastrophic disturbance of the atmosphere, he would have
> assimilated the information under the simple idea of dirty
> weather, and no other, because he had no experience of
> cataclysms, and belief does not necessarily imply
> comprehension. (p. 20)

And his similies and analogies mock MacWhirr's first encounter with the typhoon: 'He went through all the movements of a woman putting on her bonnet before a glass, with a strained, listening attention, as though he had expected every moment to hear the shout of his name in the confused clamour that had suddenly beset his ship' (p. 36). His awkwardness and apparent unfitness are emphasised: 'He stood for a moment in the light of the lamp, thick, clumsy, shapeless in his panoply of combat, vigilant and red-faced' (p. 37). But the man who could not imagine a storm beyond his own experience proves equal to his responsibilities.

When the storm first develops, Jukes is anxious, but then so is the captain. Yet by the third chapter, Jukes goes through a period during which his confidence is shaken and he becomes virtually paralysed. The narrator dramatises how his thoughts become less complex until they are almost childish oversimplifications of the actual situation:

> 'She's done for,' he said to himself, with a surprising mental agitation, as though he had discovered an unexpected meaning in this thought. One of these things was bound to happen. Nothing could be prevented now, and nothing could be remedied. The men on board did not count, and the ship could not last. This weather was too impossible. (p. 45)

When the storm proves to be more than he had imagined, he is completely overwhelmed. Like his opposite, the unimaginative man, the imaginative and high-spirited man is finally left with nothing but facts. It is not only that Mr Jukes's condescending flippancy and good-natured perception of the failings of less intelligent men are useless, but his proclivity to imagine what will happen becomes a distinct liability. For all his apparent sophistication, this cerebral ironist is momentarily reduced to repeating 'my God', and to flailing his arms and legs like an infant. Even before he discovers who it is, he instinctively returns the captain's embrace and welcomes the captain's presence. Moments later, the Captain's voice steadies him, and the narrator, not without some irony, tells us why:

> And again he heard that voice, forced and ringing feebly, but with a penetrating effect of quietness in the enormous discord of noises, as if sent out from some remote spot of peace beyond the black wastes of the gale; again he heard a man's voice—the frail and indomitable sound that can be made to carry an infinity of thought, resolution and purpose, that shall

be pronouncing confident words on the last day, when heavens
fall, and justice is done. (p. 44)

Jukes is in greater trouble than he realises. That he'aspires to peace'
and that he recalls the example of his father (a man who died of
'resignation') imply how Jukes's defences have collapsed. But his
surrogate father's call rallies him and he goes below to lead the
expedition to restore order among the Chinamen. Despite his inner
doubts, the memory of the captain's voice inspires him to respond
instinctively to the actual demands of the situation as the captain
would. Once he controls his own impulse to rebel 'against the
tyranny of training and command', he adopts the MacWhirr
principles of mutual responsibility, self-discipline, and courage even
while he still is plagued by anxiety and doubt.

In Chapter 3, we see the successive stages of Jukes's distress until
finally he is threatened with complete psychic collapse. Like Jim on
the *Patna*, Jukes imagines the possibilities with a preoccupation which
makes them harrowing *actualities*. Sympathetic to Jukes's experience of
the gale, Conrad renders Jukes's excited and exaggerated perceptions in terms of a series of rapidly changing analogies that give the
reader the essence of his irrational impressions of the situation:

> The motion of the ship was extravagant. Her lurches had an
> appalling helplessness: she pitched as if taking a header into a
> void, and seemed to find a wall to hit every time. When she
> rolled she fell on her side headlong, and she would be righted
> back by such a demolishing blow that Jukes felt her reeling as
> a clubbed man reels before he collapses. The gale howled and
> scuffled about gigantically in the darkness, as though the entire
> world were one black gully. At certain moments the air
> streamed against the ship as if sucked through a tunnel with a
> concentrated solid force of impact that seemed to lift her clean
> out of the water and keep her up for an instant with only a
> quiver running through her from end to end. And then she
> would begin her tumbling again as if dropped back into a
> boiling cauldron. (pp. 42–3)

Conrad stresses the rapid disintegration perceived by Jukes by using
verbs of violent flux as well as participles and adjectives that suggest
turmoil and destruction:

The *Nan-Shan* was being looted by the storm with a
senseless, destructive fury; trysails torn out of the extra gaskets,
double-lashed awnings blown away, bridge swept clean,
weather-cloths burst, rails twisted, light-screens smashed—and
two of the boats had gone already. They had gone unheard
and unseen, melting, as it were, in the shock and smother of
the wave. (p. 44)

To Jukes, this is a vision of the end of the world, not as apocalypse,
but as eternal chaos where things and living creatures become
interchangeable: 'Jukes had a vision of two pair of davits leaping black
and empty out of the stolid blackness, with one overhauled fall flying
and an iron-bound block capering in the air . . .' (p. 44). Jukes's
surrealistic personifications are those of a romantic consciousness
which perceives reality in terms of subjective impressions. He even
imagines that the movements of the ship's engines are alive:
'Sometimes all those powerful and unerring movements would slow
down simultaneously, as if they had been the functions of a *living
organism*. . . . The wood encased bulk of the low-pressure cylinder,
frowning portly from above, emitted a faint wheeze at every
thrust . . .' (pp. 69–70, emphasis mine).

MacWhirr is at home in the texture of the story which, as much as
MacWhirr's character, comments on Jukes's imaginative hysteria.
Straightforward descriptions become ironic comments on both
Jukes's psychic complexity and the language required to present it. At
the height of the storm, some of Conrad's comments have an almost
fabular clarity and conceptual simplicity: 'On board ship there is only
one man to whom it is worthwhile to unburden yourself' or 'The
second mate was lying low, like a malignant little animal under a
hedge' (pp. 58, 59).

While Conrad sympathetically renders Jukes's thoughts and
feelings, he still exposes the first mate's lack of inner strength:

While he was exchanging explanatory yells with his captain, a
sudden lowering of the darkness came upon the night, falling
before their vision like something palpable. It was as if the
masked lights of the world had been turned down. Jukes was
uncritically glad to have his captain at hand. It relieved him as
though that man had, by simply coming on deck, taken most
of the gale's weight upon his shoulders. Such is the prestige,
the privilege, and the burden of command. (p. 39)

In the second-to-last sentence of the above quotation, the narrator steps away and tells us more about Jukes than the mate probably could have verbalised at the time or, indeed, later. And in the final sentence, the narrator intimates the vast distinction between Jukes's responsibilities as first mate and MacWhirr's as captain.

Although the character for whom he most deeply feels is obviously Jukes, Conrad admires MacWhirr at the same time as he is amused by this uncomplex man. The ingredients of a grotesque caricature dissolve into a tribute to the man whose instinctive courage and sense of justice make civilisation possible. Conrad must have felt the incongruity of extolling a sensibility that was fundamentally at odds with his brooding, meditative temperament. But he appreciates MacWhirr's virtues: courage, a sense of fairness, and above all, professional competence. If it were not for both the narrator's earlier ironic tone toward him and his presentation of MacWhirr's rather bathetic private moments, Captain MacWhirr might be a figure of heroic dignity. What enables MacWhirr to steady himself when his defences are penetrated and his personality threatened is finding the towel in its accustomed place. This meticulous man is sustained by simple objective facts. The location of his watch and the functioning of a lock are at the centre of his mental world. If there is one anecdote that renders the essence of MacWhirr's psyche, it is his realisation that he might never use the matchbox again: 'The vividness of the thought checked him and for an infinitesimal fraction of a second his fingers closed again on the small object as though it had been the symbol of all these little habits that chain us to the weary round of life' (p. 85). To MacWhirr, concepts and things, his drowning and his losing a hat, have nearly equal significance. But his reductive perspective enables him to understand that people can be battered to pieces as well as ships, that Chinamen are humble, and that their lives and properties must be taken into account.

Jukes's last letter is a self-condemning dramatic monologue, another aspect of his original condescending attitude toward MacWhirr that the narrative has rejected: 'There are feelings that this man simply hasn't got—and there's an end to it. You might just as well try to make a bedpost understand' (p. 98). MacWhirr is the kind of man whose integrity and decency Joseph Conrad admired and whose lack of subtlety and complexity he envied. Yet he knew that the captain embodies the complacency, condescension and, yes, racism of British imperialism. He does not idealise MacWhirr's commitment to the Chinese which is based simply on his conception of the White

Man's Burden. MacWhirr insists that the coolies be given an equal chance to live and a share of their money, but does not tolerate the sentimental rhetoric of Jukes that equates Chinamen with passengers.

Conrad, the convert from the world of action to the world of the imagination, admired MacWhirr's integrity and sense of purpose and despised the ineptitude of the imaginative men, such as Jim and Jukes, who seemed incapable of 'work undertaken with single-minded devotion' (*NLL*, p. 196). During the first several years of his writing career, Conrad at times longed for the clarity and simplicity of his former life when one's ship was an absorbing activity. As he wrote in *The Mirror of the Sea*, a seaman should enter into a 'serious relation' where one gives up to his ship 'the fullest share of your thought, of your skill, of your self-love' (*MS*, p. 56). Yet it is Jim and Jukes whose imaginations and intelligence most resemble his own. Their failure to meet the sea's challenges must have made Conrad wonder whether his own withdrawal from the sea, which he still regarded as temporary and often regretted, was not the result of his temperamental inability to continue to give himself completely to the demands of life at sea.

The ultimate indictment of Jukes's loquacity is the absorption of his words into the vast emptiness that surrounds the shipboard community where Jukes is ineffective: 'His voice, blank and forced as though he were talking through hard-set teeth, seemed to flow away on all sides into the darkness, deepening again upon the sea' (p. 87). By contrast, MacWhirr 'found very little occasion to talk' (p. 9). It is true that MacWhirr's own stupidity and lack of imagination, epitomised by his tautology, 'A gale is a gale', lead him into the typhoon. And MacWhirr may seem foolish when he whines about the condition of the lock: 'Shut the door so it don't fly open, will you? I can't stand a door banging. They've put a lot of rubbishy locks in this ship, I must say' (p. 35). His monosyllabic diction, grammatical errors, and awkward syntax ostentatiously differentiate MacWhirr from the more sophisticated vocabulary and polished syntax of Jukes and Conrad's narrator. The captain's understated comment, 'I shouldn't like to lose her,' indicates a sense of commitment to abstract values that sharply contrasts with Jukes's retrogression into infantile self-immersion.

Like Jim, Jukes *creates* the world he lives in. He lives within his own illusions and fantasies, and uses irony and flippancy to distance and distort his recollection of his own behaviour and its contrast to the captain's. After the crisis, he quickly reverts to his characteristic verbal behaviour. His letter to his friend could have been written by Jim after his early, pre-*Patna* lapses. It may be instructive to see Jukes as a potential Jim who, because he is relegated to a subordinate role and finds a source of moral sustenance, escapes disgrace. One of the story's ironies is that this reasonably intelligent and imaginative man lacks the flexibility and the judgement to admit his shortcomings and to recognise the important lessons of his experience. Has he really learned anything about sincerity, responsibility, or fairness? Jukes's letter is 'calculated'—the word is significant—'to give the impression of light-hearted, indomitable resolution' (p. 97). While resuming his earlier and indeed flippant attitude, which expresses itself in his rather cavalier view of the captain's heroism, he nevertheless admits that the captain handled the situation well. The contents of his letter undercut the perspicacity of his grudging and condescending final statement: 'I think that he got out of it very well for such a stupid man' (p. 102). Clearly, Jukes does not experience a major character transformation or, to recall Wills's words, 'spiritual regeneration'.

## VI. 'TO-MORROW' (1902)

'To-morrow' is an underrated story about how the expectations of an old man and a woman neighbour, who has wasted her youth serving her father, converge and focus on the reappearance of the old man's son. The concluding story of *Typhoon* returns to Colebrook, part of the Eastbay area where 'Amy Foster' takes place. The memory of xenophobia and human pettiness informs the expectations of the reader. And the perverse relationships of 'To-morrow' again demonstrate the symbiotic relationship between community standards and personal values. Captain Hagberd deludes himself into perpetually expecting that his runaway son, absent for sixteen years and the object of continuous fruitless searches and inquiries, will return 'tomorrow'. And gradually his doubting neighbour, Bessie Carvil, notwithstanding her intellectual awareness that Hagberd has no reason whatsoever to believe in the son's return, shares his fiction. According to the captain, his son's return will be marked by his marriage to Bessie and thus the considerable possessions which he has accumulated for Harry will become Bessie's. Because she is trapped as a permanent nursemaid to her tyrannous blind father who makes her life a living hell, she is peculiarly susceptible to the captain's fantasies. Because her youth has been dissipated in the service of her unreasonable and inhumane father, Harry's return offers her the only possibility of escape.

Conrad is ironic about conventional, turn-of-the century morality that requires a woman to devote herself to the care of a barbaric father and stifles one's existence.[8] The story takes a look at the conventional view of woman's responsibility and contrasts it to man's freedom to leave home. Captain Hagberd expresses the accepted belief that a daughter's duties and needs are different from a son's: 'Of course it isn't as if he had a son to provide for. . . . Girls, of course, don't require so much. . . . They don't run away from home, my dear' (p. 253). Conrad exposes the cruelty of society's attitude which reduces Bessie, who obviously could enter into a meaningful relationship, to a mere servant to her father and a sexual object for Harry. And he implies that the pathology of social imprisonment has deprived Bessie of her potential identity and reduced her world to a monochromatic cartoon. Conrad's omniscient voice represents sanity and civilisation as he exposes various kinds of exploitative relationships, the principal ones being those in which males reduce females to instruments of their policy.

## VII. 'THE END OF THE TETHER' (1902)

'The End of the Tether' (1902) is Conrad's Mutability Canto. It is Conrad's great tale of the complex problem of ageing, and of the broader problem of man's movement through time. He writes of the one problem that cannot be solved by a revolution in psychic responses or by deliberate or subconscious commitment to a set of values and beliefs. In other sea tales, he writes of man's victory over his doubts, fears, and atavistic impulses as a means of temporarily coping with the natural world. But in 'The End of the Tether', the potentially heroic figure, Captain Whalley, is unable to deal with the ravages of time notwithstanding his generous motives, his physical vitality, and his faith in God; the sea journey with its destination and movement through time becomes a metaphor for his epistemological quest. As so often in Conrad (for example, The Nigger of the 'Narcissus', 'Typhoon', 'Youth', and 'The Secret Sharer'), the small community on board a ship, temporarily sealed from outside influences while at sea, provides Conrad with a congenial form for exploring the dynamics of a group under stress as it makes its way toward the moral and physical destination of one or more of its members.

In 'The End of the Tether', Conrad considers what he believed to be the illusion of religious faith. Ironically, the captain's conception of divine justice is a subtle function of his psychological needs for his daughter's love and for his self-esteem. He believes that his self-appointed role as provider for his daughter is blessed: 'Generally his mind seemed steeped in the serenity of boundless trust in a higher power' (p. 293). But the narrator shows—albeit with great sympathy—how faith can be as pernicious an influence on man's character as any other illusion. Captain Whalley takes his own consciousness as a synecdoche for God's. Certain that his motives and aspirations will be endorsed by God, he depends upon God's suspending the process of his physical deterioration so that he can fulfil his desires.

Whalley's faith is a vestige of an earlier age. Speaking of belief in the 'earlier decades of the nineteenth century', John A. Lester defines in general terms Whalley's *a priori* assumptions: '*Belief* appears mainly to have one meaning: It is a conviction that some larger conception of life is taken as having firm validity, a fixed part of the real nature of things, so certain that one is willing to act upon it.'[9] But like so many of the writers of the 1890s and the turn of the century (including Hardy in *Tess* and *Jude* and E. M. Forster), Conrad regarded beliefs as those necessary illusions created by one's psychic and moral needs so that he might better cope in a world indifferent to man's aspirations. For Conrad, it followed that each man must find his own 'working arrangement'—must 'willfully and knowingly, find or fabricate illusions and *believe* in them' (emphasis Lester's).[10]

Whalley inhibits another age, one evoked by the early 'ubi sunt' passages. His former achievements are virtually forgotten. The narrator provides the context in which we can respond to Whalley's discovery that the world in which he had excelled has permanently disappeared:

> Departed the men who would have nodded appreciatively at the mention of his name, and would have thought themselves bound in honour to do something for Dare-devil Harry Whalley. Departed the opportunities which he would have known how to seize; and gone with them the white-winged flock of clippers that lived in the boisterous uncertain life of the winds, skimming big fortunes out of the foam of the sea. In a

world that pared down the profits to an irreducible minimum,
in a world that was able to count its disengaged tonnage twice
over every day and in which lean charters were snapped up by
cable three months in advance, there were no chances of
fortune for an individual wandering haphazard with a little
barque—hardly indeed any room to exist. (p. 177)

The narrator's emphasis on the world's deterioration, in direct
contrast to Whalley's belief in man's progress, is demonstrated by the
ensuing narrative. Whalley has become an economic anachronism
through no fault of his own: 'He was defenceless before the insidious
work of adversity, to whose more open assaults he could present a
firm front; like a cliff that stands unmoved the open battering of the
sea, with a lofty ignorance of the treacherous backwash undermining
its base' (p. 183).

Conrad's similes not only magnify but intensify the story of
Whalley's demise. The vehicles propose other contexts which are
appropriate for viewing the original statement, but these contexts are
intensifications rather than elaborations. For example in Chapter 18,
the narrator tells us that Whalley is sweating: 'The drops rolled down
his cheeks, fell like rain upon the white hairs of his beard, and
brusquely, as if guided by an uncontrollable and anxious impulse, his
arm reached out to the stand of the engine-room telegraph' (p. 225).
The 'uncontrollable and anxious impulse' suggests his compulsive
necessity to preserve his self-esteem by providing money for his
daughter. 'As if' and 'as though' introduce not decorative comparisons, but essential analyses. In the following, it is the 'as though'
explanation which carries the full weight of meaning: 'Directly he
was spoken to, he began to smile attentively, with a great deference
expressed in his whole attitude; but there was in the rapid winking
which went on all the time something quizzical, *as though* he has
possessed the secret of some universal joke cheating all creation and
impenetrable to other mortals' (p. 236, emphasis mine). The phrasing
reveals hints of an ironic tone; the carefully chosen word 'joke' makes
us see that the narrator is pointing up the irony between Captain
Whalley's petty deception and his heroic pretensions, between his
sacramental interpretation of his motives and the chicanery to which
he has stooped.

By comparing Whalley to trees and cliffs, Conrad subtly shows
that he is part of the same world as inanimate nature and comments on
Whalley's belief in his own divine mission.[11] Although the story does

concern the devaluation of a man who hubristically thinks his actions carry God's approval, Captain Whalley is the story's most attractive figure. The narrator, a man who knows both the sea and its ships and admires Whalley's integrity and achievements, is sympathetic to Whalley's dilemma and presents his comminations in the best light. He alternates his own impressionistic sensibility, sensitive to shapes and colours, with Whalley's consciousness which has digested its collected wisdom into sententious certainties: The narrator's description of the scene when Whalley walks along the port ('The flaming sky kindled a tiny crimson spark upon the glistening surface of each glassy shell') is contrasted with Captain Whalley's reflection, 'If a ship without a man was like a body without a soul, a sailor without a ship was of not much more account in this world than an aimless log adrift upon the sea' (pp. 190, 191). A 1902 Conrad letter to David Meldrum shows that he wished to maintain sympathy for Whalley even while having us understand how his impeccable and intuitive character is becoming subtle and civilised:

> The old man does not wobble it seems to me. The Eliott episode [in which Whalley meets an old colleague] has a fundamental significance in so far that it exhibits the first weakening of old Whalley's character before the assault of poverty. As you notice he says nothing of his position but goes off and takes advantage of the information. At the same time it gives me the opportunity to introduce Massy from way back without the formal narrative paragraphs. But the episode is mainly the first sign of that fate we carry within us. A character like Whalley's cannot cease to be frank with impunity. . . . Next he conveys a sort of false impression to Massy—on justifiable grounds. I indicate the progress of deterioration the shaking the character receives and make it possible thus to by and by present the man as concealing the oncoming of blindness—and so on; till at least [*sic*] he conceals the criminal wrecking of his ship by committing suicide. And always there is just that shadow, that ghost of justification which should secure the sympathy of the reader.[12]

The narrator moves inside and outside Captain Whalley but also gives us other perspectives for brief moments. At first, he is sympathetic but increasingly his gentle irony to the captain becomes critical. His distaste for Massy and Sterne is hardly disguised: 'But it seemed as though Mr. Massy had suddenly come to doubt the efficacy of sleep as against a man's troubles; or perhaps he had found the relief he needed in the stillness of a calm contemplation that may contain the vivid thoughts of wealth, of a stroke of luck, of long idleness, and may bring before you the imagined form of every desire' (p. 313). The 'seemed as though' and 'or perhaps' assume a lack of knowledge on the part of the narrator and place him in the role of a remote observer. The narrator is nervously amused with characters like Massy, whose motives he can only speculate upon but never understand. But this discomfort identifies him as a morally respectable person and lends credibility to his opinions and judgement.

Whalley had always believed in his impulses: 'Reason was of no use. It was a matter of feeling. His feeling has never played him false' (pp. 211—12). The concise, direct syntax conveys the simplicity, yet precision, of Whalley's unsophisticated mind. But Whalley has become calculating even while listening to his friend's tale of the *Sofala*, and he allows Massy to receive false impressions of his physical condition. When he returns from his first visit to the *Sofala*, before sealing the bargain, he is no longer relying on his impulses:

> He would now consider calmly the discretion of it before saying the final word tomorrow. . . . The honesty of it was indubitable: he meant well by the fellow. . . .
> The discretion of it. Was there a choice? He seemed already to have lost something of himself; to have given up to a hungry spectre something of his truth and dignity in order to live. But his life was necessary. Let poverty do its worst in exacting its toll of humiliation (p. 213).

The straightforward, declarative syntax is unchanged, but now reason and logic have a place in the consciousness of the man who had always depended on his instinctive knowledge of right and wrong. In a crystallising image, his shadow mocks his transformation: 'Periodically his shadow leaped up intense by his side on the trunks of trees, to lengthen itself, oblique and dim, far over the grass— repeating his stride' (p. 213).

That Conrad means to universalise Whalley's experience, means us to see him as type as well as an individual, is indicated by his suggestions that Captain Whalley is a patriarchal figure from another era and by his use of language to generalise and expand the captain's significance. Because the emphasis is on what he had been, a biographical outline of his past is provided. But really we are only told of Whalley's life, character, and appearance in general terms that give him representative significance. At times, Whalley could be taken for a figure from Bunyan: 'He was only a lonely figure walking purposely, with a great white beard like a pilgrim, and with a thick stick that resembled a weapon' (p. 181). He is certain not only that God will deal justly with him, but that what happens to him is directly the result of God's will. Whalley believes himself favoured by God and, despite the occasional pangs from his conscience (raising doubts about the ethics of his behaviour), imputes to God's will tacit permission to deceive Massy. At the time of the original deception, when he allowed Massy to think he was a man of means, the narrator tells us the reason for Whalley's 'superb confidence in his body': 'In the midst of life we are in death, but he trusted his Maker with a still greater fearlessness—his Maker who knew his thoughts, his human affections, and his motives. His Creator knew what use he was making of his health—how much he wanted it' (p. 271). But the narrative shows that Whalley's Christian epistemology is a delusion.

Conrad's narrator shares Van Wyck's impression of Whalley: 'It was as if nobody could talk like this now, and the over-shadowed eyes, the flowing white beard, the big frame, the serenity, and the whole temper of the man, were an amazing survival from the prehistoric times of the world . . .' (p. 287). For a moment we share Whalley's optics. Although such a self-conception is beyond his power of articulation, we realise that for Whalley the 'as if' of the previous sentence collapses until tenor and vehicle are one, until he almost believes he is a 'patriarchal' figure with typological significance. Whalley speaks in biblical language, describing his blindness as a 'visitation' and 'the sign of God's anger' (p. 301). He defines his commitment to his daughter by citing the Old Testament: 'Bone of my bone, flesh of my flesh; the very image of my poor wife' (p. 293). That he conceives himself as a potential Samson implies his belief that his time and space are informed by significance rather than the tick-tock of passing time: "It seems to me, like the blinded Samson, I would find the strength to shake down a temple upon my head" (p. 301). Whalley's hubris is paradoxically in his faith, in his belief that he lives in space imbued with Divine blessing because God endorses his motives and works his will through him. He believes that he is part of a universal history, directed by God, that stretches from the creation of the world to the fulfilment of the Covenant. According to such a view, as Erich Auerbach has explained, 'Everything else that happens in the world can only be conceived as an element into this sequence; into it everything that is known about the world . . . must be fitted as an ingredient of the divine plan.'[13]

Part of Whalley's magnitude derives from Conrad's juxtaposing him with petty and niggling men; it is revealed by contrasting descriptions of the specific details of Whalley's world with Massy's or Sterne's. The contrast between the humanity of Whalley's generation and the bloodless isolation of the successor is illustrated by the descriptions of the shipboard living quarters. Massy's room is 'not so much severe as starved and lacking in humanity, like the ward of a public hospital, or rather (owing to the small size) like the clean retreat of a desperately poor but exemplary person' (p. 260). But then we recall Whalley's stateroom, decorated by his wife, or his subsequent room on the *Fair Maid* after his wife's death:

> He had the cabin arranged in accordance with his simple
> ideal of comfort at sea. A big bookcase (he was a great reader)
> occupied one side of his stateroom; the portrait of his late wife,
> a flat bituminous oil-painting representing the profile and one
> long black ringlet of a young woman, faced his bedplace.
> Three chronometers ticked him to sleep and greeted him on
> waking with the tiny competition of their beats. He rose at five
> every day. The officer of the morning watch, drinking his
> early cup of coffee aft by the wheel, would hear through the
> wide orifice of the copper ventilators all the splashings,
> blowings, and sputterings of his captain's toilet. These noises
> would be followed by a sustained deep murmur of the Lord's
> Prayer recited in a loud earnest voice. (p. 171)

Whalley's room is dominated by his living presence; his books, his words, the sounds of his washing, and the portrait of his loving wife. Objects exist in harmonious relationship with the man to whom they belong. By contrast, the essence of Massy's room is emptiness; to describe it is to note what is lacking; everything is closed, as if humanity and feeling had no place there:

> The absence of the usual settee was striking; the teak-wood top
> of the washing-stand seemed hermetically closed, and so was
> the lid of the writing desk, which protruded from the partition
> at the foot of the bed-place, containing a mattress as thin as a
> pancake under a threadbare blanket with a faded red stripe, and

a folded mosquito-net against the nights spent in harbour. There was not a scrap of paper anywhere in sight, no boots on the floor, no litter of any sort, not a speck of dust anywhere; no traces of pipe-ash even, which, in a heavy smoker, was morally revolting, like a manifestation of extreme hypocrisy; and the bottom of the old wooden arm-chair (the only seat there), polished with much use, shone as if its shabbiness had been waxed. (p. 261)

At one point, the chatty narrator of 'Freya of the Seven Isles' remarks: 'I suppose praiseworthy motives are a sufficient justification almost for anything' (*'Twixt Land and Sea*, p. 179). 'The End of the Tether' explores precisely this statement as it concerns a fundametally decent man. Each of the three men knows Whalley's secret, and each uses the secret to his advantage. Massy is tortured by Sterne who understands him intuitively because they operate on a similar motivational level; both will use people as instruments. But Captain Whalley is also haunted by Sterne's presence. Central to Whalley's belief that the human experience is a *significant* one is his theory of mankind's gradual perfectability; man had progressed, he thought, 'in knowledge of truth, in decency, in justice, in order—in honesty, too, since men harmed each other mostly from ignorance. [The world] was, Captain Whalley concluded quaintly, more pleasant to live in' (p. 288). (The narrator's use of the word 'quaintly' becomes a sardonic comment on the growing disjuncture between Whalley's rhetoric and behaviour.) As he does in 'Falk: A Reminiscence' (completed in 1901) and 'Heart of Darkness' (1899), Conrad whole-heartedly rejects this optimistic rereading of Darwin's theory of evolution which took such forms as the Shavian Life-Force. Whalley's self-serving duplicity, just as much as the predatory behaviour of the succeeding generation of Europeans such as Sterne and Massy, refutes the notion of mankind's progressive evolution.

Whalley thinks that man's justice and God's justice are the same and that the ways of God are explicable to man:

He had drifted into [his falsehood] from parental love, from incredulity, from boundless trust in divine justice meted out to men's feelings on this earth. . . . Surely God would not rob his child of his power to help, and cast him naked into a night without end. He had caught at every hope; and when the

evidence of his misfortunes was stronger than hope; he
tried not to believe the manifest thing. (p. 324)

But in spite of his certainty that his motives are understood, he cannot
deny the fact of his blindness. His optimism, his faith, even his belief in
verbal forms become shaken: 'In the steadily darkening universe, a
sinister clearness fell upon his ideas. In the illuminating moments of
suffering he saw life, men, all things, the whole earth with all her
burden of created nature, as he had never seen them before' (p. 324).
His prayers for death are unanswered: 'All the days of his life he has
prayed, for daily bread, and not to be led into temptation, in a
childlike humility of spirit. Did words mean anything? Whence did
the gift of speech come?' (p. 325). That Whalley trusted in the
magical powers of words to create reality is shown by his faith that
prayer *enables* him to request God's beneficence. But Whalley
discovers that optative does not become indicative. Words are not
capable of incantation, but are just the *names* of hopes and things.
Whalley never repents his sin: The 'recrudescence of moral suffering'
that he feels in Massy's presence is not remorse (p. 325). Whalley
discovers that, like all men, he is defined by time and must reach the
end of the line, what he calls 'the end of the tether'. Once his Christian
epistemology is discredited, it is apparent that Whalley's process of
ageing has been a gradual process of, to use Kenneth Burke's term, an
'inturning towards a nonexistent core'.[14] But he perceives the loss of
light in terms of an act of God that deprives him of his place in the
creation. What could be more excruciating for the man of Faith than
a vision of God's withdrawal until only the 'dark waste' of chaos
remains? 'God had not listened to his prayers. The light had finished
ebbing out of the world; not a glimmer. It was a dark waste; but it was
unseemly that a Whalley who had gone so far to carry a point should
continue to live. He must pay the price' (p. 333). Conrad shows that
Whalley instinctively reverts to an older tradition of ending his life
nobly.[15] But there is an element of self-deception in his notion of a
seemly death because it is based on carefully planned commercial
arrangements by which he provides for his daughter.

   Whalley's death does accomplish his wish of saving his money for
his daughter, and it also draws Van Wyck out of his cocoon.
Disappointed in love, Van Wyck had substracted himself from the
human community and become a rather cynical observer. But his
perception of Whalley's quality impels him to make a moral
commitment, although paradoxically, to keep Whalley's secret, he

must resort to subterfuge. He intervened on Whalley's behalf by offering to provide Sterne with the essential capital which the latter can offer Massy in exchange for the command of the *Sofala*. In exchange for this bribe, Sterne will not expose Whalley's secret. Originally, Whalley's rhetoric appealed to him: 'What men wanted was to be checked by superior intelligence, by superior knowledge, by superior force, too—yes, by force held in trust from God and sanctified by its use in accordance with His declared will' (p. 289). But, finally, Whalley becomes a significant figure for Van Wyck *because* he understands (just as Marlow in 'Heart of Darkness' does when he lies to the Intended) that no man can live by self-created absolutes:

> The fact of Captain Whalley's blindness had opened his eyes to his own. There were many sorts of heartaches and troubles, and there was no place where they could not find a man out. . . . It seemed necessary that he should come out into the world, for a time at least. . . . It weighed on him now— and Captain Whalley appeared to him as he had sat shading his eyes, as if, being deceived in the trust of his faith, he were beyond all the good and evil that can be wrought by the hands of men. (pp. 315–16)

The traditional metaphor of a voyage through time replaces the typological perspective of a contemporary man as a patriarch. After his death, the lawyer stresses what Whalley had seemed to imply about himself:

> The old fellow looked as though he had come into the world full grown and with that long beard. . . . He looked indestructible by any ordinary means that put an end to the rest of us. His deliberate, stately courtesy of manner was full of significance. It was as though he were certain of having plenty of time for everything. Yes, there was something indestructible about him; and the way he talked sometimes you might have thought he believed it himself. (pp. 336–7)

But Whalley's fate demonstrates the impossibility of suspending durational time; for Conrad, a human life is not a significant event within a pattern of history informed by God.

## NOTES

1. In his *Conrad: A Reassessment* (Cambridge: Bowes and Bowes, 1952), Douglas Hewitt suggests that the title figure's effect on the narrator is an extremely important part of 'Falk: A Reminiscence' (pp. 40–5). Despite his penetrating comments, the disregard of the narrator's role has led to the misunderstanding and relative neglect of this excellent tale. See also Bruce Johnson, 'Conrad's "Falk": Manuscript and Meaning', *Modern Language Quarterly*, vol. xxvi (June 1965). In his important article Johnson underestimates the importance of the narrator's relationship with Falk and thus writes that 'the story is ill-suited for the intellectual and emotional burden it simultaneously carries and avoids' (p. 276).

2. It may well be that Conrad's references to the tale as 'Falk' in his Author's Note are primarily responsible for the traditional foreshortening of the title.

   We might recall that Conrad wrote in the same note, 'If we go by mere facts then the subject is Falk's attempt to get married; in which the narrator of the tale finds himself unexpectedly involved both on its ruthless and its delicate side.' But Conrad may well be mocking any attempt to 'go by mere facts'.

3. John A. Lester, jun., *Journey Through Despair 1890–1914: Transformations in British Literary Culture* (Princeton: Princeton University Press, 1968), p. 41.

4. In a splendid article, Robert Andreach, 'The Two Narrators of "Amy Foster"', *Studies in Short Fiction*, vol. ii (1965), pp. 262–9, argues that Dr Kennedy diminishes his own guilt. Karl discusses the biographical implications of Amy Foster', particularly the 'exogamous marriage, a continuing aspect of Conrad's work'. See *Joseph Conrad: The Three Lives*, pp. 513–15.

5. As Andreach puts it, 'The classical allusions are Kennedy's attempt to remove the necessity for seeking a natural explanation for the events, and the excess of rhetoric—repetition, questions, negatives—demonstrates that he cannot comprehend what he witnessed' (ibid., p. 262).

6. See my 'The Narrator as Character in Hardy's Major Fiction', *Modern Fiction Studies*, vol. iv (Summer 1972), pp. 155–72, and 'Speaking of Paul Morel: Voice, Unity, and Meaning in *Sons and Lovers*', *Studies in the Novel*, vol. viii (1976), pp. 255–77.

7. John Howard Wills, 'Conrad's "Typhoon": A Triumph in Organic Art', *North Dakota Quarterly*, vol. xxx (1962), pp. 62–70.

8. For views of women and sexuality in the period, see Hynes, *The Edwardian Turn of Mind* (Princeton: Princeton University Press, 1968) chaps. 5, 6, 8.

9. Lester, pp. 177–81.

10. Ibid.

11. See William Moynihan, 'Conard's "The End of the Tether": A New Reading', *Modern Fiction Studies*, vol. iv (Summer 1958), pp. 173–7; reprinted in Robert W. Stallman, *The Art of Joseph Conrad: A Critical Symposium* (East Lansing: Michigan State University Press, 1960), pp. 186–91; See pp. 187–8.

12. William Blackburn (ed.), *Joseph Conrad: Letters to William Blackwood and David S. Meldrum* (Durham: Duke University Press, 1958), Autumn, 1902, pp. 169–70.

13. Erich Auerbach, *Mimesis: The Representation of Reality in Western Literature*, trans. Willard Trask (Princeton: Princeton University Press, 1953), p. 13.

14. Kenneth Burke, *The Philosophy of Literary Form*, rev. ed. (New York: Vintage, 1957), p. 71.

15. Lawrence Graver, *Conrad's Short Fiction* (Berkeley and Los Angeles: University of California Press, 1969) argues that Whalley's end is not heroic, for 'Whalley, like Kurtz, sees the horror of his life and his memory perpetuated by an enormous lie' (p. 118; see pp. 113–19).

# Part Two
# Politics

# 7 Conrad's quarrel with politics: The disrupted family in *Nostromo*

## I

Conrad's novels about politics have been viewed both as nihilistic statements and dramatisations of a political vision. While the subject of these novels—*Nostromo, The Secret Agent*, and *Under Western Eyes*—is often politics, their values are not political. The novels affirm the primacy of family, the sanctity of the individual, the value of love, and the importance of sympathy and understanding in human relations. Conrad's friendships with Cunninghame Graham, Wells, and Shaw show that he put personal relationships before political ideology. His concern for the working class derives not from political theory but from his experience as a seaman and from his imaginative response to the miseries of others. Conrad's humanism informs his political vision. In his political writings, it is the abstractions upholding private virtues that carry conviction. He wrote in 'Autocracy and War' (1905) that it was to 'our sympathetic imagination' that we must 'look for the ultimate triumph of concord and justice' (*NLL*, p. 84). In 'Autocracy and War' the paramount values threatened by Russian autocracy are 'dignity', 'truth', 'rectitude', and 'all that is faithful in human nature' (*NLL*, p. 99). Thus, Russia is 'a yawning chasm open between East and West; a bottomless abyss that has swallowed up every hope of mercy, every aspiration towards personal dignity, towards freedom, towards knowledge, every ennobling desire of the heart, every redeeming whisper of conscience' (*NLL*, p. 100).

In discussing the political novels I shall take very seriously a number of contentions made by Avrom Fleishman in his influential study of Conrad's politics. Despite Conrad's conservatism, I find little evidence to support his thesis that Conrad regards the state as 'a source, perhaps the only source, of the values by and for which [individuals] live'.[1] Nor do I believe Conrad emphasises 'the primacy of the community, which gives individual life its possibility and its value'.[2] Perhaps on board ship the community must take precedence over the individual in moments of crises. But Conrad's fiction argues for the *primacy* of the individual and perceives social organisations as necessary evils. My readings of the specific novels rejects Fleishman's contention that 'the alienated man is either redeemed or not only insofar as he is able to identify his personal career with the life of a community'.[3]

The ideas expressed in 'Autocracy and War' (1905) are pivotal to Fleishman's arguments. Yet these ideas are not dramatised in the political novels.[4] In that essay, Conrad proposes abstract ideals rather than political theory, shibboleths rather than working programmes; for example, he writes: 'The common ground of concord, good faith and justice is not sufficient to establish an action upon; since the conscience of but very few men amongst us, and of no single Western nation as yet, will brook the restraint of abstract ideas as against the fascination of material advantage' (*NLL*, p. 111). But the essay boils down to two central points. Above all, Conrad is opposed to autocracy. Secondly, he uncharacteristically affirms a belief in the evolution of both nations and mankind:

> The true greatness of a State . . . is a matter of logical growth,
> of faith and courage. Its inspiration springs from the
> constructive instinct of the people, governed by the strong
> hand of a collective conscience and voiced in the wisdom and
> counsel of men who seldom reap the reward of
> gratitude. . . . A revolution is a short cut in the rational
> development of national needs in response to the growth of
> world-wide ideals. (*NLL*, pp. 91, 101)

But the political novels belie this optimism and reduce it to fustian. In the political novels Conrad is disillusioned with materialism, and imagines that 'industrialism and commercialism' may foster wars between democracies. Like Dostoevsky, Conrad disavows the 'Crystal Palace', the Victorian symbol of science and progress: 'The dreams sanguine humanitarians raised almost to ecstasy about the year 'fifty of the last century by the moving sight of the Crystal Palace—crammed full with that variegated rubbish which it seems to be the bizarre fate of humanity to produce for the benefit of a few employers of labour—have vanished as quickly as they had arisen' (*NLL*, p. 106). His famous image of a universe created by an indifferent knitting machine is an ironic comment on the pretensions of industrial machinery to wear the mantle of human progress: 'It knits us in and it knits us out. It has knitted time, space, pain, death, corruption, despair and all the illusions—and nothing matters. I'll admit however that to look at the remorseless process is sometimes amusing' (20 Dec. 1897; *LL*, vol. i, p. 216). In such a mechanistic, amoral world, Conrad understands the necessity for political and social organisation. While he dissects flaws in various systems, states, and communities he does not propose alternative programmes. But he does insist on preserving the freedom of the individual to live his own life as long as he does not pose a physical threat to others.

II

Criticism that insists upon discussing *Nostromo* from a predominantly political perspective often seems to confuse the novel's subject matter with its novel's values.[5] When Conrad created imagined worlds with a political and historical dimension, as he did most notably in the three consecutive novels generally classified as political novels—*Nostromo* (1904), *The Secret Agent* (1907), and *Under Western Eyes* (1911), he was concerned less with political theory than with the cost of politics in terms of disruption of family ties, of personal relationships and, ultimately, of personal growth. To be sure, Conrad was fascinated by political doctrines, movements, and ideals. But he despaired that political activity could make a difference in a world he regarded as a 'remorseless process'. He sadly realised that political activity fails because most men are selfish; those who are not selfish are victims of their own obsession, and thus are incapable of sustained activity on behalf of the community. I shall not deny that Conrad considers how, why, and for what values men organise themselves into nations, communities, parties, factions, and interest groups. But I shall argue that Conrad indicts political activity as both suspect in its causes and pernicious in its effects. In his view, Costaguana's oscillation between revolution and autocracy, between succession and federation, has little to do with the governance of men. Even at the close, when Gould's vision for the mine is fulfilled and Sulaco flourishes, the conditions for the next revolutionary uprising are growing, like poisonous mushrooms, in the discontented hearts of Captain Fidanza and his comrade, the malevolent 'blood-thirsty' photographer.

With deep regret, Conrad came to believe that political activity was a threat to the traditional paradigms on which civilisation depends: heterosexual relationships, family relations between parents and child as well as siblings, and personal relationships—between all those who seek to understand and to be understood, to love and to be loved. Thus, in the political novels, Conrad posits interpersonal relationships and family ties as *alternative* values to political doctrines, while he demonstrates that man can be destroyed when he allows political abstractions to subsume his private self. In *Nostromo*, even when high-minded characters espouse ideals, political principles are thinly veiled disguises for the desire to control the enormous treasure of the San Tomé mine. Because of their own obsessions and moral weaknesses, the Goulds, Decoud, Antonia, Nostromo, and even the Viola family are engulfed by politics created by the insistent demands of materialism. *Nostromo* is the story of men who, while seeking to define their own lives in bold and heroic terms, become entrapped by the circumstances that they seek to control and the political activity in which they engage.

The disrupted chronology, the rapidly shifting focus, and the ominous instability of the ending dramatise a world which has lost its moral centre, a world in which 'the best lack all conviction, while the worst/Are full of passionate intensity'.[6] The form is a correlative to a narrative about a civilisation that lacks a moral centre. Like *Dubliners*, *Nostromo* is really a series of episodes in the moral history of a nation; Costaguana and Sulaco are metaphors for a nation and a major city under siege. Despite the hectic activity—the political machinations, the riots and uprisings, the marches and retreats—the novel moves towards climactic moments when the major characters are isolated and must discover the essential self that has survived the public self. The scenes in which Mrs Gould gradually and incompletely awakens to her loneliness, Gould to his position as an adventurer, Nostromo to the awareness that he has been manipulated by those who do not care for him, are all the more effective because they are in stark contrast to the rapid and confusing external events. Decoud's excruciating discovery of his moral emptiness and his subsequent suicide are rhetorically and structurally climactic because each of the major characters has already discovered an inner self, distinct from the position which society defines for him. No matter what illusion or abstraction to which a character has committed himself—whether it be Viola's republicanism, Monygham's devotion, Gould's idealism, Nostromo's 'good name'—each major character returns to a position in which he is alone, stripped of his public self, and exposed to the the vicissitudes of an indifferent cosmos. At first, each major character is depicted as part of the social and political order of Sulaco; only then is he examined in his private facet and shown to be serving not the community but dimly understood psychic needs and unacknowledged obsessions. Conrad reveals that each of the major characters—even idealists like the Goulds upon whom civilisation depends—has given himself to serving an external political or economic entity and, in doing so, has sacrificed his or her own possibilities for love, friendship, and self-development.

## III

If we first consider the Goulds, we shall see that *Nostromo* stresses how fanatic commitment to economic goals and concomitant political action can destroy the relationship between man and wife. Moreover, we shall see how Gould's public self derives from private needs and psychological causes that he neither understands nor acknowledges. Gould's plan to revive the mine illustrates the way that a man gives the the *names* of ideals to his psychic needs and libidinous impulses. He has an irrational need to revive the mine, to perform a ritualistic act of slaying the dragon which slew his father. An infantile but understandable anger at the death of his absent but revered father, and the shock to his own identity now that he has no father figure to sustain him, are causes of his wilful disobedience of his father's wish that he not return to Costaguana. Gould defines his goals to his wife in terms of moral abstractions which he *must* believe:

> I pin my faith to material interests. Only let the material
> interests once get a firm footing, and they are bound to impose
> the conditions on which they alone can continue to exist.
> That's how your money-making is justified here in the face of
> lawlessness and disorder. It is justified because the security
> which it demands must be shared with an oppressed people. A
> better justice will come afterwards. That's your ray of hope.
> (p. 84)

But this speech, filled with non sequiturs and with wishes posing as logic, shows how Gould seeks to transform his own subjective needs into a viable political theory. As he had idealised his father, he now idealises his own motives. Yet Conrad is not without sympathy for those such as Gould, or even the subservient Tekla and the fanatic Haldin in *Under Western Eyes*, all of whom believe that political action can make a difference. As Decoud understands of Gould, 'He could not believe his own motives if he did not make them first a part of some fairy tale' (p. 215). Gould's irrational and subconscious needs to assuage his conscience because of his absence while his father was victimised, and to revenge himself on the forces that he consciously blames for the death of his father, have entrapped him into compulsive behavior that prevents him from fulfilling his wife sexually or emotionally.

In a crucial passage the narrator makes clear that Gould's material and political ideals derive from his obsession with his father's defeat.

It hurt Charles Gould to feel that never more, by no effort of will, would he be able to think of his father in the same way he used to think of him when the poor man was alive. His breathing image was no longer in his power. This consideration, closely affecting his own identity, filled his breast with a mournful and angry desire for action. In this his instinct was unerring. Action is consolatory. It is the enemy of thought and the friend of flattering illusions. Only in the conduct of our action can we find the sense of mastery over the Fates. . . . He resolved firmly to make his disobedience as thorough (by way of atonement) as it well could be. The mine had been the cause of an absurd moral disaster; its working must be made a serious moral success. He owed it to the dead man's memory. (pp. 65–6)

While Gould might believe in his idealistic abstractions, his 'faith' in material interests derives in large part from an irrational need to defeat the forces that defeated his father. The narrator's analysis of Gould's motives for disobeying his father's express wish that his son avoid the 'curse' of the mine stresses the irrational and emotional basis for that decision.

Mrs Gould, as an orphan, responds to Gould because he is an authoritarian Victorian father figure who provides resolution and direction to her life. Living a drab life with a nearly destitute and eccentric aunt, she is psychologically ready to be 'inspired by an idealistic view of success' that professes to be interested in the mine because it will create the appropriate conditions for 'law, good faith, order, security' (pp. 67, 84). She lacks the will to oppose his indomitable ego because she needs to apotheosise him. She believes his abstract parables because they give her 'a fascinating vision of herself' as a companion in heroic activities (p. 65). She is attracted to Gould's 'unsentimentalism' and, as the narrator notes facetiously, 'that very quietude of mind which she had *erected in her thought* for a sign of perfect competency in the business of living' (p. 50, emphasis mine).

Gould's libidinous energies are engaged by the mine instead of his relationship to his wife. The first silver that the mine produces is described in terms that suggest a demonic birth: '[Mrs Gould] laid her unmercenary hands, with an eagerness that made them tremble, upon the first [spungy lump] turned out still warm from the mould; and by her imaginative estimate of its power she endowed that lump of metal with a justificative conception, as though it were not a mere fact, but something far-reaching and impalpable, like the true expression of an emotion or the emergence of a principle' (p. 107). Mrs Gould is midwife to silver rather than mother to children. Just as the uncorrupted waterfall becomes galvanised into a silver-fall, Gould's sexual substance becomes a stream of silver and his offspring a lump of silver: '[Mrs. Gould] heard with a thrill of thankful emotion the first wagon load of ore rattle down the then only shoot; she had stood by her husband's side perfectly silent, and gone cold all over with excitement . . . when the first battery . . . was put in motion for the first time' (p. 107). She has sublimated her sexual needs and has tacitly permitted the production of the silver to become his homage to her and to substitute for intercourse. The result is not only a childless marriage, but her becoming a lonely, isolated, sexually frustrated woman. Potentially tender moments climax not with intimacy but with Gould's return to the mine at night. For the spongy lump grows into a wall that divides her from her husband:

> She had watched . . . [the mine] turning into a fetish, and now
> the fetish had grown into a monstrous and crushing weight. It
> was as if the inspiration of their early years had left her heart
> to turn into a wall of silver-bricks. . . . He seemed to dwell
> alone within a circumvallation of precious metal, leaving her
> outside with her school, her hospital, the sick mothers, and the

feeble old men, were insignificant vestiges of the initial inspiration. (pp. 221–2)

Mrs. Gould's solitude and personal deprivation are progressive conditions, evolving and increasing in intensity as a direct response to the success of the mine and the growth of Gould's public identity as Señor Administrator and as the King of Sulaco. It is almost as if by a process of grotesque metamorphosis Gould was turned into 'the mysterious weight of a taciturn force' (p. 203). Part of Gould's tragedy is that his position as 'King of Sulaco' and his concomitant identification with the mine have transformed him into an extension of the inanimate world. Because he has *become* synonymous with the mine, it is ironically appropriate that he uses silence as a means of communicating its power and force: 'Behind [his silences] there was the great San Tomé mine, the head and font of the material interests, so strong that it depended on no man's good-will . . .' (p. 203). Because Gould's libidinous needs are fulfilled through the 'flow' of the mine, he plans to respond to a challenge to his position by destroying it. For all his high-minded ideals, Gould's real interest is in dominating and controlling the mine. His fantasies of playing what he calls 'my last card' and 'send[ing] half Sulaco into the air if I liked' reveal him as a rogue, a 'hustler' and a megalomaniac on the model of Kurtz (pp. 67, 204, 206). The self-controlled and repressed Gould may at first glance seem Kurtz's opposite, but Gould's subordination of ends to means is a repressed and respectable version of Kurtz's reversion to savagery. Both are imperialists who espouse the highest ideals, but their actions undermine the stability and morality of the indigenous culture that they expect to civilise. Yet Conrad is grimly sympathetic to Gould, while he regards Kurtz as a man who lacks all 'restraints in the gratification of his lusts'. Just as Kurtz turns from his Intended, once he has made his political, materialistic and sexual conquests, Charles Gould turns from his wife to the mine when she is no longer required to fulfil his ego. (The reader understands that she is really the first external entity that he has conquered and dominated.)

Mrs Gould embodies an English tradition of manners and morals for which Conrad's respect grew throughout his career. Like Woolf's Mrs Ramsay, she perpetuates personal warmth, generosity and hospitality; in doing so, she creates an alternative to the turmoil of political ructions and materialistic greed. Even while repressing her own sexuality, she provides warmth, understanding, and sympathy not only to her husband, Monygham, and the Viola family, but to Decoud, Sir John, and finally to Nostromo himself. After five chapters in which cultivated behaviour and civilised discourse between two individuals have been ostentatiously absent, she is presented without irony as a woman 'guided by an alert perception of values. She was highly gifted in the art of human intercourse, which consists in delicate shades of self-forgetfulness and in the suggestion of universal comprehension' (p. 46). By circumstances rather than choice, she dedicates herself to perpetuate Agape rather than Eros. Conrad understands that Mrs Gould's character is partially determined by the frustrations of her marriage. The repeated juxtaposition of her with the statue of the Madonna on the staircase and the image of her as a good fairy emphasise the connection between her asexuality and her position as a viable alternative to her husband's values. Her sexless and loveless marriage is stressed upon her return from Europe by the presence of the icon of Madonna and Child, which 'seemed to welcome her with an aspect of pitying tenderness', and by the emphasis on the fecundity of Basilio and Leonardo p. 505). The failure of the doctor to develop his interest beyond worshipful devotion anticipates the narrator's poignant summary, a summary which almost seems an epitaph for a woman whose life has been all but completed: Mrs Gould is 'wealthy beyond great dreams of wealth, considered, loved, respected, honoured, and as solitary as any human being had ever been, perhaps, on this earth' (p. 555). Although Mrs Gould's public role as the 'first lady of Sulaco' remains unchanged, 'the silver threads' beneath her 'fair hair' indicate metaphorically how she, too—like Nostromo and her husband—has become a slave of the mine (p. 555).

Notwithstanding her role in resurrecting Dr Monygham, her dignity, harmony and warmth are not effectual. Nor does her social position fulfil her. As Mrs Gould gradually becomes aware of the mine's gruesome effects upon her husband, and turns towards Dr Monygham for some crumbs of human relationship, her own feeling of solitude increases. When Gould announces that he will openly support the plan of separation, Mrs Gould is no longer concerned with participating in his imaginative world. Although it is the narrator who makes the harsh judgement about Gould's sanity, she intuitively knows more than she can acknowledge to herself:

Mrs. Gould watched his abstraction with dread. It was a
domestic and frightful phenomenon that darkened and chilled

the house for her like a thunder-cloud passing over the sun.
Charles Gould's fits of abstraction depicted the energetic concentration of a will haunted by a fixed idea. A man haunted by
a fixed idea is insane. He is dangerous even if that idea is an
idea of justice; for may he not bring the heaven down pitilessly
upon a loved head? (p. 379)

Before Dr Monygham leaves Mrs Gould in the scene in which both
fail to seize the opportunity of passionate love because of their
acceptance of social conventions, the narrator notes that Mrs Gould's
'immobility' and 'grace' give 'her seated figure the charm of art, of an
attitude caught and interpreted forever' (p. 520). The narrator
emphasises that Monygham is sexually attracted to her. But both
repress their sexual needs in a peculiar psychodrama in which
Monygham's libido finds an outlet in 'an augmented grimness of
speech' (p. 513). Her entirely uncharacteristic 'smile of gentle malice'
shows Conrad's awareness of libidinous, but sublimated needs; yet
her passion in this interview remains repressed as she contents herself
with discussing the sexual activities of others.

   Mrs Gould's response to Antonia's loss of Decoud reflects her own
plight. While Mrs Gould is consciously empathising with a woman
whose deprivation seems an alternative to her fulfilment, she
subconsciously sees Antonia's life as a version of her own just as surely
as Brierly (and, to a lesser extent, Marlow) judges himself when he
had been asked to judge Jim's case. But Mrs Gould's complex
defences will not allow her to look too deeply into her own case:
' "What would I have done if Charley had been drowned while we
were engaged?" she exclaimed mentally, with horror. Her heart
turned to ice, while her cheeks flamed up as if scorched by the blaze of
a funeral pyre consuming all her earthly affections' (p. 379).
Ironically, the funeral pyre is for the values that Mrs Gould represents
and which are defeated by materialism and political machinations.
Mrs Gould's final meditation on her husband dramatises her
continued need to believe in her husband's sanctimonious abstractions, despite her knowledge that something has gone egregiously
wrong in the behaviour of the man she apotheosised. Always
idealising and sentimentalising like her husband (whom *she* now had
difficulty thinking of except in his public position as Senor
Administrador), she needs to place his behaviour in the context of a
comfortable theory: 'There was something inherent in the necessities
of successful action which carried with it the moral degradation of the

idea' (p. 521). (Since the entire paragraph is her meditation, this speech should not, as some critics have argued, be thought of as Conrad's message.) Yet, in a moment of poignant honesty and profound cynicism, she acknowledges her isolation and the deterioration of her hopes and dreams when she tells Giselle: 'I have been loved, too' (p. 561).


IV


Nostromo, the man garbed in silver trappings, is the offspring of the mine. Virtually anonymous, with only the vaguest claims to a personal past or national identity, he is metaphorically the spongy lump of silver metamorphosed into a fully grown adult. Nostromo is the child of materialism and imperialism; he is created by the needs of Mitchell and, later by Gould, as a human instrument which can be depended upon to place the interests of those he serves before his own. That he belongs to the imperialists and their political interests is implied by the title that has been conferred upon him by those he serves: Nostromo, 'our man'. Such a name deprives him of a personal identity in the eyes of those he serves. When he flippantly promises the chief engineer that he will 'take care' of Sir John 'as if [he] were his father', he acknowledges the patrimony of materialism and concomitantly neglects his own need for human relationships (p. 43).

Nostromo's relation to the cargadores and natives parallels Gould's position with the aristocrats. Both are motivated by intense vanity which is related to their needs to compensate for a disrupted family. Both rely on taciturnity and detachment to maintain that position, and both are treated almost like royalty by obsequious followers because of the power they are perceived to hold. When Nostromo gradually drifts into bondage to the treasure, he becomes Gould's double. The following might just as well be written of Gould: '[Nostromo] sat down on the soft earth, unresisting, as if he had been chained to the treasure, his drawn-up legs clasped in his hands with an air of hopeless submission, like a slave set on guard' (p. 495). The terms on which he rebels only establish the dominance of the paternity of material interests. He wants to overthrow the flourishing regime he helped to establish. He supports a socialist party which seeks to undermine the authority figures whom he allowed to become his political fathers in place of Viola; he wants to assuage his guilt for betraying the trust of the people, specifically the cargadores, even though Sulaco's prosperity has clearly brought tangible benefits to the people. His rightful name, Fidanza, is an ironic suggestion of *fidanza*, the Italian word for 'confidence', the quality for which he is recognised by others but which in its most profound sense he lacks, and of the Latin root, *fidelitas*, or loyalty, the value he has implicitly renounced.

The most important facts in shaping Nostromo's prior life are that he is an orphan and that he had been exploited by an abusive uncle. But he has found in the Violas a surrogate family to whom he is deeply attached. The Violas address him by his rightful name, offer him a home, and treat him as a replacement for the son whom they had lost. Amidst the political turmoil that ensues upon Don Ribiera's overthrow, he makes his first appearance 'protecting his own', the Violas (p. 16). He allows Teresa to berate him as a mother would a son because he instinctively realises that she is concerned with his welfare, concerned lest he become the chattel of the English.

That he places great value on his relationship with his surrogate mother is emphasised by the guilt he feels for refusing to get Teresa a priest. His is the response of a man to whom family claims are of very great importance. He takes his failure to fulfil her request hardly less seriously than Jim takes his jump from the *Patna* or Razumov takes his betrayal of Haldin. Because at this point he desperately needs to have her love and understanding, Nostromo calls Teresa 'mother' and offers explanations that contrast with his usual taciturnity. He had with Teresa a strange love-hate intimacy which at times was almost Oedipal in its passionate intensity. Just as Gould needs to atone for his father's death, so Nostromo must atone for a 'burden of sacrilegious guilt' (p. 420) which makes him believe that he has prevented the salvation of Teresa's eternal soul by placing his duty to the mine ahead of his duty to his surrogate mother. As soon as he is on the lighter, he begins to fret about not fulfilling her wishes, even though he tries to rationalise that with Father Corbelàn away, no priest would have come. He is obsessed with his refusal, and as Jim does to Marlow, he becomes loquacious to Decoud because he seeks to justify himself *to himself* and also establish a personal tie to Decoud. Explaining to Decoud why he had not killed Hirsch, Nostromo shows how his primitive superego acknowledges and seeks fraternal ties: 'I could not do it. Not after I had seen you holding up the can to his lips, as though he were your brother' (p. 284).[7]

It is after he has violated Teresa's wishes that he has a radical conversion experience and adopts Viola's political values and

Theresa's religious epistemology. Since, despite his physical prowess, he is an emotional and moral child Nostromo requires both an authority figure and someone who will respond to his needs for understanding and sympathy. Therefore he seeks Giorgio. For the first time, praise is not enough and Nostromo requires extrinsic values. He pathetically builds his entire existence upon a few bromides: Viola's judgement that the poor are 'dogs' of the rich and Teresa's curse of 'poverty, misery, and starvation'. These reductive formulae become the basis for his behaviour; when he acknowledges the legitimacy of their advice, he does so completely. The restoration of Nostromo to his surrogate father, while the latter is lost in desolation, provides a striking dramatic alternative to the political ructions and selfishness that rage around the Casa Viola. But Viola cannot fulfil Nostromo's need for an understanding and responsive auditor; Nostromo, to whom words have become important now that the paean of public praise is seen as sham, is certain that 'the old man understood nothing of [his] words' (p. 469). Even while somewhat resentful of the comparison to the imagined character of the deceased son, Nostromo responds to Viola's 'strong voice' because Viola's approval of him as a surrogate 'grown-up son' still matters.

The last chapters with their arabesque plot are written more as romance than as mimetic novel; they illustrate how materialism corrupts family ties and prevents passionate love. Since Nostromo is an adopted son, on the face of it his love for either sister is not incestuous. But Nostromo perceives that Linda seems to play the roles of mother to Giselle and wife to Viola: 'Linda, with her mother's voice, had taken more her mother's place. Her deep vibrating "Eh, Padre?" seemed, but for the change of the word, the very echo of the impassioned, remonstrating "Eh, Giorgio?" of poor Signora Teresa' (p. 529). Although Linda would willingly be submissive, Nostromo can perceive her only as a younger version of Teresa. Because the Violas have shaped whatever superego he has, Linda serves as a constant reminder to him that he both betrayed the trust of his surrogate parents by stealing the treasure and denied Teresa's last request. While Giselle is passive, quiescent, and submissive, Linda is a replica of her parents: 'Linda, with her intense, passionately pale face, energetic, all fire and words, touched with gloom and scorn, a chip off the old block, true daughter of the austere republican, but with Teresa's voice, inspired him with a deep-seated mistrust' (p. 524).

Just like Gould, Nostromo is perceived in terms of an illicit sexual relationship to the materialistic world. He has anthropomorphised the treasure into a beloved object: 'He yearned to clasp, embrace, absorb, subjugate in unquestioned possession this treasure, whose tyranny had weighed upon his mind, his actions, his very sleep' (p. 529). The narrator renders his bondage to the silver in psychosexual language that obliquely suggests Nostromo's need (not unlike the doctor's) to abase himself. Nostromo cannot simply carry off Giselle because 'The slave of the San Tomé silver felt the weight as of chains upon his limbs, a pressure as of a cold hand upon his lips' (p. 539). When Giselle asks what stands between her and him, he answers 'a treasure' (p. 540). The silver has become an invisible wall that divides the two lovers. The parallel to the Goulds is evident. Because Nostromo is submissive to the silver, it is all the more important to him that he choose a woman who will allow him to be dominant. If he could tell Giselle his secret, he feels that he could break the spell of the treasure which holds him in bondage and win his release. But his psyche *requires* the libidinous bondage to the silver: 'The spectre of the unlawful treasure arose, standing by her side like a figure of silver, pitiless and secret with a finger upon its pale lips. . . . It seemed to him that [Giselle] ought to hear the clanking of his fetters—his silver fetters—from afar' (pp. 542, 546). This perverse bondage causes his death. Because he is wedded to the silver, because 'he had welded that vein of silver into his life', Nostromo chooses the very kind of light-headed woman that he formerly patronised (p. 526). He is sexually attracted to her because he can compensate for his bondage to the silver by being the dominant authoritative figure that he cannot be for Linda. While Linda 'pronounces [his] name with her mother's intonation' which makes Nostromo experience 'a gloom as of the grave', Nostromo thinks of Giselle as a 'child' to whom he can minister (p. 532). (At one point with Giselle he becomes 'gentle and caressing, like a woman to the grief of a child' [p. 538]).

Nostromo's death derives from the conflict between materialism and its morals with an older tradition in which the family's honour is a paramount value and in which courtship must take place under the auspices of the father's approval. While the mine has created conditions in which Nostromo cannot fulfil his positions as betrothed and as adopted son, the reason for his failure is that, as Marlow says of Jim, he is not good enough, that is, he is psychically and morally flawed. Politically, Nostromo is not a man of principle but a *tabula rasa* until educated by materialism. Had Nostromo not been in bondage to the silver, he might in his role of adopted son have already taken his place beside Viola and be in the position of defending the family

honour against unwanted intruders. In the traditional family, Giorgio
would have become the charge of his married daughter and son-in-
law as he approached senility. After Viola's shot separates him from
his father and love, he turns desperately to Mrs Gould as a
replacement for Teresa; she becomes for him a mother figure to
whom he turns to make a dying confession and thus undo Teresa's
curse. Ironically, he requires the kind of personal solace that he had
failed to provide for Teresa in a similar position. Their final dialogue,
in which Mrs Gould's 'genius of sympathetic intuition' responds to
Nostromo's needs and in which he finds for the first time a woman in
whom he can confide, dramatically illustrates the efficacy and value of
personal relationships (p. 560).

## V

Decoud's parents are alive, but they are remote from his thoughts,
possibly because he regards the mother and father who are 'ruled' by
his sister, as ineffectual (p. 223). As we learn when Decoud faces
suicide, he cannot sustain an image of his past relationships because he
does not believe in himself. In Costaguana, he unconsciously seeks to
compensate for his lack of parental authority by seeking the approval
and authority of Don José and Mrs Gould. After his impassioned
speech to the Notables from the Assembly in which he argues against
surrender, it is Don José's exhortation, 'In God's name, then, Martin,
my son!' which gives him the energy to pursue his plan for separation
(p. 236). (Although Decoud interprets Don José's words as specific
endorsement for his plan, what he approved is his idea of resisting the
Montero brothers.) The emphasis that Decoud puts upon Don José's
sanction is demonstrated by his not only excitedly repeating it to
Antonia, but repeating it with the important embellishment that
reflects his own need to intensify and to specify the completeness of
his approval: 'Your father told me to *go on* in God's name' (p. 238,
emphasis mine). The parallels to Nostromo's case are significant. Like
Nostromo, Decoud is a surrogate son to the father of his beloved.
Like Linda, Antonia is motherless and has become a virtual nurse of an
invalid, senile father. It may be that Antonia's attraction to Decoud,
like Linda's to Nostromo, is intensified by her father's acknowledge-
ment of paternal feelings for her beloved. Furthermore, Decoud
offers Antonia the completed family that she lacks: 'My sister is only
waiting to embrace you. My father is transported with joy. I won't

say anything of my mother! Our mothers were like sisters' (p. 182).

Decoud, the man who is alternately cynic and romantic, alternately pragmatist and idealist; the man whose perceptive analysis of others often goes beyond the narrator's understanding; the man who uses the written word to rescue his identity is, like Marlow, a character from whom Conrad is at times barely able to distance himself. Decoud is Conrad's mirror, and the distance between Conrad's voice and his character dissolves when he narrates Decoud's complete inability to cope with his solitude.[8] Decoud's final nihilism and self-hate objectify qualities that Conrad despised in himself.

Decoud is deeply committed to Antonia, in direct contradiction of the narrator's remark that he had 'no faith in anything except the truth of his own sensations' (p. 229). He has idealised his love into a sustaining illusion as Gould does the mine and Nostromo his reputation. For Decoud politics is always a disguise for personal motives. But after five days of solitude and silence, he no longer draws 'strength' and 'inspiration' from her love because he ceases to believe in the value of his own existence or in the possibility that others might care for him. His mind becomes his hell, a hell without the people and relationships that are for him the only source of value. Decoud depends upon Don José, Antonia, and his sister to define him. Like the Captain in 'The Secret Sharer', like Marlow in 'Heart of Darkness', Decoud desperately needs a responsive human being who will understand, share, and hopefully approve his motives and feelings. In a passage that qualifies the narrator's own allegation that Decoud is a cynic, the narrator defines an interpersonal relationship that Decoud seeks as an alternative to the pursuit of wealth and power: 'Friendship was possible between brother and sister, meaning by friendship the frank unreserve, as before another human being, of thoughts and sensations; all the objectless and necessary sincerity of one's innermost life trying to re-act upon the profound sympathies of another existence' (p. 223). His love for Antonia depends in part on his belief that he can find in the same person both a heterosexual partner and a responsive consciousness. For him, the climactic moment in his relationship with Antonia is when he penetrates her austerity and provokes her to respond to his melodramatic vision of his own death. But once apart from her his belief that she understood him gradually fades.

Like Nostromo, Antonia is disenchanted with the stability of the Occidental Republic, and feels compelled to support the plan of her uncle, Father Corbelàn, to annex Costaguana. After Decoud's and her father's death, Antonia requires as a surrogate father her unbending and authoritarian uncle. Lacking a passionate love, she turns her libidinous energies to political 'remedy'. She now identifies her interests with an abstraction, 'our countrymen', as surely as her uncle identifies his interest with the welfare—and especially the economic welfare—of the Catholic Church.

The theme of the disrupted family is reinforced by the character of Hernandez, whose intervention is essential for the establishment of the Occidental Republic. The latter became a kind of Robin Hood figure after his wife and children were murdered when he had been forcefully impressed into service. Thus his life of action is as much a psychic compensation as Charles Gould's. The narrator focuses upon the disruptive effects of political turmoil on minor characters and upon the anonymous people of all classes. The attention to background details—the woman with two frightened daughters clinging to her arm; the exodus of those who fear the arrival of Pedro Montero; the woman searching for her missing son who is probably dead; the wife watching her husband die—incorporates into the fabric of the novel a panorama of representative vignettes which illustrate the cost of military and political action deriving from misunderstood and unacknowledged motives. Such family groupings as the following dramatise more effectively than any narrative analysis how the family, the fundamental unit of civilisation, is threatened by actions taken in the name of material progress and concern for the people: 'Three women—of whom one was carrying a child—and a couple of men in civilian dress—one armed with a sabre and another with a gun—were grouped about a donkey carrying two bundles tied up in blankets' (p. 359).

## VI

When Conrad returns to write an Author's Note in 1917, how characteristic it is that he seeks to define the persona as an intimate of Don José and as a reader of his unpublished manuscript, 'History of Fifty Years of Misrule'. He obviously wants to reinforce the authority and authenticity of his speaker. It is the narrator who establishes the alternative values to materialism, solipsism, and ambition. The attitudes he expresses and the values he espouses make him a self-dramatising example of the civilised man. The narrator is committed to tolerance, moderation, and propriety. He understands the relationship between a man's public behaviour and barely acknowledged psychic needs. He shows how the interests of the people are barely taken into account by those acting in their name. He maintains an ironic and critical detachment as he presents each character's perspective. And it is he who affirms that the family is the primary unit of civilisation, even while he regrets the failure of political activity and the disappointment of man's idealistic aspirations.

As the novel progresses, the narrator's detachment, rationality, scrupulous fairness, and reluctance to probe into psychosexual problems or to meditate upon psychic motives gradually evolve into a voice in whose balance of mind, decorum, and restraint the Edwardian reader would have had confidence.[9] He observes Edwardian literary and social amenities by sidestepping sexual matters, involved psychological analyses, and prolonged interior monologues. The efficacy of the novel's satire of imperialism and materialism depends upon the narrator conveying an alternative to zeal, intemperance, and self-delusion. The speaker's restraint contrasts with Gould's seething turbulence, Decoud's bitter irony deriving in part from his own self-loathing, Mitchell's complacency, and Monygham's obliqueness. Yet so offended is he by sottishness and meanness that on occasion he is capable of becoming an outraged moralist when his standards are breached; for example when describing the pretensions of General Montero, each phrase seems to carry an accretion of outrage from its predecessor: 'The imbecile and domineering stare of the glorious victor of Rio Seco had in [it] something ominous and incredible; the exaggeration of the cruel caricature, the fatuity of solemn masquerading, the atrocious grotesqueness of some military idol of Aztec conception and European bedecking, awaiting the homage of worshippers' (p. 122). But such vituperation is the more striking because of its rarity.

Conrad's narrator undermines the heroic pretensions of his characters and disabuses the reader of the notion that materialism has its heroes.[10] By using such legendary material as a quest for treasure and by including isolated acts of courage by those who are potential heroes, Conrad raises expectations of heroic behaviour. But he deflates them as he gradually reveals the limitations and ineffectuality of his potential heroes: Gould, the king of Sulaco; Nostromo, the Adamic man; and Mrs Gould, whose innocence and moral purity suggest the Madonna. The bathetic denouement of the romance plot which comprises the last three chapters is itself a comment on the possibility of reinvigorating the larger-than-life world of love and heroism embodied in romance or epic. Indeed, the heroic image that a man creates for himself—for example Gould's image of himself as the bringer of justice and security, and Nostromo's image of himself as the man of incorruptible reputation—really has little to do with the basic interests of the community. Rather than heirs to an heroic tradition where men risked everything to save the community, these are men whose acts are corrupted by their motives. Throughout the novel, characters inflate their motives into self-serving pieties, but the narrator gradually deflates the pretensions of those who—usually deluding themselves—wrap their behaviour in pious abstractions. Although Decoud and Nostromo are on the lighter in the name of politics and the welfare of Sulaco, the narrator ironically observes: 'There was no bond of conviction, of common idea; they were merely two adventurers pursuing each his own adventure, involved in the same imminence of deadly peril' (p. 295). 'Adventurers', the term that Gould reluctantly admits describes his position in Sulaco, is a pejorative word because of its association with the 'impious adventurers' of the first chapter who, according to legend, have become captives of the treasure that they discover. Within the context of the novel, 'adventurer' comes to mean a self-indulgent solipsist. And gradually the reader sees that the gringo adventurers of Chapter 1 are the appropriate archetypes for the principled Gould, the amoral Nostromo, and the cynical Decoud.

The speaker does not use bitter, scathing irony to separate himself from a world he adhors. He is not, like the narrator of *The Secret Agent*, a man who, as we shall see, uses verbal aggression as an outlet for his frustration at being unable to change the world he describes. With his vast knowledge of Costaguana's history and geography and his familiarity with the characters, he speaks both as historian and journalist. The very care with which the narrator makes distinctions, in contrast to the glib use of abstractions by those political paternalists who seek to disguise their motives in moral bromides (Gould, Sir John, Holroyd, Mitchell), is itself an important statement about the narrator's values. For example, he understands the difference between the motives if not the consequences of Gould's high-minded principles and Holroyd's pious megalomania. The narrator wants to re-establish and redefine qualities that seem to be losing their original meaning in the backlash of economic adventurism. Although *Nostromo* may appear to those who live within Sulaco, including even Monygham, to be courageous and selfless, the narrator carefully indicates that it is his vanity which 'called out his recklessness, his industry, his ingenuity, and that disdain of the natives which helped him so much upon the line of his work and *resembled* an inborn capacity for command. It made him *appear* incorruptible and fierce' (emphases mine).[11]

The narrator avoids the kind of intense psychological analysis of the turn-of-the-century Marlow tales and *The Secret Sharer* because Conrad wants gradually to display the private characters beneath the public rhetoric and social amenities and to show that the characters have fundamentally different identities from the ones that they originally imagined themselves to have. 'Heart of Darkness' and *Lord Jim* are predicated on dramatising the process of Marlow's discovering the subtleties of another character, and *Nostromo* bears some important vestiges of Conrad's interest in the epistemological problem of how we can possibly understand and empathise with another man. He places the reader in the position Marlow once occupied. The narrator creates the moral context in which the reader makes his judgements; for example, take his extended metaphor of wealth as a poisoned sword that turns upon its bearer: 'More dangerous to the wielder, too, this weapon of wealth, double-edged with the cupidity and misery of mankind, steeped in all the voices of self-indulgence as in a concoction of poisonous roots, tainting the very cause for which it is drawn, always ready to turn awkwardly in the hand' (p. 365). At the point where the characters come closest to self-discovery, the narrator symphathetically renders their plights but he does not draw conclusions or propose alternative abstractions to the ones that have been discredited by the characters' actions. The reader must do that for himself.


## VII

Conrad understood, as Stephen Marcus wrote in a different context, that 'It is when the super-ego sanctions us to act freely and punitively in the name of some of humanity's highest ideals—whether it be the Deity, or the Nation, or Democracy, or Revolution, or Science itself—that the greatest horrors of human aggressiveness, violence and destruction are unleashed.'[12] *Nostromo* shows that history is composed of personal dramas, acted out not in service to political ideals—no matter what the actor espouses as his motive—but out of dimly understood needs that are transferred by rationalisation into public rhetoric. Conrad often sympathised with idealists who sought

change through politics even while he dramatised not only the futility
of political action but its dehumanising quality. He had to convince
himself that turning his back on his country and, in particular, his
father's revolutionary heritage was a proper decision. The political
novels are a means by which Conrad can atone for his neglect of
political involvement, and exonerate himself at the same time, by
showing the ultimate futility of a life based on preserving or
reforming society. Through such diverse characters as the Professor,
the Monteros, Haldin, and even the respectable Don José and Charles
Gould, Conrad implies that those who are zealously committed to
political ideas sacrifice their potential for personal growth. In *The
Secret Agent* and *Under Western Eyes*, too, characters whose active
lives revolve around upholding the *status quo* or destroying it have
sacrificed their humanity to a ritualistic hunt in which values and
ideals are subsumed by the chase and in which each character is
bathetically both hunter and prey.

It is not necessary to agree with Jocelyn Baines that Costaguana is a
disguised version of Poland to understand *Nostromo* as a sublimated
act of self-justification on Conrad's part.[13] Conrad was deeply
troubled over accusations that he had abandoned Poland. He
suspected his motives for settling in England and turning his back
upon both his country and his family heritage. Once he left the sea
and became a writer, the justification that Poland lacked the facilities
for his chosen career was difficult to sustain. It may be that *Nostromo*
also reflects Conrad's subconscious resentment towards a father who
neglected family for politics and ultimately left him an orphan, after
inflicting exile, disgrace, and economic hardship upon his family. If
*Nostromo* is subconsciously written to atone for Conrad's turning his
back on his father's tradition, it is hardly surprising that the
catalytic act that generates the novel's plot and the decisive act in
the history of Costaguana is Gould's return to the land of his father's
defeat for the purpose of reviving the mine. By castigating the
possibility of change through politics, Conrad convinced himself of
the rectitude of his own decision to desert Poland, to which his father
had made a complete political commitment. Given his father's
zealotry and Conrad's consciousness of it, it is hardly too much to say
that politics becomes a paternal abstraction to which Conrad must
atone, palliate, and explain himself. The means of palliation are his
political novels. *Nostromo* justifies the choice of personal fulfilment
over political involvement because it shows politics as a maelstrom
that destroys those it touches and shows, more importantly, that

one inevitably surrenders a crucial part of one's personality when one commits oneself to ideology.

The search for a restored family is an underlying motif in Conrad's fiction. An orphan since childhood, an expatriate living in an adopted country with a tradition of strong family ties, a man who did not become a husband or father until middle age, Conrad was preoccupied with the value and meaning of traditional family ties and figurative variations of them within interpersonal relationships.[14] His fiction abounds with homeless young men from disrupted families searching for putative fathers and brothers as well as for compatible women to relieve the pangs of isolation and excruciating loneliness. Within the shipboard community in the early sea tales, including 'Youth', *The Nigger of the 'Narcissus'*, 'Typhoon' and 'The End of the Tether' the captain is a patriarchal figure with whom younger men have a complex father-son relationship. In the sea tales, the shipboard community with its defined responsibilities and camaraderie becomes an important substitute for men who either lack family ties or who, because of their profession, must of necessity turn from them while on ship. Conrad's conception of the shipboard community as an extended family in which each man's place within the hierarchy defines his duties and responsibilities provides an important alternative to the political anarchy in *Nostromo*. *The Mirror and the Sea* (1906) was begun while he was still writing *Nostromo* and it may be that his eulogy of the sea contains as much of his political philosophy as 'Autocracy and War' (1905). Conrad perceived the love a man has for a ship in terms of analogies to family and passionate love; the men who sail a ship 'learn to know [her] with an intimacy surpassing the intimacy of man with man, to love with a love nearly as great as that of man for woman, and often as blind in its infatuated disregard of defects' (MS, p. 58). Conrad's vision of idyllic shipboard life affirms the values of family and personal relations, while placing commitment to community on other than materialistic terms. It is to these values that we must juxtapose the compulsive quest for wealth and power in *Nostromo*.

NOTES

1. Avrom Fleishman, *Conrad's Politics: Community and Anarchy in the Fiction of Joseph Conrad* (Baltimore: The John Hopkins Press, 1967), p. 57.
2. Ibid., p. 56.

3. Ibid., p. 71.

4. For further discussion of the importance of 'Autocracy and War', see Fleishman, especially pp. 32–7 and pp. 68–9.

5. If I were to select paradigmatic statements of the view of *Nostromo* with which I would take issue, it would be the following from Eloise Knapp Hay's learned *The Political Novels of Joseph Conrad* (Chicago: The University of Chicago Press, 1963): (1) 'Everything illustrates the author's theory of history' (p. 175); (2) 'Evil . . . is exterior and is not, even, moral' (p. 183).

6. William Butler Yeats, 'The Second Coming', ll. 7–8.

7. As the perspicacious Decoud notices, Nostromo's loquacity is a subconscious symptom of his lost self-respect: 'The usual characteristic quietness of the man was gone. It was not equal to the situation as he conceived it. Something deeper, something unsuspected by everyone had come to the surface' (p. 282).

8. One could cite a number of the 1895–8 letters to show how Decoud's final crisis approaches states of mind that Conrad experienced. Take for example the following from a 1896 letter to Garnett which I cited earlier:

> I am paralyzed by doubt and have just enough sense to feel the agony but am powerless to invent a way out of it. . . . I knock about blindly in it till I am positively, physically sick—and then I give up saying—tomorrow! And tomorrow comes—and brings only the renewed and futile agony. I ask myself whether I am breaking up mentally. . . . Everything seems so abominably stupid. You see *the belief* is not in me—and without the belief—the brazen thick headed, thick skinned immovable belief nothing good can be done. (Aug. 5, 1896; Garnett, pp. 64–5).

9. Because Conrad creates a voice concerned with the moral and psychological lives of his characters, the novel's texture does not support a view that the novel is fundamentally mythic. For example, the narrator's bathetic rendering of Monygham's psychosexual difficulties hardly supports Dorothy Van Ghent's reading that Monygham's past corresponds to the 'phase' of 'self-knowledge' within the heroic ideal: 'The doctor, with a lifting up of his upper lip, as though he were longing to bite, bowed stiffly in his chair. With the utter absorption of a man to whom love came late, not as the most splendid of illusions, but like an enlightening and priceless misfortune, the sight of that woman . . . suggested ideas of adoration, of kissing the hem of her robe' (p. 513). (Introduction to *Nostromo* [New York: Holt, Rhinehart and Winston, 1961], p. xvi.) For a provocative and brilliant mythopoeic reading, see Claire Rosenfield's *Paradise of Snakes* (Chicago and London: The University of Chicago Press, 1967), pp. 43–78.

10. My argument here specifically takes issue with Royal Roussel's interesting contention that 'The anonymity of the narrator [of *Nostromo*] is thus the deliberately chosen stance of a consciousness which has abandoned the adventure and, with it, any hope for a positive self.' *The Metaphysics of Darkness* (Baltimore and London: The Johns Hopkins Press, 1971), p. 113.

11. Holt, Rhinehart edition, pp. 342–3. This quotation appears in the 1904 text. The Holt, Rhinehart edition (based on the 1925 American edition) includes this and other passages that have been deleted from the final standard 1926 edition.

See Van Ghent, p. xxvii and Rosenfield p. 46, footnote 12.

12. Steven Marcus, review essay of Stanley Milgram's *Obedience and Authority, The New York Times Book review* (13 Jan., 1974), p. 3.

13. See Jocelyn Baines, *Joseph Conrad: A Critical Biography* (New York: McGraw-Hill, 1960), pp. 313−14.

14. Lawrence, Woolf, and Joyce also are preoccupied with revivifying family paradigms, particularly in their major works *The Rainbow, To the Lighthouse,* and *Ulysses*. If Lawrence, Woolf, and Joyce were immersed in the British novel and a cultural tradition that stresses the value of close family ties, Conrad's personal history and psychic needs made him deeply concerned with revivifying personal and family relationships. Conrad, Lawrence, Woolf, and Joyce focus on the family as the basic unit of civilisation during a time when political ideology and religious belief seemed ineffectual to them. From Richardson (*Clarissa*) and Fielding (*Tom Jones*) through Dickens (*Bleak House*) and Hardy (*Jude the Obscure*), the British novel is preoccupied with family paradigms: the relationships between fathers and sons, the plight of disowned children and orphans, and the quest for intimate friendships. A recurring pattern is that of a homeless or a rejected child desperately searching for either a father or a heterosexual partner who would compensate for the sense of loneliness caused by the loss of parents. (That the British novel remains a fundamentally private genre concerned with a grammar of motives and with nuances of private relationships undoubtedly has to do with its middle-class roots.)

# 8 Language as value in *The Secret Agent*

I

We must not allow our insistence on discussing the inevitable relationship between technique and meaning to blur the distinction between on the one hand, the written, linear language on the page (the means of mimesis), and on the other, the imaginary events and characters (the objects of mimesis) for which language is a catalyst. Criticism of *The Secret Agent* has rarely distinguished between the object of mimesis and the means of mimesis; between the 'monstrous' town of London and the language that Conrad creates to describe it. For example, Joseph I. Fradin and Jean W. Creighton argue that Conrad creates a language 'stripped of moral energy and commitment to the community of men' in order to reflect 'a morally neutral and incoherent universe'.[1] I will argue the very opposite; namely, that the language is constantly evaluating, controlling, and restraining the nihilism of the imagined world. For *The Secret Agent* depends upon a tension between disintegration of the content (Conrad's perception of turn-of-the-century London) and integration and cohesion of the form (the language and the tightly unified narrative). Conrad creates a language that is moral, civilised, and rational, and a narrator with the intelligence and moral energy to suggest alternatives to the cynicism, amorality, and hypocrisy that dominate and prevail in political relationships within London. Although the narrator to whom the entire language of the book is assigned at first seems isolated and detached from a world he abhors, he gradually reveals himself as a multi-dimensional figure whose concern and sympathy for those trapped within the cosmic chaos become part of the novel's values.

The major character is the narrator; his *action* is to attack a world he despises. The satire in *The Secret Agent* depends upon the immense ironic distance between a civilised voice that justifiably conceives of himself as representing sanity, rationality, and morality; and the personae of London who are for the most part caught in a maelstrom of violence and irrationality beyond their control. In order to convince the reader of an unbridgeable schism between himself and the people he describes, the narrator at times feels compelled to use language that is intemperate, zealous, and unreasonable. Conrad's narrator wants to awaken his audience to a world where public life has contracted to a bizarre game between police and political extremists, while private relationships mirror the secrecy and subterfuge of politics. For him, the essentials of civilised life— whether they be religion, education, or art—have been debased. Especially for the first seven chapters, virtually every description is an ironic evaluation. Because every phrase is the function of an established moral perspective, the narrator speaks in language that is simultaneously proleptic and parodic of the action. For example, Verloc is depicted in language that anticipates the corpse he will become; ensconced in his bed, 'his prominent, heavy-lidded eyes rolled sideways amorously and languidly, the bedclothes were pulled up to his chin' (p. 7). It is as if Verloc's death had already occurred, as indeed it has for the retrospective narrator. Always informed by foreknowledge of already completed events, the narrator's view of each character at first seems static and is immune to moments of doubt or impulses for re-evaluation. The preterite itself becomes the ultimate synthesising tool.

The narrator depicts London as a city where human personality is deprived of its poential for growth and freedom of decision. Commitment to the twin creeds of anarchy and counter-revolution simultaneously displaces the motives and values for which men live, and, like a spreading epidemic, squelches the vitality and potential of each individual. Gradually and barely perceptibly, as the narrator ostensibly concentrates on the incestuous relationship between police and anarchists and on the perverse domestic life of the Verlocs, he conveys a picture of a blighted civilisation by means of an accretion of unobtrusive details which seem to be mere background: the 'fraudu-lent cookery' of the Italian restaurant; the mechanical piano that plays without human participation, the secondhand furniture store with its ghostly merchandise that implies a world without people; the street which 'in its breadth, emptiness, and extent . . . had the majesty of inorganic nature, of matter that never dies' (p. 14). Perhaps the narrator's unwillingness to make distinctions, his desire to take a syncretic view, reveals something about Conrad's urge to define himself in opposition to the city he abhors.

But the probing narrative transcends the parochialism of the narrator's irony and the manipulation of Conrad's verbal game. Conrad creates—and I use this word deliberately—an independent reader who observes London through the eyes of the narrator and who simultaneously judges the narrator's 'activity' of satirising that world. If the narrator's language reduces all characters to the same level, the *action* counterpoises that reduction. As the reader progresses through the novel, he experiences arousal of his sympathies only to have these sympathies deflated. Eventually he finds himself resisting the narrator's efforts to homogenise the characters, and unwilling to become an accomplice in the narrator's equation of the dehumanising aspects of urban life in London with the people who live there. If the details I cited above separate us from London and momentarily invite us to regard London superciliously with disgust, other images engage the reader's sympathy and pity even when they do not seem to affect the narrator: the 'troop of assorted children . . . [who] ran and squabbled with a shrill, joyless, rowdy clamour' (p. 62); or Mrs Neale, the alcoholic servant, who is reduced to 'all fours amongst the puddles, wet and begrimed, like a sort of amphibious and domestic animal living in ashbins and dirty water' (p. 184).

Moreover, Conrad's obsessive need to distinguish himself from the characters is only one aspect of his response to the grotesque world he observes. Beneath his contempt for London as a symbol is an interest in the individual emotional and moral lives of its inhabitants: Stephen's compassion and morality; Mrs Verloc's obsessive love for her brother; her hatred of Verloc after she knows what has occurred to Stephen; her anxiety about the gallows; her subsequent revived hopes with Ossipon; and her despairing suicide. Commenting retrospectively on the choice of method, Conrad wrote: 'Even the purely artistic purpose, that of applying an ironic method to a subject of that kind, was formulated with deliberation and in the earnest belief that ironic treatment alone would enable me to say all I felt I would have to say in scorn as well as in pity' (Author's Note, p. xiii). But perhaps because the narrator's satiric and dogmatic tone convinces his audience that London is without redeeming values, it has been customary to ignore this claim of 'pity' and to insist that Conrad writes about most of these characters without real feeling. The truth is that his narrator frequently departs from his bitterly ironic tone and sympathetically shares the perspective of the characters, whom Conrad perceives to be as much victims as culprits.

Conrad creates a narrator who despises the devaluation of language in contemporary life. The narrator's verbal behaviour is distinguished from that of the rest of the characters. The stylised syntax, the puns, the proleptic and echoing phrases, the verbal leitmotifs, and the image clusters combine to form an alternative to the language of London. The debased quality of language within London takes the form of the Verlocs' marital dialogue of the deaf, the political clichés of the anarchists' conversation, and the pervasive newspapers which seem to be a metonymy for the world they describe: 'the rags of the dirty men harmonized excellently with the eruption of the damp, rubbishy sheets of paper soiled with printers' ink. The posters [advertising the papers], maculated with filth, garnished like tapestry the sweep of the curbstone' (p. 79). Newspapers, both a cause and symptom of the devaluation of language, are a major means by which people communicate within the novel, but the information is always incomplete and distorted. Immune to the significance of events, the newspapers create rather than mirror reality. The newspaper reporting Stephen's death is ironically described as 'a good-sized, rosy sheet, as if flushed by the warmth of its own convictions, which were optimistic' (p. 70). The one detail that the newspapers report about hangings, that 'the drop given was fourteen feet', has impressed itself upon Mrs Verloc to the point where it becomes a fixation just as if that detail 'had been scratched on her brain with a hot needle' (p. 268). Similarly, Ossipon is haunted by the factual report of her death. At times, the narrator deliberately parodies the popular journalistic style (used for short obituaries and feature stories) of summarising a man's significance in a sequence of appositions: 'Alexander Ossipon, anarchist, nicknamed the Doctor, author of a medical (and improper) pamphlet, late lecturer on the social aspects of hygiene to working men's clubs, was free from the trammels of conventional morality— but he submitted to the rule of science' (pp. 296–7).

After *Almayer's Folly* (1895) and *An Outcast of the Islands* (1896), Conrad tried to perfect a meditative style which renders every nuance of the major character's consciousness. This phase climaxed with *Lord Jim* (1900). Both the presence of an omniscient narrator as an ultimate standard and Marlow's sending of undigested data about Jim's demise indicate that Conrad could no longer comfortably work within the form of the epistemological quest. In 'The End of the Tether' (1902), and 'Typhoon' (1902), Conrad began to use the traditional omniscient narrator to establish an ironic distance between, on the one hand, the narrator and reader and, on the other, the characters within the narrative. *The Secret Agent*, which exploits the subtlety of this technique, is the culmination of this phase. The language of *The Secret Agent* is itself an ironic comment on the action. Establishing his own moral superiority and perspicacity to his characters by implicitly denigrating them, the narrator develops a relationship with the reader that depends upon shared disdain for certain kinds of behaviour.

We might consider briefly how the narrator uses language as an instrument of aggression to ridicule his characters and to deprive them of their humanity. That each of the narrator's observations is discrete from the preceding and subsequent ones emphasises the isolation of each individual. In the following passage, each subject belongs only to its predicate, and is disconnected from other subjects except by physical proximity:

> [A] milk cart rattled noisily across the distant perspective; a butcher boy, driving with the noble recklessness of a charioteer at Olympic Games, dashed round the corner sitting high above a pair of red wheels. A guilty-looking cat issuing from under the stones ran for a while in front of Mr. Verloc, then dived into another basement; and a thick police constable, looking a stranger to every emotion, as if he, too, were part of inorganic nature, surging apparently out of a lamp-post, took not the slightest notice of Mr. Verloc. (p. 14.)

Repetition of syntactical patterns may underline the narrator's disdain for the mindlessness or compulsiveness of a character's behaviour: '[Ossipon] looked in without a thought, without intention, without curiosity of any sort. He looked in because he could not help looking in. He looked in, and discovered Mr. Verloc reposing quietly on the sofa' (p. 284). Sometimes, the narrator's repetition of phonic patterns mocks the content of passages:

> By exercising his agency with ruthless defiance [the professor] procured for himself the appearances of power and personal prestige. That was undeniable to his vengeful bitterness. It pacified its unrest; and in their own way the most ardent of revolutionaries are perhaps doing no more but seeking for peace in common with the rest of mankind—the peace of soothed vanity, of satisfied appetites, or perhaps of appeased conscience. (p. 81.)

The plethora of explosive 'p's' creates a sound almost like spitting that, along with the slow-moving, bathetic sequaciousness of the final phrases, reinforces the narrator's contempt for the professor. From the very first page, images are not really comparisons of the world within the novel to an extrinsic one with which narrator and reader are familiar, but rather they are part of the process of subverting the reader's 'familiarity' with the London being described. As if it had an independent will of its own, the bell 'clatter[ed] . . . with impudent virulence'; Verloc 'wallowed . . . on an unmade bed'; the people who visit the Verlocs' shop are described in terms that deliberately obliterate the distinction between their bodies and the shabby clothes they wear (p. 4).

The vehicles of a metaphor do not simply express a quality to be associated with the tenor, but replace the tenor as the essential quality of the imagined world. Thus, although literally the light from the carters' eating-house has nothing to do with Verloc's bleeding corpse, its 'soiled blood-red light' extends the corrupting energy of the trickle of blood from which Mrs Verloc has sought to escape (pp. 266, 269). In a world where virtually every character is involved in a parasitic relationship—where Verloc seeks to thrive on the corpse of Stephen; and then Mrs Verloc wishes to build a life on the corpse of her husband; and finally Ossipon seeks advantage from the corpse of Mrs Verloc—Yundt's talk about eating people's flesh becomes not only a self-indicting speech but part of the physical reality from which the reader desperately and eagerly wishes to disassociate himself. If vehicle displaces tenor, then the real importance of the oft-noted bestial images is their suggestion that a bizarre and grotesque metamorphosis is a lurking possibility within the Bosch-like nightmare that the narrator presents.

## II

In *The Secret Agent*, Conrad takes issue with a common Edwardian view that time inevitably equals progress. Such writers as Butler and Shaw proposed the concept of an upwardly evolving Life Force.[2] Conrad regarded as cant the political euphoria of the Fabians and his socialist friend, Cunninghame Graham, that a 'benign' and 'congenial' future awaits us once we locate and ameliorate the problems of civilisation.[3] Conrad's sense of history as a process inexorably indifferent to man's aspirations was shaped partly by his despair and indignation at the continuous suppression of Polish freedom. Thus, even the dedication to the utopian H. G. Wells has its ironic aspect. *The Secret Agent* proposes no solutions for the oppressive economic system and negligent political system.

In this section, I shall explore how the narrator's disciplined use of ironic language manipulates his audience to accept his satiric indictment of contemporary London. As Norman Holland has noted, the very first paragraphs obfuscate more than they disclose, and leave the reader awaiting the narrator's disclosure of the mystery behind such words as 'nominally', 'ostensible', and 'discreetly'.[4] Because the elusive method of presenting data (including the scrambled chronology) makes the reader dependent on the narrator's whim in revealing information, the reader is especially vulnerable to rhetorical manipulation. The first-time reader soon finds himself accepting the narrator's judgements even when they are not supported by argument. The narrator of *The Secret Agent* deliberately implies the moral interchangeability of the characters within this dehumanised world by applying similar descriptive terms to both the moral nihilists and those of whom one might be tempted to approve. For example, the Assistant Commissioner is systematically equated with those he opposes. The Assistant Commissioner's 'sense of loneliness and evil freedom' are not so different from the Professor's 'sinister freedom': '[A spy's] occupation is free from all restraint. He's without as much faith as is necessary for complete negation, and without that much law as is implied in lawlessness' (p. 140). He lingers near the Verlocs' shop, 'as though he were a member of the criminal classes' (pp. 150–1). His political responses derive from secret motives (he responds to Heat's plan to arrest Michaelis: 'If the fellow is laid hold of again . . . [the lady patroness] will never forgive me' [p. 112]). Although the Assistant Commissioner does solve the crime and might have emerged as an implacable detective hero in the tradition of Dickens's Bucket, Conrad refuses to let us take him seriously. The Assistant Commissioner's view that he is the victim of an 'ironic fate', chained to his desk, is mocked by the selfish motives of his quest. While some critics would have us take him as the hero, one can legitimately ask whether ridding England of Vladimir really solves the political and social issues raised by the novel.[5] And does he not find temporary 'joyousness and dispersion of thought' (p. 150) when he narcissistically rediscovers the primitive pleasure of 'tracking down' secret societies? His 'instinct for self-preservation' (a term later used to characterise Mrs Verloc) is a corrupted version of an impulse for 'work and excitement'. This impulse has been debased by his marriage, his chivalric service to the Lady Patroness, and his participation in a bureaucracy where moral distinctions are impossible and where his own urge for activity is gradually being stifled.

Conrad's narrator implies that civilisation has undergone progressive devolution. He stresses the primordial mud and fog; he focuses on man's resemblance to animals; as if they were fossilised, he compares the Verlocs to rocks and stones (for example, Verloc is 'steady like a rock—a soft kind of rock' [p. 13]; Mrs Verloc's head is compared to stone). Civilisation seems to be returning, metaphorically if not actually, to jungle and wilderness. The professor's house is 'lost in a wilderness of poor houses'; a furniture store encloses 'a bizarre forest of wardrobes, with an undergrowth tangle of table legs, a tall pier-class glimmered like a pool of water in a wood' [p. 82]. Walking the city streets, the Assistant Commissioner felt lighthearted as if he were 'alone in a jungle', which is the one place where he feels comfortable [p. 150]. The fault for this devolution appears to rest with those who are responsible for sustaining civilisation. The narrator does not exclude any of the social order from his scorn. Heat shares with Ethelred, Toodles, and even the Assistant Commissioner the habit of confusing political philosphy with the personal comfort the system affords them. Heat's concern is that Verloc's exposure threatens *his* system; thus he opposes arresting the guilty party because his reputation rests upon secret knowledge. Although Ethelred and his myrmidon Toodles consider themselves rather enlightened reformers, they respond to threats to the *status quo* only because they identify their self-interest with that of the political system. Notwithstanding their reflex opposition to the anarchists, those who uphold the political *status quo* do not implicitly or explicitly represent alternative values to those articulated by the revolutionaries or reactionaries. Indeed, are not the words describing Verloc's compulsive concern for his own safety applicable to the motives of the forces of legality? 'All these people had to be protected. Protection is the first necessity of opulence and luxury. They had to be protected; and their horses, carriages, houses, servants had to be protected; and the source of their wealth had to be protected in the heart of the city and the heart of the country' (p. 12). And other similarities extend the subtle equation between the underground political world of London and those whose mission is to uphold civilisation; thus Ethelred's and Heat's heaviness equates them with such moral and physical indolents as Verloc and Michaelis. When

Heat is threatened by the Assistant Commissioner, he responds with the same combination of 'indignation' and anxiety with which Verloc had reacted to Vladimir:

> He felt at the moment like a tight-rope artist might feel if suddenly, in the middle of the performance, the manager of the Music Hall were to rush out of the proper managerial seclusion and begin to shake the rope. Indignation, the sense of moral insecurity engendered by such a treacherous proceeding joined to the immediate apprehension of a broken neck, would, in the colloquial phrase, put him in a state. And there would be also some scandalized concern for his art, too, since a man must identify himself with something more tangible than his own personality, and establish his pride somewhere, either in his social position, or in the quality of the work he is obliged to do, or simply in the superiority of the idleness he may be fortunate enough to enjoy. (pp. 116–17.)

(How applicable is the last sentence to every character except Winnie's mother and brother.)

The narrator stresses that those who should protect society are as oblivious to the objective world outside themselves as those who would destroy it. Ethelred, the 'great man' and 'presence', is handicapped by poor vision; he expresses himself in a vigorous manner but in his haughtiness refuses to concern himself with—has indeed a physical horror of—details. A not entirely unsympathetic caricature of an Edwardian progressive, Ethelred takes seriously his business as a reformer and lives as if time were measuring progress toward social goals. Whatever our present attitudes to ecology, Conrad would have wished us to see that the energy devoted to the bill for the nationalisation of fisheries was misspent and that Ethelred, with his obvious leadership capacities—his 'powerful' touch and vigorous tone are stressed—is exhausting himself with trifles. (His fastidious and ineffectual counterparts are the Count and narrator of 'Il Conde' and the narrators of 'An Anarchist' and 'The Informer'.)[6]

The narrator compares the Verlocs' domestic 'secrecy' with the pervasive subterfuge that informs the tacit, yet taut arrangements between not only anarchist and police, but also among the forces of legality themselves.[7] Told 'to its anarchistic end of utter desolation, madness and despair', Winnie Verloc's story reflects Conrad's desire to stress the symbiotic relationship between political and private life

(Author's Note, p. xv). Brett Square is the symbolic centre of London's moral turpitude and physical wasteland. When Verloc looks from his door, the physical images are intensifications of the fragmentation and ugliness that beset London: 'A fragile film of glass stretched between him and the enormity of cold, black, wet, muddy, inhospitable accumulation of bricks, slates, and stones, things in themselves unlovely and unfriendly to man' (p. 56). Winnie as 'protector' and 'guardian' of Stevie plays the same role as Verloc and the police imagine themselves playing for society. She conceives of marriage as a 'bargain' which commits her to surrendering her 'freedom' to Verloc's autocratic rule; once she is betrayed, she feels that there is 'something wanting on her part for the formal closing of the transaction': her revenge (p. 259). The narrator stresses how the Verlocs' mask of domestic respectability parallels the surface order with which society is protected by the police. Describing the Verloc home, the narrator might be describing the arrangements that make life possible in London itself as well as in the offices of the Assistant Commissioner, Heat, or Ethelred: 'For it had been respectable, covering by a decent reticence the problems that may arise in the practice of a secret profession and the commerce of shady wares. To the last its decorum had remained undisturbed by unseemly shrieks and other misplaced sincerities of conduct' (p. 264).

Finally and paradoxically, those most committed to political movements are the most selfishly concerned with either their own physical or psychic gratification. The narrator exposes 'secrecy' as a concept by which individuals substitute purely personal needs, whether conscious or not, for the interest of either political goals or the larger community. And 'private' comes to mean insidious or invidious and ultimately becomes synonymous with 'secret'. The narrator also redefines 'freedom'. 'Freedom' means to be without personal or community ties and, finally, without values by which to act. 'Freedom' becomes a state of personal anarchy in which the individual has, from fear or greed, liberated himself from the demands of his superego and stepped into a kind of moral vacuum; has, like Kurtz or Leggett, 'kicked himself loose of the earth'. For Conrad, the rigid social order of ship life with its hierarchy, discipline, and clearly defined duties provides a contrast to the concept of 'freedom' toward which these characters strive. Conrad would not have understood the existentialist concept of 'freedom'. When Winnie Verloc is released from her domestic tyranny, the reader watches 'freedom' and 'knowledge' become equated with *madness* and *despair*. At this point, the narrator uses 'freedom' facetiously as a term synonymous with 'complete irresponibility' and 'endless leisure' and shows how Mrs Verloc's 'knowledge' replaces her illusions about Verloc with a 'maddening' fixation for revenge that drives her to murder. Yet, Mrs Verloc engages our sympathies as she rediscovers repressed and latent impulses for self-preservation, passion, and even self-gratification.

Let us return to Fradin's and Creighton's argument that the language imitates the void of a 'morally neutral and incoherent universe'. Satire depends on the potential agreement between reader and narrator about norms and values. The narrator insidiously establishes a complicit relationship with his audience at the expense of his human subjects. The narrator is the ultimate secret agent, the man who has lived in contemporary London and learned of its intricate political arrangements, its physical ugliness, and its moral and spiritual atrophy; and now he has withdrawn to use all his artistic and intellectual resources to indict the city that he knows so well. The reader shares the moral superiority, detachment, and condescension of the narrator. Conrad expects us to juxtapose the narrator's ironic redefinition of such terms as 'freedom' and 'knowledge' with definitions established by social and moral tradition. He is satirising, among other things, the elasticity of language in London. The reader undergoes the process of experiencing a world in dissolution. But this experience is counterpointed by his perception that civilisation survives in the narrator's evaluation. By writing a novel that relies on the reader's endorsing the narrator's judgements, Conrad is affirming that moral abstractions are still viable if only we would return to them. The *control* and *discipline* of his language, as opposed to the language of London, create an alternative to the world observed.

## III

As I have argued, pervasive irony between what the narrator perceives and what each character understands is essential to the satiric technique. Yet, at times, the narrator invites the reader to share something of the humanity of these characters who are caught in a *Zeitgeist* beyond their perception and control. He isolates the characters from the continuum of moral anarchy to which their behaviour contributes and somewhat sympathetically examines their motives. As the Verlocs are overwhelmed and snuffed out by political circumstances, they are viewed by the narrator with compassion. By withholding crucial details about the deadly events Mr Verloc will set in motion and by showing him being bullied and intimidated by Vladimir, the narrator creates sympathy for Verloc who has become obsolete because of a management change. When the narrator switches to Verloc's feelings of insecurity and doubt and tells us he was 'startled and alarmed', we do not endorse Vladimir's epithets for Verloc—'vulgar, heavy, impudently intelligent'—because Verloc is the victim (pp. 26–7). Clearly the narrator is manipulating the reader to sympathise temporarily with the working man who cannot cope with the absurdities of the arrogant and urbane manager; thus he sets the stage for the revolutionary rhetoric of the next chapter in which he begins with Michaelis's laissez-faire Marxism that is only gradually revealed as nonsense as the chapter proceeds. But even the re-reader, sharing the narrator's knowledge of Verloc's arrangements and knowing the events that Verloc's fright unintentionally has set in motion, cannot ignore the sympathetic situation which causes the narrator to suspend the scathing irony with which Verloc is rendered. Despite deliberate verbal echoes, the vigilance and protection of the police and its agents are not the same as Mrs Verloc's obsessive 'maternal vigilance' of Stevie. Winnie is an example of how the potential for love, fidelity, and passion becomes warped and destroyed both by human brutality and economic conditions. Ironically, her rage at Stevie's demise enables her to discover in an act of homicide the atavistic energy that modern man seems to have lost: 'Into that plunging blow, . . . Mrs Verloc had put all the inheritance of her immemorial and obscure "descent, the simple ferocity of the age of caverns and the unbalanced nervous" fury of the age of bar-rooms' (p. 263). Suddenly the narrator invites the reader to see a hint of kinship with a woman who can only separate herself from moral and psychological conditioning in the act of murder.

On several occasions, most notably when the narrator speaks in the first person, Conrad lifts the veil of anonymity from the narrator. When he has his speaker abruptly shift from third to first person as he describes those who have the 'air of moral nihilism', it is almost as if Conrad wanted to create the illusion of a speaker telling us more than he wishes about himself (p. 13). At first, it seems that the narrator's occasional shifts to the first person are merely to narrow the distance between himself and his audience. But it is clear that in a passage such as the one that follows, the narrator sympathetically reaches out to acknowledge a kinship with the characters he has been satirising, and—for a brief moment—the ironic distance collapses: 'It is only when our appointed activities seem by a lucky accident to obey the particular earnestness of our temperament that we can taste the comfort of complete self-deception' (p. 112). Given the relationship between author and reader, moments of self-revelation and ironic self-consciousness inevitably raise questions about the *reader's* purity. (We might recall how the speaker in *The Waste Land* insists on including the reader in his indictment: 'You! hypocrite lecteur!—mon semblable—mon frère!.') When the professor doubts his ability to move men, the narrator writes: 'Such moments come to all men whose ambition aims at a direct grasp upon humanity—to artists, politicians, thinkers, reformers, or saints. A despicable emotional state this, against which solitude fortifies a superior character . . .' (p. 82).

Chapter 8 separates the Verlocs from the political events and examines them as a not unsympathetic family portrait. The Conrad who praised Anatole France for wishing men to 'believe and hope, preserving in our activity the consoling illusion of power and intelligent purpose', would not anaesthetise himself to the human needs of the characters.[8] The people of London are more than grotesque caricatures, after all. In this chapter, the narrator shifts his perspective and sympathetically renders Mrs Verloc's mother's heroic self-denial; the dimensions of Winnie's passionate commitment for her brother; the charity of Stevie; and Mr Verloc's haunted consciousness. The more compassionate perspective makes all the more compelling the descriptions of poverty and misery in London. The progress of the cab of death corresponds to the gradual revelation of both Mrs Verloc's mother's heroic self-sacrifice and the dimensions of Stevie's humanity. To the narrator and the re-reader, the funeral cortège is not only for Stevie who by Chapter 8 is already dead, but for Winnie's mother for whom this is the last journey; and, indeed, for Winnie and Verloc who will soon join Stevie among the dead. Trapped in their private world of secret motives and private accomodations, Winnie, her mother, the cabman, and even Verloc are now seen as poignant victims of circumstances beyond their control. When at the end of the chapter Verloc goes out, 'leading a *cortège* of dismal thoughts along dark streets', the narrator establishes a proleptic connection between the cab and this inept, tortured man embarked on a course which will soon end in his murder (p. 177, emphasis mine).

The narrator subverts the reader's complacency by abruptly proposing as a hero in Chapter 8 an apparently retarded young man and suggesting as heroine an infirm old woman (the mother of

Winnie and Stevie) who gives up her comfort to ensure continued care for her helpless son. The narrator presents Stevie as a moral barometer, an index of how society cares for those who do not quite fit its preconceived patterns. As if to imply a parasitic relationship in which he is the host, Conrad makes Stevie frail in contrast to the well-fed rotundity of the other characters except Yundt, the Professor, and the Assistant Commissioner. He is used as an instrument of violence by Verloc, the very man he idealises. He is ironically associated with St Stephen, the first Christian martyr. (When he protests against the driver's whipping, the narrator calls attention to 'walls of St. Stephen' [p.157].) He is the one character who idealistically observes the world with the expectation that right and wrong should exist. Significantly, the character described as a 'moral creature' is retarded, incoherent to his fellows, and dead. Stevie is the last righteous man, the heir to the Christian tradition of mercy, charity, and love. But while the narrator recognises Stevie as a prophet and shaman, the other characters regard him as deranged. The purity and simplicity of his judgements are ignored (an example: 'Bad world for poor people') because Stevie's concepts of justice and goodness have become anachronisms.

While the Professor is society's self-created scourge, Stevie is its discarded conscience. At the very centre of the novel, Stevie's in-genuous response to the wretched cabman and his miserable horse is a sad, yet comic, manifestation of his need—and the need of all whose motives have not been corrupted—to love and be loved: 'He could say nothing; for the tenderness to all pain and misery, the desire to make the horse happy and the cabman happy, had reached the point of a bizarre longing to take them to bed with him' (p. 167). Autistically locked in his own silence, Stephie's inarticulateness separates him from a world in which verbal behaviour takes the place of feeling. As Michaelis, Verloc, and Ossipon prolixly debate the appropriate revolutionary posture, Verloc opens the door upon 'the innocent Stevie, seated very good and quiet at a deal table, drawing circles, circles, circles; innumerable circles, concentric, eccentric; a coruscating whirl of circles that by their tangled multitude of repeated curves, uniformity of form, and confusion of intersecting lines suggested a rendering of cosmic chaos, the symbolism of a mad art attempting the inconceivable' (p. 45). That the compassionate and sensitive Stevie lacks verbal facility distinguishes him not only from the anarchists, but even from the narrator who coldly and rationally dissects the world he observes. Yet, the articulate narrator is sympathetic to Stephie's plight and desires. The narrator's arabesque construction of his tale, with its arbitrary time shifts and obsessive repetitions of verbal patterns, is a kind of correlative to the 'repeated curves' and 'intersecting lines' with which Stevie renders the 'cosmic chaos'.

## IV

T. S. Eliot's remark about the use of myth in *Ulysses* as a 'way of controlling, of ordering, of giving a shape and significance to the immense panorama of futility and anarchy which is contemporary history' also describes one of Conrad's principal methods of evaluating contemporary urban life in *The Secret Agent*.[9] Conrad does not develop a continuous parallel to literary works and to religious traditions, but in brief allusions he nostalgically evokes departed cultural values to which he juxtaposes those of modern London. The narrator provides religious and mythical allusions as both a method of judgement and a means of proposing alternative values to the moral anarchy of London. Cumulatively, such allusions work as they do both for Joyce and Eliot to posit historic alternatives to the urban wasteland. They serve to emphasise how far Western man has strayed both from his biblical heritage and his epic tradition. By qualifying his zeal with a note of urbanity, and suggesting by reference to Old Testament, Greek, and Elizabethan civilisations that civilisations are ephemeral, the narrator raises the possibility that London's moral darkness may be temporary.

That the characters are as completely unaware of the narrator's allusions as the characters in *Ulysses* (1922) are of the Homeric pattern emphasises the gulf that divides the civilised narrator and the world he describes. The narrator often places the Verlocs within a literary or cultural context that becomes an obvious bathetic comment on their quality. Describing Verloc's return, he writes, 'And across the length of the table covered with brown oilcloth, Winnie, his wife, talked evenly at him the wifely talk, as artfully adapted, no doubt, to the circumstances of this return as the talk of Penelope to the return of the wandering Odysseus' (p. 183). One need not dwell on the ironic distinction between Ulysses and Verloc, or between Penelope and Mrs Verloc; yet the presence of her suitor, Ossipon, and Verloc's cunning approach to danger give the allusion the barest touch of credibility that is essential. Mocking the quality of their domestic life, the narrator facetiously observes that Winnie 'did not expect from her husband in the daily intercourse of their married life a ceremonious amenity of address and courtliness of manner; vain and antiquated forms at best, probably never exactly observed, discarded nowadays even in the highest spheres, and always foreign to the standards of her class' (p. 190). Biblical and romance allusions also underline the ironic disjunction between the traditional archetypes of Western civilisation and the quality of present life. After learning that she has lost her brother, Mrs Verloc manifests 'the biblical attitude of mourning—the covered face, the rent garments; the sound of wailing and lamentation filled her head' (p. 246); as if she were an epic queen, her ring glittered 'with the untarnished glory of a piece from some splendid treasure of jewels' (p. 213). Later, the narrator ironically confirms Winnie's view of Ossipon as 'her saviour' and as a 'messenger of life' by speaking of his 'Apollo-like ambrosial head' (p. 310).

Conrad uses language borrowed from Shakespeare's great trage-dies to emphasise the distance between, on the one hand, Shakespeare's tragic universe and the men who inhabited it, and on the other, the quality of contemporary life. The allusions to significant murders in Shakespeare's major tragedies are especially resonant. Othello's speech before murdering Desdemona and sub-sequently committing suicide is recalled by Mrs Verloc's twice repeated question 'Shall I put out the light?' and Verloc's response 'put it out' (an order she later repeats to Ossipon after she has permanently subdued Verloc's light). After Othello reiterates 'Put out the light', preparatory to killing his wife, he then turns to Desdemona and exclaims, 'But once put out thy light . . . I know not where is that Promethean heat / That can thy light relume.' Winnie as Desdemona inverts Shakespeare's tragedy by killing Verloc (Othello) and then committing suicide when deserted by her lover. Verloc's poignant and regretful 'What's done can't be undone' (p. 240) echoes Lady Macbeth's similar weary reference to the past ('What's done cannot be undone'). Verloc, like Lady Macbeth, has generated a concatenation of violent events beyond his wildest dreams. The 'funereal baked meats' (p. 253) recalling Hamlet's objections to his mother's premature marriage are hardly gratuitous when we recall the Oedipal relationship between Mrs Verloc (Gertrude) and Stevie (Hamlet). Stevie is a parodic version of both Hamlet and King Hamlet. Like Hamlet, he is a moral creature in a perverse world which patronises him; like King Hamlet, he is murdered by a close, trusted relative. Verloc (Claudius) is sexually aroused on the very day of Stevie's death. In contrast to Shakespeare's tragedies, in *The Secret Agent* moral equilibrium is not restored; there are no figures like Fortinbras, Macduff, Malcolm, or Cassio to rebuild the community and to set the world right.

Religious language is persistently used to describe the activities of secular, and at times solipsistic, attitudes and responses: Michaelis's 'faith revealed in visions'; the 'meditations' of Verloc; the 'meditative' attitude of Ethelred; the 'providentially' blessed crusades of the Assistant Commissioner; and the sudden 'illuminations' of Heat (who considers the anarchists as 'his special flock' [p. 93]). Such language continually suggests the absence of one source of values which, in the view of the former Catholic but now agnostic Conrad, had traditionally provided the necessary illusions to make life purposeful. Conrad begins Chapter 2 with what I believe is an ironic echo of Donne's 'Good Friday, 1613, Riding Westward'. (We might especially recall the following lines: 'Hence is't, that I am carried towards the west / This day, when my soul's form bends toward the east. / There I should see a Sun, by rising set, / And by that setting endless day beget' [ll. 9–12].) Just as Donne's speaker is 'carried towards the west' by his commitment, so Verloc, too, is propelled westward by a call from his employer: 'Mr. Verloc was going westward through a town without shadows in an atmosphere of powdered old gold' (p. 11). Like Donne's speaker, Verloc's soul bends to the East, only the East for him is the source of autocratic conspiracy. Rather than the prayer and devotion to which Donne's speaker responds, Verloc for the moment focuses his passions on the political conspiracies of the autocratic regime represented by Vladimir. Using the conventional pun, the speaker of Donne's meditative poem asks of the sun (Son) to 'Burn off my rusts, and my deformity, / Restore thine image, so much, by thy grace'. But Mr Verloc looks approvingly upon the 'rustiness' produced by the sun upon the town's opulence, and devotes himself to preserving the facade of wealth he observes. (Since it cannot be proven that Conrad knew this poem, it is possible that he is simply making ironical use of traditional Elizabethan and metaphysical imagery.) The religious language burlesques Verloc's purpose:

> Mr. Verloc retraced the path of his morning's pilgrimage as if
> in a dream—an angry dream. This detachment from the
> material world was so complete that, though the mortal

envelope of Mr. Verloc had not hastened unduly along the streets, that part of him to which it would be unwarrantably rude to refuse immortality, found itself at the shop door all at once, as borne from west to east on the wings of a great wind. (p. 37).

Compulsively concerned with the protection of a society that offers the possibility of 'hygienic idleness', he lacks not only religious faith, but the ability to imagine a world outside himself (p. 12).

Mrs Verloc's perception of the trickle of blood as a 'destroying flood' inverts the apocalyptic flood from which Noah emerged to redirect mankind's destiny:

[Winnie Verloc] had become aware of a ticking sound in the room. . . . It grew upon her ear, while she remembered clearly that the clock on the wall was silent, had no audible tick. What did it mean by beginning to tick so loudly all of a sudden? . . . Mrs. Verloc cared nothing for time, and the ticking went on. . . . Dark drops fell on the the floorcloth one after another, with a sound of ticking growing fast and furious like the pulse of an insane clock. At its highest speed this ticking changed into a continuous sound of trickling. Mrs. Verloc watched that transformation with shadows of anxiety coming and going on her face. It was a trickle, dark, swift, thin. . . . Blood! (pp. 264–5).

(The narrator's grotesque verbal play on blood–flood recalls an earlier passage in which the Assistant Commissioner, speaking with Heat about Stephen's demise, 'looked down into [a] wet and empty [street] as if swept clear suddenly by a great flood' [p. 100].)

There is no Covenant after this flood, no promise of rebirth. Chronological time has been replaced by the nightmare of a perpetual wasteland. The descent of night, London's ironic response to Verloc's repeated request to 'put out the light', emphasises the symbolic movement of life towards death within the novel. 'Night, the inevitable reward of men's faithful labours on this earth, night had fallen on Mr. Verloc, the tried revolutionist' (pp. 287–8). The descent of night (prelude to a new dawn as well as the ironic displacement of Verloc by Apollo-Ossipon) emphasises the cyclical nature of human life.

As the novel ends, the Professor, armed with his device and his credo 'Blood. Death.' (p. 304) stalks the streets, transformed by his own grotesque will into a force. But even here there is a hint of hope. In the guise of providing explanations for the Professor's plight, the narrator has shown that the man who prides himself on control over his fate has been reduced to a role synonymous with the destructive device he carries. He has revealed the Professor as an emotional spastic whose destiny is really in the hands of the police and whose every action is determined by his past. While the police have not completely erased the anarchists, neither do the latter flourish; they cannot affect the ennui and malaise of society by a few murders.

Let me conclude by pursuing the comparison between *Ulysses* and *The Secret Agent*. Both concentrate on the quality of urban life within one crucial day. As in *Ulysses*, the precise formality of structure (a product of the selection and arrangement of language) is an ironic comment on the lack of purpose within the urban wasteland that is the subject. As in *Ulysses*, characters who have obvious and easily ridiculed shortcomings gradually engage our sympathies and become separated from the sterility of the described world. In *Ulysses*, the form humanises Bloom; for example, in the 'Ithaca' section, Joyce deliberately posits his· most detached style, only to show us how Bloom's humanity even triumphs over the scientific catechism which at first seems at odds with the essence of the human spirit. Bloom transcends the mythic pattern in the 'Hades' section and creates a contrapuntal movement towards life that denies the endless echoes of death and affirms the values of generosity, charity, love, and above all, 'warm fullblooded life' (*Ulysses*, p. 115). Similarly, in *The Secret Agent*, the narrator's essential humanity creates alternatives to perceiving the world one-dimensionally. His rationality, moral values, and humane responses—his tolerance and sanity— dramatically testify to the viability of civilisation and refute both the nihilism within the imagined world and his own tendency to view London as an urban inferno.

NOTES

1. Joseph I. Fradin and Jean W. Creighton, 'The Language of *The Secret Agent*: The Art of Non-Life', *Conradiana*, vol. i, no. 2 (autumn 1968), pp. 23–35.
   In preparing this chapter, I have found the following studies especially stimulating in addition to those I cite elsewhere: Joseph I. Fradin, 'Anarchist, Detective, and Saint: The Possibilities of Action in *The Secret Agent*', *PMLA*, vol.

lxxxiii (Oct. 1968), pp. 1414–22; Elliott B. Gose, Jr., ' "Cruel Devourer of the World's Light": *The Secret Agent*', *Nineteenth-Century Fiction*, vol. xv (June 1960), pp. 39–51; Albert J. Guerard, *Conrad the Novelist* (Cambridge: Harvard University Press, 1958), pp. 219–31; Eliose Knapp Hay, *The Political Novels of Joseph Conrad* (Chicago: University of Chicago Press, 1963), chap. 6; Irving Howe, *Politics and the Novel* (New York: Horizon Press and Meridian Books, 1957), pp. 76–113; Claire Rosenfield, *Paradise of Snakes: An Archetypal Analysis of Conrad's Political Novels* (Chicago: University of Chicago Press, 1967), chap. 3; and R. W. Stallman, 'Time and *The Secret Agent*', *Texas Studies in Literature and Language*, vol. i (Spring 1959), pp. 101–22; reprinted in R. W. Stallman (ed.), *The Art of Joseph Conrad: A Critical Symposium* (East Lansing: Michigan State University Press, 1960), pp. 235–54.

2. See John A. Lester, jun., *Journey Through Despair 1880–1914: Transformations in British Literary Culture* (Princeton: Princeton University Press, 1968), pp. 81–6, 184.

3. Robert L. Heilbroner, *The Future as History* (New York: Grove Press, 1961) uses these terms. See p. 17.

4. See Norman N. Holland, 'Style as Character: *The Secret Agent*', *Modern Fiction Studies*, vol. xii (Summer 1966), pp. 221–31.

5. For example, in his *Conrad's Politics: Community and Anarchy in the Fiction of Joseph Conrad*, Avrom Fleishman argues that 'The Assistant Commissioner is rendered as a moral ideal' (p. 192).

6. *The Secret Agent*, written in 1906, was completed immediately after 'An Anarchist' and 'The Informer' and immediately before 'Il Conde'. All were written between November 1905 and December 1906.

7. See Fleishman's perceptive discussion of the 'secrecy' motif, pp. 190–3.

8. See 'Anatole France' in *Notes on Life and Letters*. The cited passage comes from the 1904 section of that essay, p. 34.

9. T. S. Eliot, 'Ulysses, Order, and Myth', *The Dial*, vol. lxxv (1923), pp. 480–3; reprinted as 'Myth and Literary Classicism' in *The Modern Tradition*, eds. Richard Ellmann and Charles Feidelson, jun. (New York: Oxford University Press, 1965), pp. 679–81; see p. 681.

# 9  *A Set of Six*: Marionettes

## I

Except for 'The Brute', the six stories in *A Set of Six* (1908) address the subject matter of the three major political novels: revolution, class struggle, the cost of political activity, and how individuals may become caught in the web of history. Written in the 1905–7 period after *Nostromo* and either immediately before or after *The Secret Agent*, the five political stories stress how human impulses for love and tenderness are stifled by political ideology, arbitrary traditions, and established customs. In all six tales, Conrad explores the psyche and values of idiosyncratic personalities; except for 'The Brute' these personalities are defined by their political position, even if as in 'The Duel' that position takes the form of commitment to an anachronistic code of honour. Most of these stories examine the kind of fanatical and irrational behaviour which is at the heart of political activity in *Nostromo, The Secret Agent,* and *Under Western Eyes.* Throughout the volume, Conrad's tone is one of ironic detachment. In the Preface to *The Shorter Tales,* he wrote: 'The volume called *A Set of Six* . . . is very different in its consistent mood of clear and detached presentation from any other volume of short stories I have published before or after.'[1] But Conrad was adamant that detachment did not imply cynicism: 'The fact is that I have approached things human in a spirit of piety foreign to those of humanity who would like to make of life a sort of Cook's Personally Conducted Tour—from the cradle to the grave' (28 Aug. 1908; *LL*, vol. ii, p. 82). In the same letter, he takes umbrage at 'those who reproach me with the pose of brutality, with the lack of all heart, delicacy, sympathy—sentiment—idealism'.

While the use of an imperceptive and self-indicting narrator has a long literary heritage, Conrad's interest in creating idiosyncratic and ineffectual tellers seems to be most influenced by his reading of James and Maupassant. Conrad's literary criticism frequently defines *his* literary values, not so much because he distorts other writers, but because he focuses on qualities in other writers that mirror his own aesthetic goals. He most frequently experimented with the well-meaning, but morally obtuse narrator during the same period when he wrote essays in praise of Maupassant (1904) and James (1905). In such stories as 'Mademoiselle Perle' and 'Les Soeurs Rondoli', Maupassant provides the precedent of a man reminiscing on past experience that reveals more about himself than he realises. Conrad particularly admired Maupassant's dramatisation of a perceiving consciousness in whose mind the facts have taken an independent shape:

> In Maupassant's work there is the interest of curiosity and the moral of a point of view. . . . His facts are so perfectly rendered that, like the actualities of life itself, they demand from the reader the faculty of observation which is rare, the power of appreciation which is generally wanting in most of us who are guided mainly by empty phrases requiring no effort, demanding from us no qualities except a vague susceptibility to emotion. (*NLL*, pp. 26–7)

Conrad's humanistic attitude to his speakers' self-deceit, folly and half-truth follows the attitude he ascribes to Maupassant: 'He is merciless and yet gentle with his mankind; he does not rail at their prudent fears and their small artifices; he does not despise their labours. It seems to me that he looks with an eye of profound pity upon their troubles, deceptions and misery' (*NLL*, p. 29).

Conrad praised James for his presentation of 'the fine consciences, in their perplexities, in the sophism of their mistakes' (*NLL*, p. 18). The fastidious, over-refined narrators 'of 'The Informer', 'An Anarchist' and 'Il Conde'—all written in the 1905–6 period shortly after the January 1905 publication of the James essay—show James's influence. Yet Conrad's ambivalence to James is revealed by the implicit suggestion that possibly James's characteristic choice of subject is too limited and that beneath the civilised exterior is a lack of substance: 'He has mastered the country, his domain, not wild indeed, but full of romantic glimpses, of deep shadows and sunny places. . . . And, indeed, ugliness has but little place in this world of his creation' (*NLL*, p. 17).

In four of the following tales—'The Brute', 'An Anarchist', 'The Informer', and 'Il Conde'—the speaker's present state of mind is the central subject. Barely aware of an audience, the speaker is engaged in trying intellectually to extricate himself from experiences with which he has not been able to cope emotionally and morally. Because Conrad's imperceptive narrators have pretences to decency and sensitivity, they demand our pity and compassion, despite their emotional and moral shortcomings. Our response to unreliable and/or imperceptive narrators depends upon, as Wayne Booth indicates, 'our linguistic experience, our logical and moral sense, and our past experience', and these elements vary from reader to reader.[2] What happens is described by Mark Schorer:

> The fracture between the character of the event as we feel it to be and the character of the narrator as he reports the event to us is the essential irony, yet it is not in any way a simple one; for the narrator's view, as we soon discover, is not so much the wrong view as merely *a* view, although a special one. No simple inversion of statement can yield up the truth, for the truth is the maze.[3]

In a tale told by an imperceptive narrator, the reader's role is similar to his role in a dramatic monologue. Because the speaker is the one living voice within the fictive world, the reader momentarily surrenders his own consciousness and experiences the consciousness of the speaker.[4] He brings his own, presumably larger, perspective, to a situation seen by the speaker's narrow perspective, at the same time as he shares the speaker's consciousness. The author may give hints that the speaker's values are defective, but the degree to which he posits alternative values varies.

For his epigraph to *A Set of Six*, the one volume where the prose monologue is the major form, Conrad borrows the following nursery rhyme:

> Les petites marionnettes
>    Font, font, font,
> Trois petits tours
>    Et puis s'en vont.

Conrad's passionate if quixotic preference for marionette-shows over drama may help us understand the epigraph:

> But I love a marionette-show. . . . I never listen to the text

mouthed somewhere out of sight by invisible men who are here today and rotten tomorrow. I love the marionettes that are without life, that come so near to being immortal! (6 Dec. 1897; *LL*, vol. i, p. 213.)

Especially in the political monologues, Conrad is the 'invisible man' and ventriloquist amusedly watching his puppets enact their parts in a Vanity Fair of moral and emotional myopia. Yet we must listen to *his* text.

Conrad, like his twentieth-century counterparts, struggles to find his authentic self through writing. Eliot uses Prufrock and Gerontion, and Joyce uses the anonymous boy in the early *Dubliners* stories and later, Stephen Dedalus, to clarify themselves through fictions that exaggerate characteristics of a potential self that has been rejected, or a former self that has become obsolete. Similarly, except for 'The Brute' which is a kind of crude *jeu d'esprit*, these tales help Conrad define the humanistic values that he believed make civilisation possible. Because they allow him to 'test' political and moral positions that are finally revealed as inadequate, the political monologues help define the attitudes that inform *The Secret Agent* and *Under Western Eyes*. His experiences with ironic ventriloquism in 'The Informer', 'An Anarchist', and 'Il Conde' make it possible for him to create the extremely complex self-deprecating language teacher in *Under Western Eyes*, whom Conrad gradually reveals as the one moral figure in a world beset by violence and anarchy.

## II. 'GASPAR RUIZ' (1906) AND 'THE BRUTE' (1906)

Conrad was sceptical of those who believed in any political values with passionate certainty, and he regarded political movements with deep suspicion. Notwithstanding his humanism that often qualified his pessimism, he never shared Cunninghame Graham's belief that the replacement of one political system by another would lead to a better world. Written between *Nostromo* and *The Secret Agent* and completed in late 1905, 'Gaspar Ruiz' takes its subject, but not its quality, from the South American novel. Gaspar Ruiz, a man of the people, has great strength and size, but limited intelligence and imagination. As Avrom Fleishman suggests, the plot 'serves to suggest a political nexus as binding as fate, impersonally destructive to all individuality (e.g. to Ruiz's flamboyant egoism), and incommensurate with its victims' powers of explanation.'[5]

With its satiric view of the vicissitudes of South American revolutionary and counter-revolutionary movements, 'Gaspar Ruiz' echoes *Nostromo*. The earthquake, eliciting the cry 'Misericordia', serves as an ironic comment upon man-made violence created by political differences. As a victim who derived energy from his adoration of a strong-minded woman, Gaspar recalls Dr Monygham; but as a man who struggled to wrest his private life from public and political demands, he suggests *Nostromo*. Losing his anonymity when he identified his private interest with public matters, Gaspar is also caught in the web of history and politics. In both tales, the Cordillera mountains stand apart from the destructive behaviour of mankind and take their place in a cosmic pattern which seems to reduce man to insignificance. But, sadly, there are few suggestions of *Nostromo's* subtlety in this rather melodramatic tale.

The narration is shared by General Santierra, who recalls incidents in which he took part a half-century ago, and an anonymous speaker, who eventually reveals himself as one of the general's audience. The story depends in part upon the incongruity of the urbane, civilised General Santierra describing violent and savage actions. The general's straightforward syntax and nostalgic tone suggest the memoirs of a worldly military hero. Superficially knowledgeable, but oblivious to the real moral implications of what he describes, General Santierra shows the value and limitations of an ahistorical, but personal perspective. He romanticises the past into a pattern of significance culminating in the revelation that he has given Gaspar Ruiz's daughter, Erminia, a place in his heart. The very wordiness of the general's reminiscence implies a solipsism which is part of his character. As Marlow does in 'Youth', the narrator recalls his immaturity with gentle irony and fondness, but here the cruelty and sadism of the tale ironically undercut the general's sentimentalism. His insistence that he suffered begins to seem inappropriate when we recall that he survived the victims to enjoy comfort and prosperity. The anonymous narrator's simple, succinct wisdom, confidence, and mature self-assurance are the values by which the moral collapse brought on by the civil war is measured. But if he is to supplement the general's point of view, why does Conrad make him part of the general's audience and—since the general is his only apparent source—presumably dependent entirely on the general's information? By having the anonymous narrator's detached point of view dependent upon the general's involved point of view, Conrad unfortunately created a rather limiting and circuitous situation.

Except for 'Gaspar Ruiz', the first story in *A Set of Six*, a subtitle defines the narrator's perspective; in 'The Brute', written in the 1905–6 winter, the subtitle is 'An Indignant Tale'. The source of the principal speaker's indignation is the ship which deprived his brother of his fiancée. Conrad's original subtitle was 'A Piece of Invective', suggesting the juxtaposition of the shrilly indignant principal narrator with his impassive audience. Conrad uses a calm introductory narrator to place the hysterical principal narrator in an ironic context. The tale's focus is upon the principal narrator's ludicrous, inconsistent, and simplistic interpretation of the death of his brother's fiancée on a ship, the *Apse Family*, which he recalls as a 'deadly killer'. Yet he unconsciously presents the boat simultaneously as a gigantic whore and as a hermaphroditic monster. He seems to relish describing the female boat's violation by a masculine rock: 'That brute ran up a shelving, rocky shore, tearing her bottom out, till she stopped short' (pp. 130–1). The narrator is not a detached, objective observer but one whose experience has been affected by his private grief and by his discomfort with women and sexuality. As with the other dramatic monologuists to be considered in this chapter, he tells us more about himself than he does about the world he describes. An interesting if unsuccessful experiment in the use of the prose dramatic monologue, 'The Brute' ranks with 'The Black Mate' and 'The Partner' as the poorest Conrad.

While 'The Brute' purports to be a study of Edwardians trying to cope with sexuality, it actually reveals an instance of Conrad's own bad taste in dealing with sexual materials. Dismayed at the English tendencies to legislate private morality, and especially to purify drama, Conrad wrote in 1907 in a short piece entitled 'The Censor of Plays': '[The Censor] must be unconscious. . . . He must be obscure, insignificant and mediocre—in thought, act, speech, and sympathy. He must know nothing of art, of life—and of himself' (*NLL*, pp. 79–80). 'The Brute' may be his joke at the expense of those who would support censors, but it reveals his difficulty in dealing with sexual matters. That the principal speaker is assigned a unique style shows that Conrad's use of the sexual metaphor is deliberate. Yet the entire effort to place sexual innuendoes in socially permissible contexts demonstrates Conrad's own leering enjoyment of adolescent sexual humour, perhaps a vestige of the bachelor ethos of maritime life. Both his proclivity to view sexuality as a threat to masculine independence and his use of elaborate formal devices in the cause of crude sexual puns indicate, in this tale, an immature view of psychosexual relations.

## III. POLITICAL MONOLOGUES: 'AN ANARCHIST' (1906), 'THE INFORMER' (1906) AND 'IL CONDE' (1908)

The three political monologues not only give us insight into Conrad's novels about politics, but they are splendid stories in their own right. The narrators of 'An Anarchist', 'The Informer', and 'Il Conde' reveal emotional and moral deficiencies, even while thinking of themselves as urbane and detached observers of the events they report. What distinguishes these three tales from Conrad's other fiction is that they are dramatic monologues told by imperceptive and self-deluded narrators whose efforts to impose specific interpretations on the events they report and to define their own roles in relation to these events are undermined by the obvious inadequacy and one-sidedness of their versions of events. The narrators of these tales believe themselves to be sophisticated, objective, and even dispassionate observers speaking to a sympathetic audience that shares their values. It is inconceivable to any of them that their sensibilities or values are deficient. As in a dramatic monologue, the reader is expected to sympathise with the speaker at the same time as he judges the speaker's deficiencies. Over the course of a story the speaker unconsciously presents a self-portrait quite different from the impression he wishes to create for his audience. Conrad uses a variety of subtle methods to expose the inadequacies of his speakers. The narrator may be unable to recognise the moral implications of the actions he narrates. The narrator may make statements that have little cognitive value and are obvious reflections of the narrator's own psychic needs, or seemingly insignificant details may be introduced so that the reader will be able to draw relationships that escape the teller. Often these devices work in concord as when the narrator of 'Il Conde' recalls that he had first met the Count at a *Resting Hermes*. In this case, a seemingly objective statement about an apparently insignificant detail becomes a transparently subjective one in which the speaker unconsciously indicates his preference for passivity and inaction, a preference he shares with the Count whom he purports to discuss dispassionately. Without realising it, the narrator points out a

symbol of the milieu to which he and the Count belong: the god of
eloquence and learning displayed in a condition of stasis. The speakers
of these stories are cultured men of some means who imagine that
they speak for a civilisation under seige. The Count of 'Il Conde'
embodies their ideal; neither dilettante nor connoisseur, 'He said the
right things. . . . Nothing profound. His taste was natural rather
than cultivated' (p. 269). These stories, like *The Secret Agent* (written
between 'An Anarchist' and 'The Informer' on one side, and 'Il
Conde' on the other), stress the devolution of the manners and values
of Western civilisation.[6] Those who are potentially capable of
defending civilisation, including even Sir Ethelred whose compelling
interest is in his fisheries bill, fail to defend actively the civilisation
they purport to value. ('No details please,' he insists to the Assistant
Commissioner.) Serious moral dereliction on the part of those who
opt for an ivory-tower life, for their avocation, and the *art* of living,
enables the revolutionaries and anarchists to become a pervasive
threat.

The first of these stories, 'An Anarchist', was completed in late
1905. At first glance, the story seems to be composed of two unrelated
sections: a prelude depicting the relationship between the narrator, a
lepidopterist, and his adversary Harry Gee, and a principal section
containing the pathetic history of Paul, the former French anarchist.
Indeed, most of the critics who have commented on the tale have
virtually restricted their comments to the story of Paul's downfall.[7]
But one cannot ignore the narrator's encounter with Harry Gee,
which occupies over one third of the story, especially if one recalls the
importance of the introductory sections and the frame devices in
Conrad's other shorter fiction. Conrad juxtaposes the narrator's
recollection of his relationship to Harry Gee with the violent story of
the engineer, who had been a fellow victim of Gee's barbarism.
Conrad does this, I think, to show that telling a tale can be a device to
satisfy one's own psychic needs; specifically, the telling enables the
narrator not only consciously to avenge Harry Gee's aggressive abuse
by means of ridiculing him to his audience, but also unconsciously to
vent his frustrated and repressed antipathy to him.

When he recalls how Paul murdered his enemies, he is working out
his repressed urge for revenge by verbalising his unconscious fantasy
of dealing violently with the man he despises. The subtitle of this
undeservedly neglected tale, 'A Desperate Tale', refers not only to
Paul's history, but to the hypersensitive narrator's desperate psychic
need to avenge himself for the abuse suffered at the hands of Harry

Gee. He has been deeply frustrated by his inability to deal with Gee. His fastidious nature resented 'chaff' in the 'absence of all friendly feeling' and cringed before the manager's insults (p. 138). Not surprisingly, the narrator took umbrage at being marked by Gee as 'Ha, ha, ha!—a desperate butterfly-slayer. Ha, ha, ha!' (p. 137). In the first few pages he harps on Gee's abuse by repeating the various insults he had received. Obviously he still resents Gee's 'wearisome repetition of descriptive phrases applied to people with a burst of laughter' (p. 138). He lacks the emotional and moral equipment to function in a world dominated by 'warden hunts', 'convict hunts', and other forms of brutality. He is like the narrators of 'Il Conde' and 'The Informer', both of whom also protect themselves from involvement in public affairs by withdrawing into something of an hermetic existence. The lepidopterist, like the collector of 'The Informer' and both the narrator and the Count of 'Il Conde', becomes a passive collaborator with those who, like Harry Gee, would reduce civilisation to a Darwinian struggle of the survival of the fittest.

While the satiric thrust at Gee is a scathing critique of the corporate morality, the lepidopterist's sympathetic presentation of the anarchist derives in part from his willingness to identify with anyone who is Gee's adversary. In his retelling, the narrator's method is to let the manager and the anarchist speak in defence of their own conduct and to assume that his audience's reactions to them will be the same as his own. The narrator recognises that the manager's defence of his treatment of the anarchist exposes the manager's brutal profiteering and justifies what he, the narrator, has told the reader about the manager. But he himself is imperceptive about the anarchist's character. Notwithstanding the moral delicacy he applies to other matters, he offers no condemnation of Paul's conduct or evaluation of Paul's sanity. While Paul may deserve some sympathy as a psychotic personality, surely the recital of Paul's own excuses is not sufficient to preclude adverse judgements upon his behaviour. The speaker does not understand that he is fascinated by Paul's capacity for passion, rage, and violence because his only weapon, namely his rhetoric, has proved ineffectual.[8]

Written in the 1905–6 winter before *The Secret Agent*, 'The Informer' is a splendid story, as well as a testing ground for both the ironic tone and the subject matter of the major novel. (Since, originally, Conrad thought of *The Secret Agent* as a short story, perhaps it was to be a sequel to 'The Informer'.)[9] 'The Informer' depends upon a narrator who does not understand either the implications of his encounter with the anarchist, Mr X, or Mr X's motives for telling his tale of anarchists. The reader shares X's joke at the expense of the narrator, at the same time that Conrad invites the reader to watch the narrator condemn himself out of his own mouth. The narrator of 'The Informer' is frightened by Mr X's urbanity and sophistication and does not try to disguise his shock at finding that he and X are not as antithetical as he would like to believe. X belongs to a noble family, looks 'fashionable', and visits the same 'very good restaurant' where they dine together and share a bottle of champagne. To the narrator's grudging admiration, X can share the narrator's enthusiasm for porcelains and bronzes. The narrator is horrified by his perception that X could be mistaken for him and, indeed, could superficially appear to be his double.

But the narrator does not realise that he presents himself in a rather unfavourable light. The narrator's fanatical obsession with his avocation is indicated at the outset by his insistent repetition of variations on the root word 'collect' and by his metaphor to describe how his friend stores up his experience (he 'puts the memory away in the galleries of his mind' [p. 73]).[10] Collecting has become his *raison d'être*, the yardstick by which he measures human experience. For him and his friend who 'collects acquaintances', *objets d'art* and human beings are equally interesting for the private pleasure of contemplating their uniqueness. The narrator's epistemology is based on his collections. He discusses this new phenomenon, an urbane anarchist, in the only language he can understand. He compares Mr X with some of his Chinese bronzes which are 'monstrously precious'.

Mr X provokes the narrator into rebuking him for his luxurious life. This gives X the opening he desires. He reminds the narrator pointedly that the 'well-fed' bourgeois, by devouring his polemics 'with wonder and horror', underwrite his standard of living. The tale that follows is a direct thrust at the obtuse narrator whose entire monologue verifies the truth of X's assertion to the narrator that 'you, too, like to see mischief being made' (p. 78). The 'world at large' does not have 'an inkling' of X's activities, partly because those who could warn it—namely, the narrator and his friend—tacitly collaborate with their enemies (p. 74). The narrator may not be swayed by demagogy, but he too is guilty of the very 'amateurism' which, X implies, undermines society's structure (p. 78). Turning the screw ever tighter on his listener, he explains, in the vocabulary to which the narrator can respond, the difference between gesture and sincerity: 'Just as good and otherwise harmless people will join you in ecstasies over your collection without having the slightest notion in what its marvellousness really consists' (p. 78). The extent to which X puts the narrator off guard and makes him self-conscious is illustrated by his confused reaction to X's indictment: 'I felt the need to say something which would not be in the nature of assent and yet would not invite discussion' (p. 79).

X's tale, motivated by the 'petty malice' of aggravating the narrator, illustrates how the poses and gestures of the aristocracy, far from being harmless, actually destroy a sincere man. Although a police agent posing as an anarchist, Sevrin is admired by X because he is a man who acts from passion and conviction. X implies that such men, whether police or anarchist, have much in common, and that the real contrast is between men of conviction and those, like the narrator, for whom passionate commitment is impossible. X cynically implies that it is appropriate that the police masquerade as anarchists and vice versa because they are bound by intensity of conviction and are different in kind and quality from the brother, sister, and the narrator, who lack the character to either uphold or destroy civilisation. But, for the reader, not only the ability of Sevrin to move from revolutionary to police agent and of X to move from anarchist to aristocrat, but the similarity between ideologically opposite fanaticisms suggests the moral *equivalence* of terrorist and police agent. (That police and anarchists are similarly motivated is a major theme in *The Secret Agent* where members of both groups serve their private interests while espousing public or political values.) The emotions and values that the narrator respects are systematically divested of their significance; X reduces everything that makes the narrator's life significant to one verbal common denominator: 'gesture', the word he uses to suggest the amorality of the leisure classes.

Although not the major focal point, the story surely judges the urbane anarchist. X himself makes few material sacrifices and lives as a member of the very class he despises. Even allowing for the distortion due to the narrator's prejudice, our impression of X is as a rather macabre figure. 'All bony ridges and sunken hollows', he is completely expressionless; and yet he fully enjoys the very civilisation he seeks to destroy. His enjoyment of watching the Hermione Street squirm and his sending Sevrin's diary to the girl testify to his sadistic impulses. Merely because he readily admits to drawing upon the 'fund of secret malice' which 'we all have' does not extenuate his behaviour. Surely one who controls his potential for malice is morally superior to one who does not. He displays this fund of malice in every aspect of the grotesque comedy he stages for his own benefit. He even drops details solely to provoke the narrator into a pompous, self-righteous position. Such is the case when he drops the names of some 'advanced' publications, not because the names are relevant to his story, but to intimidate the narrator.

Thus 'The Informer' is more than an 'ironic tale' (to recall Conrad's descriptive subtitle for the story in *A Set of Six*) about Sevrin's heroic sacrifice for a girl who cannot perceive anything but 'gesture and grimace'. Rather, it is one of Conrad's dramatic monologues in which the narrator damns himself out of his own mouth. The narrator does not realise he has been a victim of the anarchist's mordant wit and that his discomfort—he ceases dining at the 'good' restaurant—has been manipulated and staged to indulge X's zest for petty malice. The 'Informer' becomes, then, not only Sevrin, but the narrator who exposes himself as ineffectual *and* Mr X who reveals himself as a malicious, petty aristocrat despite his alleged concern for the 'amendment' of mankind by means of 'terror and violence' (p. 77).

Critics have neglected the importance of the narrator in discussions of 'Il Conde', although a number of provocative analyses of this subtle story, written in 1906 after the completion of *The Secret Agent*, have appeared since 1955.[11] The narrator is another of Conrad's imperceptive speakers. He thinks he stands outside the story he narrates as a dispassionate objective narrator. On occasion, he both recognises the Count's shortcomings and takes an ironic view of his behaviour. But within Conrad's broader perspective, he is seen to be narrow and limited. Conrad invites his reader to see the close similarity between the narrator and the Count. Far more than he knows, the narrator identifies and sympathises with the Count and becomes for the reader the 'secret sharer' of the Count's plight and the indignities he suffers.

To begin with superficial resemblances: both narrator and Il Conde visit the same museum, admire the same *objets d'art*, and stay at the same hotel ('good, but not extravagantly up to date' [p. 269]). The narrator obviously admires the scrupulous pains the Count takes with his appearance and assures his audience that he is a 'perfectly unaffected gentleman' (p. 269). Yet the reader knows that the Count's dyed moustache and perfume are foppish. The narrator admires him for not being part of the 'hateful tribe' in which he includes both dilettante and connoisseur. In the narrator's world a 'fairly intelligent man of the world' is preferable to an expert (p. 269). The Count is a good European because he speaks four languages (p. 272)—which is exactly how many languages the narrator uses in the tale (English, French, Italian, and Spanish).[12]

Yet there are more fundamental resemblances, too. The very words the narrator uses to describe the Count apply equally well to him. Like the Count, he is a 'man of moderate feelings and toned-down vocabulary' (pp. 274–5). Typical of how the narrator's punctilious behaviour and fastidious rhetoric fuse into one gesture is his circumlocution, 'I did not think I was intruding', in explaining how he came to introduce himself (p. 270). His self-effacing account is interrupted occasionally by fussy parentheses and stammerings induced by over-delicacy (as when he describes the Count's anxieties when the knife is pressed in his stomach [p. 283]). What the narrator says of the Count, when the latter tells him of his encounter, is wonderfully appropriate to his own method of telling: 'He was systematically minute in his narrative, simply in order . . . not to let his excitement get the better of him' (p. 275).

The narrator and Il Conde are the same type of person. After the narrator seeks him out as his companion, they soon become fast friends. The former tells us that the Count's 'existence' was 'correct, well-ordered and conventional, undisturbed by startling events' (p. 270). And there is nothing in the speaker's limited perspective to indicate that he has a wider breadth of experience than the Count. Indeed, upon rereading, we can only smile when the narrator describes the Count's life: 'It was a kindly existence, with its joys and sorrows regulated by the course of Nature—marriages, births, deaths—ruled by the prescribed usages of good society and protected by the State' (p. 272). For this, ironically, describes the narrator, whose only actions are visiting a sick friend and seeing off the train he describes as the Count's funeral cortège. His defence of the Count's way of life ('his idleness was always ready to take a kindly form' [p. 273]) becomes a defence of his own. In both men, we see what Paul Wiley, speaking of only the Count, calls 'a form of subtle egotism, an overrefinement of feeling'.[13] In this regard, the speaker believes that the making of one's fortune requires 'roughness' and implies that to have the right-sized inheritance is far more 'proper' than to earn one's livelihood (p. 272).

The narrator shows himself to be only partially reliable in several ways other than his failure to recognise that he is the same sort of man as the Count. The narrator, like his double, also fears having his world punctured by unknown terrors. The narrator wants to believe that the Count's only reason for leaving Naples is that, as the narrator puts it, 'his delicate conception of his dignity was defiled by a degrading experience' (p. 288). *He* denies that timidity played a part in the Count's exit, though the *Count* indicates he is afraid. And he wants to romanticise the Count's departure as equivalent to the Japanese *hara-kiri*, 'a form of suicide following upon dishonour, upon an intolerable outrage to the delicacy of one's feelings' (p. 280).

The Count has been touched by the dormant passions and instinctive behaviour that he, like the narrator, has distilled out of his life. In symbolic terms, the Count, the over-civilised aesthete, is haunted by his repressed passions, objectified by the *Cavaliere*. His assailant seems a ubiquitous threat. The Count thinks he sees him everywhere because the *Cavaliere* is, on one level, his instinctive self; the latter *is* from a good family and *is* a university student. (The *Cavaliere*, like our own instinctive urges, appears and disappears without the Count's being conscious of him). His encounter with this irrational opposite permanently transforms the Count; he actually behaves more instinctively after his encounter with the *Cavaliere*. He gets into a tramcar 'by a sort of instinct', beckons to a pedlar in the Café 'on a sudden impulse' and experiences a 'simply ravenous' hunger that demands attention (pp. 284, 286). When the Count looks in the mirror and sees the brutal face of the *Cavaliere* rather than his own image, the reader sees that not only the elitist 'culture' of the Count, but the very social fabric that preserves community from anarchy is under siege. Naples—and by implication, Western Europe—is threatened by destruction no less catastrophic than that which Herculaneum and Pompeii had suffered from natural forces, unless it restrains the pervasive violence implied by the ubiquitous *Cavaliere* (p. 269).

While Avrom Fleishman has discussed 'Il Conde's' resemblance to Thomas Mann's 'Mario and the Magician',[14] the more striking similarity is with *Death in Venice* (1912)—specifically, Aschenbach's recurring encounters with characters that objectify the libidinous energies he has repressed: the stranger in Munich, the old dandy on the boat, the gondolier, and the performer are the major examples. Both Aschenbach and the Count have devoted their lives to creating a style of life. But the Count, like Aschenbach, cannot escape passions and instincts. However, once Aschenbach discovers his latent passions, he follows his impulses to death, while the Count is repelled by the possibility of aroused passions. He turns his back on his enlarged perspective and departs to certain death: '*Vedi Napoli e poi mori!*' ('See Naples and then die').

Both 'The Informer' and 'Il Conde' examine the implications of an over-delicate aristocracy comprised of men who protect themselves from involvement in meaningful public or private relationships by withdrawing into an ivory tower to meditate upon the beauty of *objets d'art*.[15] These men, 'expert in the art of living', in the words of the narrator of 'Il Conde', seek to base their lives, as the narrator of 'The Informer' puts it, 'upon a suave and delicate discrimination of social and artistic values' (p. 77). Yet society is ravaged by the barbarians and anarchists for whom life is the survival of the fittest and to whom traditional values mean nothing. Because the traditional guardians of *res publica* retire to self-indulgent private activities, they become passive collaborators with those who consciously seek to undermine society.

In a 1904 letter to R. B. Cunninghame Graham, Conrad had expressed misgivings about the kind of life lived by the artist, G. F. Watts: 'And so poor Watts is coming to the end of his august career. What a full and rounded life. And yet it seems poor in stress and passion which are the true elixirs against the majestic overpowering tediousness of an existence full of allegoric visions' (2 July 1904; *Cunninghame Graham*, p. 154). 'Il Conde' is a critical examination of the effects of living by gestures and conventions and the concomitant neglect of instincts and emotions. The unreliable narrator is oblivious to Il Conde's faults and unconscious of his resemblance to this man, to whom he occasionally tries to take a condescending attitude. But the reader sees that the narrator is Innocence posing as Experience revealed as Innocence. 'A Pathetic Tale', the descriptive subtitle with which Conrad introduces the story in *A Set of Six*, implies not only the Count's demise and the tone of the narrator, but also the narrator's failure to perceive that he, too, as the Count's 'secret sharer' is threatened by the ubiquitous barbarians.[16]

## IV. 'THE DUEL' (1908)

Conrad was increasingly fascinated by the Napoleonic era, which serves as the setting for 'The Duel', 'The Warrior's Soul', *The Rover*, and *Suspense*, the novel that he left incomplete at his death. In 'Autocracy and War' (1905), Conrad writes:

The degradation of the ideas of freedom and justice at the root
of the French revolution is made manifest in the person of its
heir; a personality without law or faith. . . . The subtle and
manifold influence for evil of the Napoleonic episode as a
school of violence, as a sower of national hatreds, as the direct
provocator of obscurantism and reaction, of political tyranny
and injustice, cannot well be exaggerated. (*NLL*, p. 86)

In 'The Duel', written in 1907, a basically sensible man, D'Hubert,
becomes entangled in an absurd rivalry initiated by a choleric fellow
soldier named Feraud. But adherence to a narrow conception of
honourable behaviour prevents his extricating himself from a
prolonged feud which persists against the background of the
Napoleonic era and shapes the lives of its participants. The code of
honour, seemingly apolitical, is actually the essence of the military
sensibility. Until Napoleon's final defeat, the lives of both participants
are defined in terms of a continuing senseless rivalry. The subtitle, 'A
Military Tale', is ironic because the duel, Feraud's 'war of his own', is
Conrad's parody of military struggle. 'To the surprise and admiration
of their fellows, two officers, like insane artists trying to gild refined
gold or paint the lily, pursued a private contest through the years of
universal carnage' (p. 165). War, Conrad implies, creates the appetite
for this other form of combat. Conrad's gently ironic omniscient
narrator stresses how war and hatred exhaust potentially meaningful
lives.[17] The narrator's tone of civilised tolerance creates the alternative to the waste of human energy exacted by the lifelong duel.
Passionate love is the redeeming value in 'The Duel'. It enables
D'Hubert to discover another self, a lyrical, subjective self beneath the
man who had nearly sacrificed private life for a career. Through his
attachment to Adèle he lives in an entirely different universe; he learns
that private relationships are what makes life meaningful.

The episode in which the two rivals are drawn together as
comrades for a moment presents fleetingly the friendship that might
have developed. Conrad often includes in the structure of his narrative
a brief look at what might have been. In 'Heart of Darkness',
the alternative takes the form of Marlow's inclination to succumb like
Kurtz to his primitive urges. The alternative to the Captain's triumph
in 'The Secret Sharer', his next story after 'The Duel', is Leggatt's
story of a breakdown in self-discipline. It may be that the relationship
between these two men was a primitive version of the psychological
doubling between the Captain and Leggatt in 'The Secret Sharer'.

Feraud and D'Hubert, completely antithetical in temperament and background—the one an irascible passionate southerner of common background, the other an urbane, rational northerner of good family—might well have been close friends. (After all, the friendship of fundamentally different men is at the heart of 'The Secret Sharer'.) In the retreat from Russia, they display heroic vitality, expending 'all their store of moral energy . . . in resisting the terrific enmity of nature and the crushing sense of irretrievable disaster'; as 'two indomitable companions in activity and endurance', they seem to possess a vigour which D'Hubert lacks and a dignity that Feraud lacks (pp. 212, 214).

NOTES

1. Conrad, *Last Essays*, p. 208.
2. Wayne Booth, *The Rhetoric of Fiction* (Chicago: University of Chicago Press, 1961), p. 308.
3. Mark Schorer, 'Introduction' in Ford Madox Ford, *The Good Soldier* (New York: Vintage, 1951), p. vii.
4. My understanding of the dramatic monologue is indebted to Robert Langbaum, *The Poetry of Experience* (New York: Norton and Company, 1963).
5. Avrom Fleishman, *Conrad's Politics Community and Anarchy in the Fiction of Joseph Conrad* (Baltimore: Johns Hopkins Press, 1967), p. 135.
6. In his fine study, *Conrad's Short Fiction* (Berkeley and Los Angeles: University of California Press, 1969), Lawrence Graver objects that we do not learn enough about character in 'An Anarchist' and 'The Informer'. Speaking of Paul, he writes, 'His situation is passive and he himself indifferent; we learn what was done to him by others, but get little sense of what he did to himself or how his ideas about life are changed by his experience' (p. 134). He goes on to complain that in 'The Informer', 'the girl and Sevrin are pasteboard figures manipulated to make a point. Even the personality of Mr X is not clearly conveyed. . . . The actual drama inherent in this predicament is not exploited' (p. 141). But Conrad wanted these characters to be representative rather than nominalistic.
7. See, for example, Graver, pp. 132–5; Leo Gurko, *Joseph Conrad: Giant in Exile* (New York: Macmillan, 1962), pp. 164–5; Jocelyn Baines, *Joseph Conrad: A Critical Biography* (New York: McGraw Hill, 1960), pp. 323–4.
8. For a more complete discussion of 'An Anarchist', see my 'The Lepidopterist's Revenge: Theme and Structure in Conrad's "An Anarchist"', *Studies in Short Fiction*, vol. viii (Spring 1971), pp. 330–4.
9. See Baines, pp. 325–7. For a fine discussion of this tale, see James Walton, 'Mr X's "Little Joke": The Design of "The Informer"', *Studies in Short Fiction*, vol. iv (Summer 1967), pp. 322–33. In *Joseph Conrad: The Three Lives*, (Farrar, Straus and Wroox), pp. 588–9, Karl has a brief but perceptive discussion of this story.

10. There are nine variations of the root word 'collect' in the first three paragraphs.
11. See John Howard Wills, 'Adam, Axel and "Il Conde"', *Modern Fiction Studies*, I (1955), pp. 22–5; repr. in R. S. Stallman, ed. *The Art of Joseph Conrad* (East Lansing: Michigan State University, 1960), pp. 254–9 and John V. Hagopian, 'The Pathos of "Il Conde"', *Studies in Short Fiction*, vol. iii (Fall 1964), pp. 30–8.

   Wills discusses the story in terms of two allegorical patterns: 'The Expulsion from Eden Allegory', and the 'Ivory Tower myth of the fin de siècle'. He speaks of the 'narrator's ironic recreation' of the Count's expulsion and assumes that the narrator improvises the aural symbolism 'to parallel and enrich the literal account'. But there is reason to believe that the aural effects are provided, not by the narrator, but by the over-refined Count who, even while being confronted by what for him is the most degrading experience conceivable, is attentive to the band's music. In an article that rebukes Wills for taking 'Il Conde' too seriously and for rather glib use of myth criticism, Hagopian assumes that Conrad shares with his narrator a sense of the Count's shortcomings and a recognition of the Count's function in the story. He speaks of an 'aloof and somewhat ironic narrator whose idiom, imagery, and narrative tone make the aging aristocrat not quite worthy of our fullest respect, admiration, or sympathy'. But the words aloof and ironic, I think, more appropriately describe *Conrad's* stance in relation to the Count *and the narrator*.
12. Hagopian, p. 32. 'Il' is Italian but 'Conde' is Spanish. Fourteen years later, Conrad in his Author's Note to *A Set of Six* implied that this had been an error.
13. Paul L. Wiley, *Conrad's Measure of Man* (Madison: University of Wisconsin Press, 1954), p. 90.
14. Fleishman, p. 142.
15. The resemblance between Conrad's Heyst in *Victory* to Prince Axel, of Villiers de L'isle Adam's drama, has been noted. See Wills, pp. 258–9 and Leo Gurko, p. 213.
16. I have discussed 'Il Conde' in greater detail in my 'The Self-Deceiving Narrator of Conrad's "Il Conde"', *Studies in Short Fiction*, vol. vi (Winter 1969), pp. 187–93.
17. I am taking issue with Karl who argues that this is a 'tale of honor, glory, and individual integrity'; and that 'the two duelists . . . give meaning and substance to their lives by means of a defense of their honor' (*Joseph Conrad: The Three Lives*, p. 628).

# 10 Affirming personal values: The significance of the language teacher in *Under Western Eyes*

## I

It may be that the fundamental importance of *Under Western Eyes* (1911), the last of Conrad's major political novels, is in its rejection of political commitment in favour of personal relationships and private commitments. *Under Western Eyes* needs to be considered as a dialectical novel whose central agon is a conflict between political and personal values. As with *Lord Jim*, *Under Western Eyes* has generally been examined as if it were a completed and static object, rather than as a dynamic process continually changing shape as it moves to its conclusion. Yet a dialectical novel, like a sophisticated argument, cannot be summarised by merely looking at its conclusion or by equating the set speech of a character with the meaning of the novel. *Under Western Eyes* deliberately begins with a self-deprecating, almost bathetic narrator, who seems to be imperceptive and obtuse. But the action of the novel gradually establishes his perceptivity, morality, and humanity, until he becomes a centre of value within the novel.

Rather than a 'fixed point measuring Razumov's growth', as Robert Secor claims, the language teacher is a dynamic character who grows in stature as he is drawn into situations requiring personal commitment and moral discrimination.[1] If, at first, the self-deprecating narrator seems to many readers a refugee from a James novel in a Dostoevskian world, he emerges as a somewhat attractive alternative to other characters who exaggerate their own emotions, idealise their motives, and glorify their actions. As the novel progresses, the over-fastidious, self-conscious language teacher who claims that he has become anaesthetised by words reveals himself as a substantial figure: a deeply committed friend, capable of perspicacious observation and sensitive to the needs of others. In striking contrast not only to Razumov but to every character in the novel, he responds to the dilemma of the Haldins. Because he is almost embarrassingly self-effacing about his role, many readers forget that he has befriended the Haldins, while their fellow Russians, the revolutionaries, are interested only in enlisting Natalie for their cause. Without gesture and verbosity, he performs valuable service for Natalie Haldin—counselling her unselfishly, speaking to Razumov on her behalf, and accompanying her on her search for Razumov. As he experiences a range of passions and attitudes beyond his former experience, the speaker becomes freed from his repressions and discovers within himself an imaginative power and emotional intensity far beyond that of which he had been formerly capable. Not unlike Axel Heyst, who also responds to the demands of his conscience and the subconscious arousal of repressed feelings, the English teacher is transformed from a character who has chosen to observe passively into one who is impelled to participate.

Paradoxically, the narrator who is independent of political movements has a highly developed sense of community responsibility, while Razumov, who weds himself to the regime, functions without commitment to any other human being. Obsessed first with personal success and later with self-preservation, Razumov is without a fundamental moral identity. Simultaneously Everyman (chameleon-like taking on every role required of him) and No Man (lacking an authentic self), he is Conrad's vision of moral damnation. The narrator's independence from arbitrary forces is fortuitous; but his own fundamental decency is responsible for his willingness to respond to others and for his subtle moral judgement. The narrator introduces seemingly obsolete standards of morality into an imagined world inhabited by political visionaries who confuse personal with public interest and who act impulsively and passionately without considering the consequences to others. He is quite intentionally depicted as a vestige of the novel of manners; his sensible and traditional behaviour seems as anachronistic as his tact and sense of propriety.

The language teacher's retrospective narrative recreates the process of coming to terms with the terrifying Dionysian world he has confronted. Conrad has the narrator introduce himself as an almost ludicrously ineffectual person: 'To a teacher of languages there comes a time when the world is but a place of many words and man appears a mere talking animal not much more wonderful than a parrot' (p. 3). He even claims that his occupation has deprived him of 'whatever share of imagination, observation, and insight an ordinary person may be heir to' (p. 3). In these first paragraphs, his garrulousness, his inclination to propose tendentious generalisations unsupported by evidence, and his self-absorption create an enormous distance between speaker and reader. But even in Part 1, Razumov's story begins to establish dramatically the accuracy of what seemed vague abstractions: 'the illogicality of [the Russians'] attitude; the arbitrariness of their conclusions; the frequency of the exceptional'; and their tendency to 'pour [words] out by the hour' without 'really understand[ing] what they say' (p. 4). By the conclusion of Part 1, we have learned enough about the fanaticism, mysticism, and irrationality of the Russians to begin to appreciate the intelligence and perspicacity with which the narrator has edited Razumov's record. In contrast to the revolutionary frenzy and the autocratic regime's fanaticism, the narrator's detachment and effort to discover the moral aspect of the tale become attractive. His work as an editor and narrator engages him in a conscientious search for 'a word which . . . may perchance hold truth enough to help the moral discovery which should be the object of every tale' (p. 67). His desire to educate his audience needs to be contrasted with the search for personal survival which becomes the primary activity of every life touched by Russian autocracy.

The narrator is both fascinated and repelled by the Russians and the politics of passion that they represent. Speaking to Natalie, he argues (almost like Mann's Aschenbach) for ratiocination, self-discipline, and practicality, standards which the narrator never abandons even as his emotional range expands: 'Life is a thing of form. It has its plastic shape and a definite intellectual aspect. The most idealistic conceptions of love and forebearance must be clothed in flesh . . .' (p. 106). Despite his continued disclaimers ('Difference of nationality is a terrible obstacle for our complex Western natures' [p. 116]), he involves himself in Natalie's affairs, and befriends her with a sensitivity and responsiveness that her Russian acquaintances lack. To illustrate: when he arrived at the Haldins only to discover Peter there and 'met a peculiar expression in [Natalie Haldin's] eyes which [he] interpreted as a request to stay, with the view, perhaps, of shortening an unwelcome visit' (pp. 126–7), he dutifully remained. That he is correct in reading her feelings is demonstrated by her confiding in him after Peter left. He acknowledges a physical attraction to her, but he regards this as inappropriate due to the difference in ages. One may attribute his avoidance of passionate involvement to his own fastidiousness. Nevertheless, his sense of propriety introduces a standard of conduct that implicitly comments on the self-indulgence exhibited by most of the Russians.

The narrator's capacity for moral outrage takes the form of a bitterly satiric view of the revolutionary Peter who poses as an aristocrat, and the aristocratic Madame de S. who assumes, for reasons of private pique, the guise of a revolutionary: 'Their airings suggested a conscious public manifestation. . . . Considering the air of gravity extending even to the physiognomy of the coachman and the action of the showy horses, this quaint display might have possessed a mystic significance, but to the corrupt frivolity of a western mind, like my own, it seemed hardly decent' (pp. 125–6). The narrator's carefully chosen ironic language isolates their behaviour from the very activities to which they believe themselves committed. While 'quaint display' and 'public manifestation' suggest something rather indecent, as if the couple were making an offensive spectacle of themselves, 'mystic significance', in co-ordination with the 'air of gravity' displayed by the coachman who presides over these rites, suggests the autistic nature of these self-absorbed revolutionaries. And the 'corrupt frivolity' which he facetiously ascribes to himself of course more aptly applies to those he describes. Worried that Natalie will become a victim of these hypocrites, he warns her in prescient language what the novel's revolutionaries (from the humane and devoted Tekla to the sybaritic Peter) confirm:

> The scrupulous and the just, the noble, humane, and devoted natures; the unselfish and the intelligent may begin a movement—but it passes away from them. They are not the leaders of a revolution. They are its victims: the victims of disgust, of disenchantment—often of remorse. Hopes grotesquely betrayed, ideals caricatured—that is the definition of revolutionary success. (pp. 134–5)

His suggestion that Natalie return to Russia is generous (although not without ironic implications, for he may subconsciously fear his own tepid sexual attraction to her and may thus want to place her at a distance).

The narrator's imaginative, humane response and his incisive ability to penetrate beneath vague complexities and render the fabric of the Russian experience show us that he has resources of intelligence and feeling that are unsuspected by himself. In a novel predicated upon misplaced confidence, he is the one character who understands the person who confides in him and deserves the trust given him. Later, when Razumov arrives during the narrator's accidental encounter with Natalie, the narrator would have left but 'Miss Haldin touched [him] lightly on the forearm with a significant contact, conveying a distinct wish' (p. 179). He felt that he had been 'entrusted' to speak to Razumov. Once engaged within the conversation, the narrator's ability to move from immersion to reflection, to observe others incisively even while participating in a conversation, enables him to come close to perceiving the cause of Razumov's spasmodic irrationality and near hysteria. Beneath the narrator's tolerance ('He is young, and his sincerity assumes a pose before a stranger, a foreigner, an old man. Youth must assert itself' [pp. 189–90]) lurks a never quite stated suspicion that perhaps Razumov may be other than what he seems ('Either the man is a hero to you, or . . .' [p. 191]). Indeed, the narrator comes close to the truth when he perceives that the stillness of Razumov's face 'was the acquired habit of a revolutionist, of a conspirator everlastingly on his guard against self-betrayal in a world of secret spies' (p. 187).

In this crucial meeting with Razumov, the narrator's poise and maturity are in stark contrast to Razumov's neurotic self-flagellation. Even if he patronises Razumov's emotional outbursts with a rather sententious superciliousness which understandably reflects his emotional discomfort, the narrator displays considerable presence and self-control. Because he understands that speech and action can be a function of another character's psychic needs, he knows that Razumov's sneers and insults do not reflect on him. The narrator disarms Razumov when he speaks of the trust placed in him by the Haldins: 'Both his mother and sister believe implicitly in the worth of your judgment and in the truth of anything you may have to say to them' (p. 190). The narrator's words convey the conviction of a man who believes he can communicate essential beliefs. But Razumov is disarmed because, as with Jim, words have become weapons penetrating his fictions—in this case recreating the identity of Victor Haldin's friend in such a way as to suggest his perfidy. For the narrator, words imply essential values: respect for the feelings of others, truth, loyalty. They belie his assertion that words have become mere sounds to him. If that were once true, it is no longer the case.

Typically, the narrator is overly analytic of his motives and denies his own perspicacity. Yet his civilised sense of responsibility, his concern for Natalie, and his own mature awareness of Mrs Haldin as one of those 'who do not know how to heal themselves' define him, at this crucial point of the novel, as a barometer of morality, sanity, and civilisation (p. 318). Despite feelings of helplessness and doubts of his efficacy, his concern for the Haldins motivates him to make an uncharacteristically late visit to them. Natalie believes in him for she recognises that he has established himself as one friend who 'understands'. Because he is uncommitted to political ideals, and he does not need to consider his every personal act in terms of service or disservice to a regime, he can accompany Natalie to the revolutionary quarters without anyone worrying about his personal safety. After listening to Razumov's confession, he is freed from his inhibitions. As he chastises Razumov he speaks firmly and decisively and with the energy of deeply felt moral convictions: 'This is monstrous. What are you staying for? Don't let her catch sight of you again. Go away! . . . Don't you understand that your presence is intolerable—even to me? If there's any sense of shame in you . . .' (p. 355). His rebuke is delivered in language that reflects the narrator's concern with decorum and propriety. While the narrator's perception of Razumov's frenzied, if not psychotic, behaviour in terms of *manners* has its comic aspect, it is nevertheless true that the narrator's traditional private values—good taste, rational judgement, consideration of others' feelings—enable him alone to respond to events in moral terms.


II


Critics have argued that Razumov—with his 'English manner' and his desire to be 'a celebrated old professor'—aspires to be what the narrator is.[2] In Russia and Geneva, Razumov lives alone, leading a 'solitary and retired existence' similar to the narrator's (p. 200). Like the narrator, Razumov originally has to separate himself from political affairs to 'keep an instinctive hold on normal, practical, everyday life' (p. 10). Neither man has family or romantic ties. But Conrad clearly presents superficial parallels only to emphasise crucial differences. The narrator is motivated by personal loyalty to make

Natalie Halden's life bearable, while the self-absorbed Razumov, caught in the throes of an obsession that he can neither understand nor control, seeks to destroy her. Even if we doubt that he would pursue his psychotic fantasies about 'stealing [her] soul', *he* believes that he is capable of such sexual Machiavellism. Hardly a celebrated scholar, really an obscure teacher without ambition, the narrator has come to terms with himself, and he speaks and acts according to internalised morals and manners that have become second nature to him. Razumov is a man with an underdeveloped superego; he lacks a moral identity and is, until he confesses, a 'secret' to himself. He writes his diary to rescue an identity from the events in which he is caught, while the narrator edits Razumov's diary and arranges his own narrative to give a moral dimension to his discoveries about Russia, Geneva, and ultimately, himself.

For Razumov, the lack of family ties becomes a reason for intensely focusing his energies on self-advancement. His atavistic 'rage for self-preservation' enables him to rationalise the betrayal of Haldin as an 'act of conscience' (p. 38). While Razumov is incapable of sympathetic response to anyone, the narrator responds with compassion and insight to Razumov's loneliness: 'Who knows what true loneliness is—not the conventional word, but the naked terror? To the lonely themselves it wears a mask. The most miserable outcast hugs some memory or some illusion. Now and then a fatal conjunction of events may lift the veil for an instant. For an instant only. No human being could bear a steady view of moral solitude without going mad' (p. 39). Ironically, their previously discussed interview (placed in the centre of the novel) stresses Razumov's disdain for 'that meddlesome old Englishman'. Although the narrator's profession and detachment from political involvement bear some resemblance to Razumov's aspirations before Haldin's intrusion, the scene emphasises the immense gulf that divides these two characters.

Deprivation of parental love, of romantic love, and of friendship is an important cause of Razumov's allegiance to the regime, as well as of his need to confess. Razumov, the man whose name is 'the mere label of a solitary individuality', desperately needs a responsive consciousness (p. 10). The compulsion to explain himself is the basis for always revealing more than necessary; although he is consciously aware of his indiscretions, he cannot control himself. Because his own identity is opaque to himself, he needs to define himself in someone else's mind in order to believe in himself. That within his surrealistic vision of himself writhing on the rack, he imagines himself as solitary and faceless is indicative of the incompleteness of his moral identity and his own lack of self-regard: 'Razumov beheld his own brain suffering on the rack—a long, pale figure drawn asunder horizontally with terrific force in the darkness of a vault, whose face he failed to see' (p. 88). He is his own harshest accuser because he magnifies the suspicions of both the autocrats and the revolutionaries. Even the deceased Haldin has an identity because others honour him in their thoughts, while he senses that, measured by the same standard, he exists for no one.

Once he betrays Haldin, Razumov is in a situation where to survive he must create another self separate from his actual self. Razumov believes in the ability of language to create reality; witness his reducing his basic beliefs to a piece of paper after the betrayal, his diary, and his letter to Natalie. He relies on language to create the necessary revolutionary self with which he can perform his mission as a spy; but the revolutionary identity denies the patriotic self upon which his betrayal is justified. This creates an impossible tension for a man whose self-image is in continual flux. While playing his role as police spy, he finds himself suddenly speaking about his real self. Confessing to Natalie is simultaneously an act of masochism and a reaching out for the human ties he desperately craves. His diabolical desire to ruin Natalie, like the violent beating of Ziemianitch and the imagined violence to Haldin and Peter, derive from his own lack of a subjective 'I'. His need to rediscover the actual 'I' beneath the subterfuge produces the original confession to Haldin of his lack of sympathy; it also produces his moments of unintentional revelations to the revolutionaries; and finally it results in his deliberate confession to both Natalie and the revolutionaries. Because he lacks an identity in which he believes, he is particularly vulnerable to the insinuations of Mikulin. Much as Dostoevsky's Porfiry Petrovitch and Gentleman Brown do to Raskolnikov and Jim, Mikulin's intimations of sympathy cause Razumov to reveal involuntarily that he can be manipulated.

When Razumov's actual self subsumes his fictive self, he speaks in a simple syntax that mirrors his nostalgia for the order and clarity of his former world. For example, in one outburst of sincerity to the narrator, Razumov makes a confession of faith: 'Look here! . . . I am a worker. I studied. Yes, I studied very hard. There is intelligence here . . . Don't you think Russians may have sane ambitions. Yes—I had even prospects. Certainly! I had' (p. 191). He is compulsively drawn to utter words which simultaneously enable him to play his role and betray himself. Speaking to Peter after the interview with Madame de S., he masochistically savours his doubleness, the confluence of actual and real self, because it enables him to desert his role and impose—if only for a second—a shape on events reflecting his real perception of himself: 'I am talking of the poisonous plants which flourish in the world of conspirators, like evil mushrooms in a dark cellar' (p. 206). Razumov, who began to keep a diary to rescue his identity and who used words as a magician uses tricks to create an illusion, finally uses language as a weapon to torture himself. The urge to confess to the revolutionaries and subsequently to be punished is an urge that goes beyond morality to pathology.

## III

The language teacher, who had originally depicted himself as without imagination and insight, emerges as an intense, ironical observer of the Russian world. But how do we account for the embarrassingly apologetic tone with which the narrator had begun to present Razumov's diary? It is possible that Conrad desired to indicate the narrator's present self-knowledge by having him recreate the discovery of his own imaginative and linguistic resources. If this were Conrad's intention, it would follow that the narrator would introduce himself in the guise of an obtuse former self, and then present his own moral growth. But, given the temperament of the narrator and his reluctance to comment on his own life, I think it is far more likely that Conrad considered the narrator's excruciating self-disparagement as an integral part of his character. The discrepancy between his self-derogation and his principled behaviour stresses the very different kind of incongruity between the inflated sense of self-importance that most of the autocrats and revolutionaries display and their petty and hypocritical behaviour. Although he never fully acknowledges the breadth of his own role or the subtleties of his insight, it is he who most frequently illustrates the fundamental private values of Western life—kindliness, self-respect, selflessness—which are the only viable alternatives to the Russian autocrats and revolutionaries.

That Natalie Haldin tells Razumov she has given the narrator her 'confidence' emphasises the parallel between the role of responsive friend that the narrator plays for her and the similar role that Haldin expected Razumov to play. The narrator's stance that he is completely separate and different from the Russians ('I was like a traveller in a strange country') is belied by the narrative which reveals that basic needs to love and be loved are shared by both East and West unless and until they become perverted by political concerns (p. 169). A permanent resident in a foreign country like his creator, the narrator has a moral existence independent of identification with a nation. That he does not take refuge in political mysticism or fictions about the omniscience of others gives him a capacity for private friendship based on integrity. Not only does he cease to feel 'helpless' and 'unrelated', but he offers the friendship and loyalty to Natalie that Razumov neither offers to her brother, nor planned to offer her. He is attracted to Natalie Halding yet his self-understanding and self-consciousness prevent runaway emotions. While his concern for Natalie expresses itself in the conscious role of surrogate parent and the sublimated role of surrogate lover, his fundamental humanity and sympathy for others shape his conduct to her.

The clinical matter-of-fact but rather flaccid prose with which the narrator introduces himself gives way to a more intense prose, fraught with images capturing *his* physical responses to the passions and complexities of Russian life. At first, due to his own limited experience, his vocabulary distorts and overwhelms the events which he describes. If language is, as he claims, a foe of reality, it is because he has become anaesthetised. His soul-searching about whether to inform Miss Haldin about the newspaper clipping reveals the claustrophobic world in which he has been living. That he thought 'it would have been a sort of treason' (p. 110) to let Miss Haldin discover the English newspaper report of Haldin's death, and is deeply fretful that he is 'mixed up with something theatrical and morbidly affected' (p. 110), is characteristic of the order and decorum of his life. Arriving early at the Haldins' apartment after spending a sleepless night anxious about them, he avows 'I felt as if I were about to commit an act of vandalism' (p. 111). The narrator steadfastly insists on fidelity to his primary source even when the dramatisation of a conversation results from his own perception. Once he abandons his original fastidiousness, his carefully edited, understated narrative contrasts with the hysterical tone of the parts of Razumov's diary that we do see. Despite the narrator's protestations about 'lack of art' and 'talent', his language renders the complexities of Razumov's emotional life.

The intensity and imaginative power of the narrator's own observations reveal the folly of indicting him, as critics have done, for 'intellectual obtuseness' or for lack of feeling.[3] For example, he describes the expression of the self-tortured Razumov as that 'of a somnambulist struggling with the very dream which drives him to wander in dangerous places' (p. 317); or, he transforms Razumov's psychic self-flagellation into a dramatic metaphor: 'It was as though he had stabbed himself outside and had come in there to show it; and more than that—as though he were turning the knife in the wound and watching the effect' (pp. 350–1). And it is he who provides the metaphor to indicate how political autocracy is a spreading epidemic that blights opponent and advocate alike:

> The shadow of autocracy all unperceived by me had already fallen upon the Boulevard des Philosophes, in the free, independent, and democratic city of Geneva, where there is a quarter called 'La Petite Russie'. Whenever two Russians come together, the shadow of autocracy is with them, tinging their thoughts, their views, their most intimate feelings, their private life, their public utterances—haunting the secret of their silences. (p. 107)

After Razumov tells Natalie Haldin of his role and departs, the narrator, drawing upon his own 'shadow of autocracy' image, subtly 'verifies' how autocracy has the blighting effect that he has previously described: 'Shadows seemed to come and go in [her eyes] as if the steady flame of her soul had been made to vacillate at last in the cross-currents of poisoned air from the corrupted dark immensity claiming her for its own, where virtues themselves fester into crimes in the cynicism of oppression and revolt' (p. 356).

Words lose meaning only for those who reduce life simply to 'a thing of form'. The growth of his commitment to Natalie is paralleled by a revival of his imaginative powers and a renewed belief in the possibility of language. The narrator discovers that language is one of man's most important gifts, the one that allows him to express a moral purpose and to communicate with his fellows. Originally, the narrator chooses 'cynicism' as a kind of verbal shorthand for the Russians; he wants to believe that the Russians are so different that their ideals are subverted by underlying rottenness. He had found it comfortable to believe that Russian behaviour can be explained in terms of neat abstractions: 'I suppose one must be a Russian to understand Russian simplicity, a terrible corroding simplicity in which mystic phrases clothe a naive and hopeless cynicism' (p. 104).

But he gives up the search for simple verbal formulae because he begins to understand that a common humanity unites all men. While the notion that a great gulf divides Russians and Westerners is a convenient fiction for his satire of Peter and Madame de S., it does not penetrate the complex psychology of Tekla, Sophia, Natalie, Haldin, or Razumov.

As the narrator abandons his vague generalisations upon Russian character, he begins to focus on personal values and private relationships and to use as his verbal symbol variations on the term 'understand'. To him, to 'understand' means to share the perspective of others and to penetrate the motives of other characters. He wishes to convey this kind of understanding to his Western audience. Within the dialectic of the novel, his concept of understanding is in conflict with that of the Russians. Speaking 'in familiar terms' to Razumov, a lonely man who is desperately seeking warmth and friendship, Mikulin adds 'an understanding between intelligent men is always a satisfactory occurrence' (p. 295). Mikulin and Razumov both tacitly realise that Mikulin refers to a shared understanding that one party holds an *advantage* based on secret knowledge concerning the other. 'Understand' to the revolutionaries means 'to know the motives and actions of a potential ally'; to the solipsistic Razumov it means 'to disclose to someone his real attitudes and feelings'. We might recall that 'understand' is also a crucial word in 'The Secret Sharer' which, as Bruce Johnson correctly notes, has much in common with *Under Western Eyes*; indeed Conrad interrupted his work on *Under Western Eyes* to write 'The Secret Sharer'.[4] Just as both Leggatt and the captain seek someone who is sympathetic to their perspective, Razumov desperately seeks a man who can share his view. As in 'The Secret Sharer', Conrad shows how both parties to a relationship imagine an acquaintance to be a responsive soul who can sympathetically respond to the other's emotional and moral life.

Autocratic politics create a world in which personal lives are distorted by the political abstractions served by proponents and antagonists. Each of the Russians creates for himself the fiction of a receptive counterpart who understands his every thought and feeling. Beneath the fanaticism of Peter, Sophia, Madame de S. and Tekla are glimmers of insecurity and sublimated needs for understanding and friendship. Sophia believes Peter is 'inspired', but needs to reveal her actual self to Razumov. Peter needs someone in whom to believe, and he finds 'inspired penetration' in a woman whose political beliefs derive from greed and private pique. Tekla's need to believe in

Razumov is based on the disconfirmation of Peter as a Messiah figure. (Her trust in Razumov is based on his simple polite act of doffing his hat.) And Natalie's faith in Razumov, based on her brother's own misconception, is another fiction. Not only is she oblivious to his most bizarre eccentricities, but she refuses to believe him when he tells her 'I understand nothing' (p. 180). Sophia, lost in her own fantasies, does not perceive the causes of Razumov's trembling or hesitation, but without any evidence believes that Razumov 'understands' her. She interprets every action according to her ideological illusions and speaks excitedly as if trying to convince herself of the motivations of Haldin and Razumov: 'That uncompromising sense of necessity and justice which armed your and Haldin's hands to strike down that fanatical brute . . . for it was that—nothing but that! I have been thinking it out. It could have been nothing else but that' (p. 261).

## IV

The narrator's querulous attitude to Geneva has troubled critics because that city's orderliness and preoccupation with private life appear to mirror his own standards. Tony Tanner has even argued, 'The narrator should be more approving of the achieved security of democratic civilization'.[5] Surely this kind of prescriptive exhortation depends on mistakenly identifying the English narrator with Geneva. Both Conrad's sensitivity to 'the obligation of absolute fairness' and the fictional needs of contrasting two cultural traditions made it imperative that the novel raise questions about the quality of life in democratic Geneva (Author's Note, p. viii). The narrator continually tests and redefines qualities that he associates with Russia and Geneva until, finally, he establishes the *moral* superiority of Western life. Like his fascination with Russian behaviour, his repressed romantic interest in Natalie, and his imaginative excitement as he describes Razumov's self-flagellation in physical images, his muted dissatisfaction with Geneva indicates a repressed and sublimated longing for more intense experience than his lonely bachelor existence provides. Moreover, Geneva's willingness to accommodate the callousness and irrationality of the refugee revolutionary community within its midst offends his sense of morality. If, Conrad implies, the self-discipline of Western life has its cost in passion, it is nevertheless true that benign government gives people the choice of whether to write fictions, teach languages, or even pursue political visions. Geneva is a drab and pedestrian depiction of political stability, but it still remains a place where such a figure as the narrator may combine a highly civilised conscience with an individuality that, in its insistence on self-denigration, approaches the idiosyncratic and quirky.

Russia finally emerges as primitive and atavistic, a kind of European version of the Congo where possibilities exist which have all but been discarded by Western countries. On the other hand, Geneva is a civilisation where the libidinous energies and the atavistic impulses may be squelched, but violence and anarchy are under control. It is very much to the point that the people, other than the revolutionaries, who reside in Geneva are engaged in shopkeeping, teaching, picnicking, walking; and that these quite ordinary activities can take place in Geneva, unlike Russia, without bombs and intimidation. Geneva may have its materialistic aspect, epitomised by the rather tasteless Chateau Borel that now stands abandoned by its absentee owners; but it makes possible the cultivation of personal affections and the fulfilment of private aspirations which the autocratic and violent Russian world blunts.

In contrast to the narrator who intuitively transforms every incident in his life into a matter of conscience, the Russians see their private lives in terms of a vague historical perspective. Thus the narrator's excerpts from Razumov's diary, Peter's autobiographical volume, and Tekla's life expand the novel's spatial-temporal dimensions. But the movement of the novel alternates between the personal, limited, and subjective perspective of the narrator and the vast, impersonal immensity of Russia with its countless anonymous citizens suffering unimagined misery that can barely be implied:

> Razumov received an almost physical impression of endless space and of countless millions.
> He responded to it with the readiness of a Russian who is born to an inheritance of space and numbers. Under the sumptuous immensity of the sky, the snow covered the endless forests, the frozen rivers, the plains of an immense country, obliterating the landmarks, the accidents of the ground, levelling everything under its uniform whiteness, like a monstrous blank page awaiting the record of an inconceivable history. (p. 33)

Conrad deliberately depicts Geneva as tediously geometric and rather claustrophobic. Razumov is contemptuous of its decorum; he regards the view of the lake as 'the very perfection of mediocrity attained at last after centuries of toil and culture' (p. 203). The narrator speaks condescendingly of the 'precise' and 'orderly' Geneva landscape, but the very precision of the narrator's description, as well as his personal subjective response to place, implicitly criticises the unlimited, amoral space of Russia: 'There was but little of spring-like glory in the rectangular railed space of grass and trees, framed visibly by the orderly roof-slopes of that town, comely without grace, and hospitable without sympathy' (p. 141). The novel confirms the value of the mind's own interior space, personal communication, and private relationships; it rejects historical and geographical explanations that seek to place moral responsibility beyond the individual conscience. The humanity and perspicacity that the narrator brings to his reminiscence 'contain' and undermine the Russian conception of a world of vast objective space.

Parts 2 and 3 contrast the man forced to commitment by external circumstances and the man whose life is independent of historical and political considerations. Speaking as a revolutionary while actually a spy and believing in neither identity, Razumov continuously informs on himself. By contrast, the narrator not only avoids dissembling, but continually reveals depths of sensitivity and insight that belie his original self-estimate. The value of his private interior perspective is an implicit comment on Razumov's continuing quest (pursued at times unconsciously) for freedom from politics. Within the novel politics gradually comes to mean a complex group of secret arrangements between self-interested and obsessed people for whom the ends justify the means. (In confessing to the revolutionaries, Razumov ironically fulfils his quest for freedom when he proclaims that he is 'independent of every single human being on this earth' [p. 368].)

While Peter and Sophia—like Mikulin and General T—speak of national destiny and political ideals, the narrator's life is concerned with personal relationships in the 'free, independent, and democratic' city of Geneva. That the hyperbole and zealotry of Peter are contained within the satiric perspective of the editor affirms the position of the narrator. Deftly, Conrad alternates the narrator's ironic, disciplined observations with the solipsism, hyperbole, and self-aggrandisement of the 'inspired' revolutionary's autobiographical testimony. Mocking Peter's efforts to disguise his reversion to savagery in terms of an esoteric theoretical statement, the narrator comments facetiously in sparse, straightforward prose: 'The rest of his escape does not lend itself to mystic treatment and symbolic interpretation' (p. 125). If at first the narrator's comments on Peter's memoirs seem rather niggling and cynical, Chapter 4 of Part 2 shows that Peter thinly disguises autocratic and sadistic impulses similar to the regime he would overthrow and is dependent upon subservient personalities, such as Tekla who for complex reasons savours a certain amount of abuse.

Finally, the narrator comes closest to deserving the epithet 'unstained, lofty, and solitary existence' that Haldin had used to describe Razumov (p. 135). In his self-possession, flexibility, and morality, the narrator has the safety and stability Razumov compulsively seeks. Razumov, product of irrational autocracy and a man of psychic complexity, is juxtaposed with the bland, controlled narrator who is the one character capable of a subtle moral response. The novel establishes the validity of the narrator's responding to Razumov's diary as a psychological rather than a political document. If Razumov is a paradigm of the personality on whom autocracy depends, the narrator is the paradigm of the independent, ordinary citizen on whom democracy depends. If he is repressed, he is also self-controlled; if he lacks charisma, he is considerate, sensitive, and rational. Diffident about his capacity to *understand* a story that baffles him, he originally distances his listeners by claiming a remoteness that is contradicted by the narrative. But he progresses toward understanding motives and emotions foreign to him. At first it seems that for the narrator words have a nearly neutral value, and that by contrast it is the Russians who really communicate by means of intensely felt language that corresponds to their emotional life. As the narrator's experience expands, his language becomes more and more incisive and sensitive. However, as the Russians continue to use language as a method of aggression and as a means of distortion, the narrator's conscientious search for the appropriate word and his respect for language become values. His concern about the relationship between language and meaning, his fastidiousness about the difference between rhetoric and reason, and his desire to proceed rationally and logically are in stark contrast with the irrationality and fanaticism of the Russians (including even Natalie Haldin whose vague sentiments about an era of concord and justice are the products of a mind seeking escape in apocalyptic visions).[6] The language teacher's own narration disproves his thesis that 'words' are 'the great foes of reality'. His civilised conscience emerges as the viable ethical alternative to anarchy and fanaticism. Sceptical, tolerant, and independent, he emerges as the epitome of morality and sanity.

## NOTES

1. Robert Secor, 'The Function of the Narrator in *Under Western Eyes*', *Conradiana*, vol. iii (1970–1), p. 37. Also see pp. 27–37.

2. See, for example, Claire Rosenfield, *Paradise of Snakes: An Archetypal Analysis of Conrad's Political Novels* (Chicago: University of Chicago Press, 1967), pp. 161–2.

3. John A. Palmer, *Joseph Conrad's Fiction: A Study in Literary Growth* (Ithaca: Cornell University Press, 1968), writes, '[The narrator] is full of theory instead of feeling, and [his] pompous abstractions often hide the book's subject, instead of bringing it closer' (p. 131). 'Intellectual obtuseness' is Rosenfield's phrase (p. 165). Eloise Hay, *The Political Novels of Joseph Conrad* (Chicago: University of Chicago Press, 1963) acknowledges that the narrator cannot be so obtuse as 'to fail in the important task of observing extraordinary passions and circumstances with some degree of understanding', but she still indicts him for coldness, dullness, and stupidity (p. 297).

4. See Bruce Johnson, *Conrad's Models of Minds* (Minneapolis: University of Minnesota, 1971), pp. 141–3.

5. Tony Tanner, 'Nightmare of Complacency: Razumov and the Western Eye', *Critical Quarterly*, vol. iv (Autumn 1962), p. 201.

6. Avrom Fleishman, *Conrad's Politics: Community and Anarchy in the Fiction of Joseph Conrad* (Baltimore: Johns Hopkins Press, 1967), discusses a 'dialectic between the . . . skepticism of the narrator and the serene idealism of Natalie' (p. 238). Although the dramatic action does not confirm Natalie's vague abstractions, Fleishman equates her vision of the future with Conrad's values.

# Conclusion

In St Paul's Cathedral is a monumental urn dedicated to those who died in the Boer War; over the urn is the following epigraph:

> I have fought a just fight.
> I have finished *my* course. (2 Tim. 4: 7)

If this quotation illustrates the poise, confidence, and optimism of those who presented this monument, retrospectively we see that it represents the last gasp of the British empire. The confidence and certainty of those who chose the epigraph inform these lines, but that confidence and certainty soon evaporate into dubiety and anxiety. With its subject, predicate, and object preceded by one bare qualifier, the straightforward King James prose stands in stark contrast to the circumlocutions, density, and complexity of modern poetry and fiction.

I think that one can explain the careers of the major writers of the 1885–1925 period as an intense struggle between the demands of their psyches and their responses to established cultural traditions. Hopkins' commitment as a Jesuit to renounce the pleasures of this world conflicts with his impulse to praise the infinite variety of nature (see 'Pied Beauty' and 'God's Grandeur'). Hardy's desire to retain orthodox beliefs conflicts with both his knowledge that the world is malevolent and his compulsive desire to bear witness to the misery of the world (see 'A Drizzling Easter Morning' and 'The Oxen'). Joyce's desire to be an iconoclastic artist struggles with his commitment to traditional humanism; put another way, *Ulysses* is an effort to resolve the Stephen and Bloom within Joyce's psyche. D. H. Lawrence's sympathy with individuality, instinct, and passion contrasts with his desire to be a prophetic figure who awakens the world to its current preoccupation with reason and logic, and their by-products, materialism and industrialism. Even while Yeats wishes to revive traditional concepts of courage, beauty, and love, he knows these concepts have archaic and feudal overtones. Because modern writers live in a world where there is no public agreement as to values and principles, they often seek either to create their own symbolism as Yeats and Lawrence have done or to reinvigorate old myths with private meaning as Eliot has done with Christianity.

The fundamental intellectual problem of the late nineteenth century was the awareness that man does not share common truths. While one can attribute the dissolution of accepted beliefs to the Enlightenment, the fragmentation of values and beliefs was certainly accelerated by *The Origin of Species* (1859) and *Essays and Reviews* (1860). To understand modern British literature, one has to understand the pervasive feeling in the late nineteenth century that each man is enclosed in his private world and isolated by his own perceptions from other men. Conrad believes that each man depends upon his own illusions to cope with the world. A crucial theme in the period, present in Conrad and many major writers, is the attempt to discover the words and values with which to cope with a meaningless cosmos. In the modern period order is evoked from within rather than from without because, as Marlow remarks in 'Heart of Darkness' (1898), 'we live, as we dream—alone'. Certainly, the quest for an epistemology is the characteristic activity not only of Conrad but of Eliot, Yeats, Joyce, and Lawrence. From 1890, British literature can be characterised by efforts on the part of artists to, as Eliot puts it, 'set my lands in order', Does not *The Waste Land* end with a virtual statement of the poem's method? Like a cubist collagist, the speaker collects fragments 'to shore against my ruins'.

Conrad is a pivotal figure for understanding the evolution of British literature and culture in the 1885–1925 period. In his political novels, Conrad takes issue with the Victorian and Edwardian view, emphasised by the Shavian life force and Fabian socialism, that progress is inevitable and that a benign and congenial future awaited man as he gradually solved the problems of civilisation. These novels raise fundamental doubts about the viability of traditional political concepts and principles, while showing how these concepts and principles often provide a guise for private obsessions. He also questions the widely accepted assumptions that both imperialism and the modern industrial city represented progress.

In a sense, Conrad's own anxieties and self-doubt were an intensification of those that beset British culture, and represent an important strand of cultural history. The transformation of Marlow from bold self-confident adventurer into self-doubting meditative voice was part of the movement of British culture from the Victorian to the Modern period. Conrad's stress on private relationships anticipated and paralleled the emphasis on interpersonal relationships in the work of Forster, Joyce, and Lawrence. His fiction focused on the intricacies of the individual psyche—its unconscious motives, its libidinous needs, its obsessions and compulsions—and turned the British novel inward. But he also discovered the potential of the novel for presenting a political and historical panorama and thus expanded the genre's breadth.

In the preceding pages, I have stressed the following major points:

(1) More than we have realised, Conrad's work must be read as an expression of his own personal life.

(2) His characters' quests for values are not only Conrad's, but represent those of his culture.

(3) To talk about that quest, one must focus on the speaker in each work.

(4) Conrad's political novels dissect the shortcomings of paradigmatic social and political communities. But they do not offer systematic programs or viable alternatives.

(5) In the political novels Conrad affirms the importance of family and sexual relationships in a world threatened by materialism, anarchy, and various forms of tyranny.

(6) He has nostalgic faith in the benign autocracy of shipboard life and in the simple values—courage, fidelity, hard work—that make life on ship possible. But he realises that shipboard life depends on a hierarchy that cannot bind a large social and political community.

(7) Conrad is a humanist and a sceptic; while at times these aspects conflict, he is not a nihilist.

Throughout his career, Conrad uses his fiction to define himself. The speaker, even when he is a character whom Conrad views ironically, is testing attitudes for Conrad. Even as he is writing his early adventure novels, *Almayer's Folly* and *An Outcast of the Islands*, Conrad experiences anxiety and dubiety. Feeling that his interior life is chaotic and perceiving the world as an alienated outsider rather than as a participant, Conrad relies upon his fiction to dispel his confusion and sense of alienation. From the outset of his writing career, Conrad regards a man's morality not as passionately held commitments to viable ethics, but psychological phenomena by which a man established a 'working relationship' with an indifferent cosmos. Thus he examines not only *what* a character believes, but *how* a man comes to these beliefs. He develops a meditative, introspective style to render the nuances and rhythms of the speaker's consciousness as he tells his tale. Marlow's obsession with the effectiveness of language reflects Conrad's fears that communication may be impossible and that he, as a writer, may be indulging in the illusion of speaking to others. As he becomes more comfortable in his new career and discovers his own working relationship with life ashore, he begins to turn to larger canvasses, but he never loses interest in the quest for values.

Beginning with 'Typhoon' and 'The End of the Tether', both based on maritime situations which Conrad evaluates in terms of a stable ethical code, he introduces into his fiction a voice who is more sure of himself. While he continues to have periodic episodes of self-doubt and despair, Conrad creates a confident, poised public self in *Nostromo*, *The Secret Agent*, *The Mirror of the Sea*, and *A Personal Record*. In *A Personal Record*, Conrad best expresses a fundamental tenet of this public self:

And the unwearied self-forgetful attention to every phase of the living universe reflected in our consciousness may be our appointed task on this earth. A task in which fate has perhaps engaged nothing of us except our conscience, gifted with a voice in order to bear true testimony to the visible wonder, the haunting terror, the infinite passion and the illimitable serenity; to the supreme law and the abiding mystery of the sublime spectacle. (*PR*, p. 92)

In his work after 1900, he seeks to define tenable moral positions with which men can live with dignity and integrity within a purposeless universe. Conrad's interest in dramatising the psychic needs of his speakers gives way to a desire to locate the values which make civilised life possible. Conrad shifts his emphasis from the introspective meditations of a dramatised consciousness to the ethical perspective of a mature conscience. While *The Secret Agent* indicts contemporary civilisation, the self-dramatising speaker of that novel emerges as a tough-minded ironist who creates a moral alternative to the nihilistic world he observes. Yet Conrad always draws back from the kind of confident omniscient narrator that dominated the Victorian novel and insists on looking at issues and characters in different lights. Indeed, quite often the narrator has sudden moments of ambivalence when one least expects it; at other times the narrative belies the narrator's generalisations.

Collectively the later novels from *Chance* through *The Rover* are not equal in stature to his prior masterpieces—the political novels, *Lord Jim*, *The Nigger of the 'Narcissus'*, 'Heart of Darkness' and 'The Secret Sharer'. After 1912, Conrad wrote only one great work: *The Shadow-Line*. In that tale, he realises that the authoritarian structure on board ship does not offer a model for organising communities on land, but he demonstrates that courage, confidence, self-control, and sense of responsibility to one's fellows are values essential to the survival of mankind. The later works are not radically different in theme or from his prior works. Like the earlier novels, they need to be understood in terms of Conrad's evolving psyche. They too are concerned with how obsessions and fixations shape man's behaviour. And they continue to develop the humanism of the political novels, particularly the emphasis on personal ties. Their greater concern with heterosexual love and their simplified form reflect not only Conrad's desire to reach a wide audience, but his own psychological and artistic needs. But that will be the subject of *Conrad: The Later Fiction*.

# Appendix

| Story and Volume | Date of Completion | Year of First Serialisation or Publication in a Collection |
|---|---|---|
| *Tales of Unrest* (pub. 1898) | | |
| 'The Idiots' | May 1896 | 1896 |
| 'An Outpost of Progress' | July 1896 | 1897 |
| 'The Lagoon' | Aug. 1896 | 1897 |
| 'Karain' | Apr. 1897 | 1897 |
| 'The Return' | Sept. 1897 | 1898 |
| *Youth* (pub. 1902) | | |
| 'Youth' | June 1898 | 1898 |
| 'Heart of Darkness' | Feb. 1899 | 1899 |
| 'The End of the Tether' | Oct. 1902 | 1902 |
| *Typhoon* (pub. 1903) | | |
| 'Typhoon' | Jan. 1901 | 1902 |
| 'Falk: A Reminiscence' | May 1901 | 1903 |
| 'Amy Foster' | June 1901 | 1901 |
| 'To-morrow' | Jan. 1902 | 1902 |
| *A Set of Six* (pub. 1908) | | |
| 'Gaspar Ruiz' | Nov. 1905 | 1906 |
| 'The Brute' | c. Dec. 1905 | 1906 |
| 'An Anarchist' | Nov.–Dec. 1905 | 1906 |
| 'The Informer' | Dec.–Jan. 1905–6 | 1906 |
| 'Il Conde' | Dec. 1906 | 1908 |
| 'The Duel' | Apr. 1907 | 1908 |
| *'Twixt Land and Sea* (pub. 1912) | | |
| 'The Secret Sharer' | Dec. 1909 | 1910 |
| 'A Smile of Fortune' | Aug. 1910 | 1911 |

| Story and Volume | Date of Completion | Year of First Serialisation or Publication in a Collection |
|---|---|---|
| 'Freya of the Seven Isles' | Feb. 1911 | 1912 |
| *Within the Tides* (pub. 1915) | | |
| 'The Partner' | Oct.–Nov. 1910 | 1911 |
| 'The Inn of the Two Witches' | Dec. 1912 | 1913 |
| 'The Planter of Malata' | Dec. 1913 | 1914 |
| 'Because of the Dollars' | Dec. 1913 or Jan. 1914 | 1914 |
| *Tales of Hearsay* (pub. 1925) | | |
| 'The Black Mate' | ca. 1886 (possibly revised 1908) | 1908 |
| 'Prince Roman' | Sept.–Oct. 1910 | 1910 |
| 'The Warrior's Soul' | Mar. 1916 | 1917 |
| 'The Tale' | Oct. 1916 | 1917 |

| Novel | Date of Completion | Year of First Publication in Serial or Bound Form |
|---|---|---|
| *Almayer's Folly* | Mar. 1894 | 1895 |
| *An Outcast of the Islands* | Sept. 1895 | 1896 |
| *The Nigger of the 'Narcissus'* | Jan. 1897 | 1897 |
| *Lord Jim* | July 1900 | 1899–1900 |
| *Nostromo* | Aug. 1904 | 1904 |
| *The Secret Agent* | Nov. 1906 | 1906–7 |
| *Under Western Eyes* | Dec. 1909 | 1910–11 |
| *Chance* | Mar. 1912 | 1912 |
| *Victory* | June 1914 | 1915 |
| *The Shadow-Line* | Dec. 1915 | 1916 |
| *The Arrow of Gold* | June 1918 | 1919 |
| *The Rescue* | May 1919 | 1919 |
| *The Rover* | June 1922 | 1923 |

# Selected Bibliography

The following list includes all critical and scholarly studies cited in the notes plus a number of items that have been particularly significant in the evolution of my thinking.

Andreach, Robert, 'The Two Narrators of "Amy Foster"', *Studies in Short Fiction*, vol. ii (1965), pp. 262–9.

Auerbach, Erich, *Mimesis: The Representation of Reality in Western Literature*, trans. Willard Trask (Princeton: Princeton University Press, 1953 [orig. ed. 1946]).

Baines, Jocelyn, *Joseph Conrad: A Critical Biography* (New York: McGraw Hill, 1960).

Beach, Joseph Warren, 'Impressionism: Conrad', in *The Twentieth Century Novel: Studies in Technique* (New York: Appleton-Century, 1932), pp. 337–65.

Blackburn, William (ed.), *Joseph Conrad: Letters to William Blackwood and David S. Meldrum* (North Carolina: Duke University Press, 1958).

Blackmur, R. P., *Eleven Essays in the European Novel* (New York: A Harbinger Book, 1954).

Booth, Wayne E., *The Rhetoric of Fiction* (Chicago: University of Chicago Press, 1961).

Bradbrook, Muriel C., *Joseph Conrad: Poland's English Genius* (Cambridge: At the University Press, 1941).

Burke, Kenneth, *The Philosophy of Literary Form*, rev. ed. (New York: Vintage, 1957).

Cassirer, Ernst, *The Logic of the Humanities*, trans. Clarence Smith Howe (New Haven: Yale University Press, 1961).

Chaikin, Milton, 'Zola and Conrad's "The Idiots"', *Studies in Philology*, vol. lii (July 1955), pp. 502–7.

Conrad, Joseph, *Complete Works*, 26 vols., Kent edition (Garden City: Doubleday, 1926).

Cox, C. B., *Joseph Conrad: The Modern Imagination* (London: J. M. Dent, 1974).

Crews, Frederick, 'The Power of Darkness', *Partisan Review*, vol. xxxiv (Autumn 1967), pp. 507–25.

Curle, Richard, *The Last Twelve Years of Joseph Conrad* (Garden City: Doubleday, 1928).

—— (ed.), *Conrad to a Friend, 150 Selected Letters from Joseph Conrad to Richard Curle* (New York: Doubleday, Doran and Company, 1928).

Daleski, H. M., *Joseph Conrad: The Way of Dispossession* (New York: Holmes and Meier, 1976).

Ellmann, Richard and Feidelson, Charles, jun. (eds.), *The Modern Tradition* (New York: Oxford University Press, 1965).

Fernando, Lloyd, 'Conrad's Eastern Expatriates: A New Version of His Outcasts', *PMLA*, vol. xci (1976), pp. 78–90.

Fleishman, Avrom, *Conrad's Politics: Community and Anarchy in the Fiction of Joseph Conrad* (Baltimore: Johns Hopkins Press, 1967).

Ford, Ford Madox, *Joseph Conrad: A Personal Remembrance* (Boston: Little, Brown, 1924).

Fradin, Joseph I., 'Anarchist, Detective, and Saint: The Possibilities of Action in *The Secret Agent*', *PMLA*, vol. lxxxiii (Oct. 1968), pp. 1414–22.

—— and Creighton, Jean W., 'The Language of *The Secret Agent*: The Art of Non-Life', *Conradiana*, vol. 1 (Autumn 1968), pp. 23–35.

Garnett, Edward, *Letters from Joseph Conrad, 1895–1924* (Indianapolis: Bobbs-Merrill, 1928).

Gee, John A., and Sturm, Paul J., *Letters of Joseph Conrad to Marguerite Poradowska, 1890–1920* (New Haven: Yale University Press, 1940).

Gillon, Adam, *The Eternal Solitary* (New York: Bookman Associates, 1960).

Glassman, Peter, *Language and Being: Joseph Conrad and the Literature of Personality* (New York and London: Columbia University Press, 1976).

Goodin, George, 'The Personal and the Political in *Under Western Eyes*', *Nineteenth-Century Fiction*, vol. xxv (Dec. 1970), pp. 327–42.

Gordan, John Dozier, *Joseph Conrad: The Making of a Novelist* (Cambridge: Harvard University Press, 1940).

Gose, Elliot B., jun., '"Cruel Devourer of the World's Light": *The Secret Agent*', *Nineteenth-Century Fiction*, vol. xv (June 1960), pp. 39–51.

Graver, Lawrence, *Conrad's Short Fiction* (Berkeley and Los Angeles: University of California Press, 1969).

Guerard, Albert J., *Conrad the Novelist* (Cambridge: Harvard University Press, 1958).

Guetti, James, ' "Heart of Darkness": The Failure of Imagination', in his *The Limits of Metaphor: A Study of Melville, Conrad, and Faulkner* (Ithaca: Cornell University Press, 1967), pp. 46–68.

Gurko, Leo. *Joseph Conrad: Giant in Exile* (New York: Macmillan, 1962).

Hagopian, John V., 'The Pathos of "Il Conde" ', *Studies in Short Fiction*, vol. iii (Autumn 1964), pp. 31–38.

Harkness, Bruce (ed.), *Conrad's "Heart of Darkness" and the Critics* (Belmont, California: Wadsworth, 1960).

Haugh, Robert F., *Joseph Conrad: Discovery in Design* (Norman: University of Oklahoma Press, 1957).

Hay, Eloise Knapp, *The Political Novels of Joseph Conrad* (Chicago: University of Chicago Press, 1963).

Heilbroner, Robert L., *The Future as History* (New York: Grove Press, 1961).

Hewitt, Douglas, *Conrad: A Reassessment* (Cambridge: Bowes and Bowes, 1952).

Hicks, John H., 'Conrad's *Almayer's Folly*: Structure, Theme, and Critics', *Nineteenth Century Fiction*, vol. xix (June 1964), pp. 17–31.

Holland, Norman N., 'Style as Character: *The Secret Agent*', *Modern Fiction Studies*, vol. xii (Summer 1966), pp. 221–31.

Howe, Irving, 'Conrad: Order and Anarchy', in his *Politics and the Novel* (New York: Horizon Press and Meridian Books, 1957), pp. 76–113. Reprinted from *Kenyon Review*, vol. xv (Autumn 1953), pp. 505–21; and vol xvi (Winter 1954), pp. 1–19.

Hynes, Samuel, *The Edwardian Turn of Mind* (Princeton: Princeton University Press, 1968).

James, Henry, *Notes on Novelists* (New York: Charles Scribner's Sons, 1914).

Jean-Aubry, Georges, *Joseph Conrad: Life and Letters*, 2 vols. (Garden City, New York: Doubleday, Page and Company, 1927).

Johnson, Bruce M., *Conrad's Models of Mind* (Minneapolis: University of Minnesota Press, 1971).

——, 'Conrad's "Falk": Manuscript and Meaning', *Modern Language Quarterly*, vol. xxvi (June 1965), pp. 267–84.

Karl, Frederick, *Joseph Conrad: The Three Lives* (New York: Farrar,

Straus and Giroux, 1979).

——, *A Reader's Guide to Joseph Conrad* (New York: Noonday Press, 1960).

Kelly, Aileen, 'Tolstoy in Doubt', *The New York Review of Books*, vol. xxv (29 June 1978), pp. 22–6.

Kimbrough, Robert, *Heart of Darkness: Text, Sources, Criticism*, rev. ed.(New York: Norton, 1971).

Kirschner, Paul, *Conrad: The Psychologist as Artist* (Edinburgh: Oliver and Boyd, 1968).

Krieger, Murray, 'Conrad's "Youth": A Naive Opening to Art and Life', *College English*, vol. xx (Mar. 1959), pp. 275–80.

Laing, R. D., *The Divided Self: An Existential Study in Sanity and Madness* (Baltimore: Penguin Books, 1965).

Langbaum, Robert, *The Poetry of Experience* (New York: Norton and Co., 1963 [original ed. 1957]).

——, *The Modern Spirit: Essays on the Continuity of Nineteenth and Twentieth Century Literature* (New York: Oxford University Press, 1970).

Langer, Susanne K., *Feeling and Form* (New York: Scribner's 1953).

Leavis, F. R., *The Great Tradition: George Eliot, Henry James, Joseph Conrad* (London: Chatto and Windus, 1948).

Lester, John A., jun., *Journey Through Despair 1880–1914: Transformations in British Literary Culture* (Princeton: Princeton University Press, 1968).

McCall, Dan, 'The Meaning in Darkness: A Response to a Psychoanalytical Study of Conrad', *College English*, vol. xxix (May 1968), pp. 620–7.

Malbone, Raymond Gates, ' "How to be": Marlow's Quest in *Lord Jim*', *Twentieth-Century Literature*, vol. x (January 1965), pp. 172–80.

Marcus, Stephen, Review essay of Stanley Milgram's *Obedience and Authority*, *The New York Times Book Review*, 13 Jan. 1974.

Martz, Louis, *The Poetry of Meditation*, 2nd ed. (New Haven: Yale University Press, 1962 [original ed. 1954]).

Meyer, Bernard C., MD, *Joseph Conrad: A Psychoanalytic Biography* (Princeton: Princeton University Press, 1967).

Miller, J. Hillis, *The Disappearance of God* (Cambridge: The Belknap Press of Harvard University Press, 1963).

——, *Poets of Reality: Six Twentieth Century Writers* (Cambridge: The Belknap Press of Harvard University Press, 1965).

Moser, Thomas, *Joseph Conrad: Achievement and Decline* (Cambridge:

Harvard University Press, 1967).

—— (ed.), *Lord Jim*, Norton Critical edition (New York: Norton, 1968).

——, 'The "Rescuer" Manuscript: A Key to Conrad's Development—and Decline', *Harvard Library Bulletin*, vol. x (1956), pp. 325–55.

Najder, Zdzislaw, *Conrad's Polish Background: Letters to and from Polish Friends* (London: Oxford University Press, 1964).

Palmer, John A., *Joseph Conrad's Fiction: A Study in Literary Growth* (Ithaca: Cornell University Press, 1968).

Perry, John Oliver, 'Action, Vision, or Voice: The Moral Dilemmas in Conrad's Tale-telling', *Modern Fiction Studies*, vol. x (Spring 1964), pp. 3–14.

Rosenfield, Claire, *Paradise of Snakes: An Archetypal Analysis of Conrad's Political Novels* (Chicago: University of Chicago Press, 1967).

Roussel, Royal, *The Metaphysics of Darkness: A Study in the Unity and Development of Conrad's Fiction* (Baltimore and London: The Johns Hopkins Press, 1971).

Said, Edward W., *Joseph Conrad and the Fiction of Autobiography* (Cambridge: Harvard University Press, 1966).

Scholes, Robert and Kellogg, Robert, *The Nature of Narrative* (London: Oxford University Press, 1966).

Schorer, Mark, 'Introduction', in Ford Madox Ford, *The Good Soldier* (New York: Vintage, 1951).

Schwarz, Daniel R., 'The Lepidopterist's Revenge: Theme and Structure in Conrad's "An Anarchist" ', *Studies in Short Fiction*, vol. viii (Spring 1971), pp. 330–4.

——, 'Moral Bankruptcy in Ploumar Parish: A Study of Conrad's "The Idiots" ', *Conradiana* (Summer 1969), pp. 113–17.

——, 'The Narrator as Character in Hardy's Major Fiction', *Modern Fiction Studies*, vol. xviii (Summer 1972), pp. 155–72.

——, 'The Self-Deceiving Narrator of Conrad's "Il Conde" ', *Studies in Short Fiction*, vol. vi (Winter 1969), pp. 187–93.

——, 'Speaking of Paul Morel: Voice, Unity, and Meaning in *Sons and Lovers*', *Studies in the Novel*, vol. viii (Autumn 1976), pp. 255–77.

Secor, Robert, 'The Function of the Narrator in *Under Western Eyes*', *Conradiana*, vol. iii (1970–1), pp. 27–37.

Sherry, Norman, *Conrad's Eastern World* (Cambridge: At the University Press, 1966).

——, *Conrad's Western World* (Cambridge: At the University Press, 1971).

Smith, John William, *The Unity of Joseph Conrad's Short Story Collections* (unpublished Ph.D. Thesis, Univ. of Arkansas, 1967, DA:28:234A '67).

Stallman, Robert W. (ed.), *The Art of Joseph Conrad: A Critical Symposium* (East Lansing: Michigan State University Press, 1960).

Tanner, Tony, 'Nightmare and Complacency: Razumov and the Western Eye', *Critical Quarterly*, vol. iv (Autumn 1962), pp. 197– 214.

Tindall, W. Y. 'Apology for Marlow', in R. C. Rathburn and M. Steinmann, jun., (eds.), *From Jane Austen to Joseph Conrad* (Minneapolis: University of Minnesota Press, 1959).

Tolley, A. T., 'Conrad's Favorite Story', *Studies in Short Fiction*, vol. iii (1966), pp. 314– 320.

Van Ghent, Dorothy, 'On *Lord Jim*', in her *The English Novel: Form and Function* (New York: Harper Torch books, 1961 [original ed. 1953]), pp. 229–44.

Walton, James, 'Mr. X's 'Little Joke': The Design of "The Informer"', *Studies in Short Fiction*, vol. iv (Summer 1967), pp. 322– 33.

Warren, Robert Penn, Introduction to *Nostromo* (New York: Modern Library, 1951). Reprinted from *Sewanee Review*, vol. lix (Summer 1951), pp. 363– 91.

Watt, Ian, 'Conrad Criticism and *The Nigger of the "Narcissus"*', *Nineteenth-Century Fiction*, vol. xii (Mar. 1958), pp. 257– 83.

——, 'Conrad, James, and *Chance*', in Maynard Mack and Ian Gregor (eds.), *Imagined Worlds: Essays in Honour of John Butt* (London: Methuen and Co., 1968).

Watts, C. T. (ed.), *Joseph Conrad's Letters to R. B. Cunninghame Graham* (Cambridge: Cambridge University Press, 1969).

Wiley, Paul L., *Conrad's Measure of Man* (Madison: University of Wisconsin Press, 1954).

Wills, John Howard, 'Adam, Axel and "Il Conde"', *Modern Fiction Studies*, vol. i (1955), pp. 22– 5. Reprinted in Stallman, *The Art of Joseph Conrad*, pp. 254–9.

——, 'Conrad's "Typhoon": A Triumph of Organic Art', *North Dakota Quarterly*, vol. xxx (1962), pp. 62– 70.

——, 'A Neglected Masterpiece: Conrad's "Youth"', *Texas Studies in Literature and Language*, vol. iv (Spring 1963), pp. 591– 601.

Wright, Walter, F. *Romance and Tragedy in Joseph Conrad* (Lincoln,

Nebraska: University of Nebraska Press, 1949).

Zabel, Morton Dauwen, 'Conrad', in his *Craft and Character in Modern Fiction* (New York: Viking, 1957), pp. 147–227. Includes revised version of 'Joseph Conrad: Chance and Recognition', *Sewanee Review*, vol. liii (Winter 1945), pp. 1–22.

——, (ed.), 'Introduction', *The Portable Conrad* (New York: Viking, 1947), pp. 1–47.

——, 'Introduction', *Joseph Conrad's The Shadow-Line*, '*Typhoon*', *and 'The Secret Sharer'* (Garden City, N.Y.: Doubleday and Co., 1959), pp. 1–27.

# Index